MORALITY AND
GLOBAL JUSTICE

MORALITY
AND
GLOBAL
JUSTICE

JUSTIFICATIONS AND APPLICATIONS

MICHAEL
BOYLAN

WESTVIEW
PRESS

A Member of the Perseus Books Group

Westview Press was founded in 1975 in Boulder, Colorado, by notable publisher and intellectual Fred Praeger. Westview Press continues to publish scholarly titles and high-quality undergraduate- and graduate-level textbooks in core social science disciplines. With books developed, written, and edited with the needs of serious nonfiction readers, professors, and students in mind, Westview Press honors its long history of publishing books that matter.

Find us on the World Wide Web at www.westviewpress.com.

Every effort has been made to secure required permissions to use all images, maps, and other art included in this volume.

Westview Press books are available at special discounts for bulk purchases in the United States by corporations, institutions, and other organizations. For more information, please contact the Special Markets Department at the Perseus Books Group, 2300 Chestnut Street, Suite 200, Philadelphia, PA 19103, or call (800) 810-4145, ext. 5000, or e-mail special.markets@perseusbooks.com.

Designed by Trish Wilkinson
Set in 10.5 point Adobe Garamond Pro

Cataloging-in-Publication data are available from the Library of Congress.
ISBN: 978-0-8133-4432-4
E-book ISBN: 978-0-8133-4513-0

10 9 8 7 6 5 4 3 2 1

I dedicate this book to my family:
Rebecca, Arianne, Seán, and Éamon

CONTENTS

PREFACE

This book aspires to challenge readers to think about a global sensibility of morality and justice. Most traditional texts in ethics and in social and political philosophy have a national perspective in mind. This is because the traditional natural unit of sovereignty is the state. International laws have been artifacts of bilateral and multilateral treaties that have largely focused upon trade, immigration, and aggression/war. Even the United Nations—a model for one kind of world government—reveals a statist sensibility, for it lacks the sovereignty or authority to enforce most of its dictums: Each state obeys according to its national interest. But these are legal issues that obscure the existence of fundamental natural rights that citizens around the world possess regardless of their ability to successfully make claims for particular goods.

However, the United Nations is much more than a first step toward world government. It creates an intellectual space in which the peoples of the world can think in global rather than merely national terms. It also facilitates discussions on health, business, the environment, and other concerns that touch many around the world. It is toward this new intellectual space that this book seeks to extend the reach of the traditional domain of ethics as well as social and political philosophy by including the international sphere. Sometimes this sort of perspective is called *cosmopolitanism*, understood in this book to refer to a different way to view a morally based system of justice: The natural unit is the world (instead of the state). This does not mean that the state becomes irrelevant, but merely that the horizons of moral applicability extend to people, as such—wherever they live.

Distributive justice is the focus of this book, just as it was in my earlier monograph, *A Just Society.* International distributive justice concerns the theory and mechanism of the way goods and services are parsed within the context of a society and within the context of the world. Various moral, political, and economic systems commend different formulae for the way these goods and services are handed out. In this book as well as in my earlier book there is an emphasis on a theoretical grounding via metaethical principles, normative ethical principles, and applied ethical principles. *Metaethical principles* refer to the theoretical foundations of ethics itself: "What primary principles are necessary to ground a system of ethics?" *Normative ethical principles* are one level more concrete. They still deal with theoretical questions, but theoretical questions that are seen in the context of creating a system that can yield definitive decisions to crucial moral problems. *Applied ethical principles* are yet one more level concrete as they use the underlying perspectives of metaethics and normative ethics to take into account actual *sorts* of moral situations.

Together, these three levels of analysis are necessary for authentic confrontation with events and our own existence in the world: With this foundation, critical problem solving becomes possible.

In *A Just Society,* the metaethical level was expressed via the *personal worldview imperative*:

All people must develop a single comprehensive and internally coherent worldview that is good and that we strive to act out in our daily lives.

and the *shared-community worldview imperative*:

Each agent must contribute to a common body of knowledge that supports the creation of a shared community worldview (that is itself complete, coherent, and good) through which social institutions and their resulting policies might flourish within the constraints of the essential core commonly held values (ethics, aesthetics, and religion).

In this book the vision expands globally to include an *extended-community worldview imperative*:

Each agent must educate himself as much as he is able about the peoples of the world—their access to the basic goods of agency, their essential commonly held cultural values, and their governmental and institutional structures—in order that he might individually and collectively accept the duties that ensue from those peoples' legitimate rights claims, and to act accordingly within what is aspirationally possible.

The application of the metaethical principles and normative principles is the principal substance of this book. In particular, this volume seeks to extend my analysis in *A Just Society* in several key ways:

- Metaethical principles: an exploration of the principles of the extended-community worldview imperative and how that influences personal behavior (Part One).

- Table of Embeddedness: the normative ethical theory is expressed via a table listing degrees of embeddedness, which is a hierarchical list of goods to which any agent would aspire in order to enable action in his quest to be good (Chapter 3).
- Normative principles: viewing the degrees of embeddedness in a wider global context that includes global justice, human rights, culture and religion, and the relationship between national and global justice (Part Two).
- Key areas of applied ethics: applied ethical principles are considered in the light of the global issues of poverty, public health, race, gender, sexual orientation, democracy, globalization, the environment, war and terrorism, and immigrants and refugees (Part Three).
- Exercises: chapter-ending Critical Applied Reasoning Exercises (CARE) help readers to the next step of assessing, evaluating, and making judgments about individual problems in the international arena.
- Directions for readers to personally get involved in advancing their considered positions in the real world through an appendix that suggests ways to put theory into practice.

For instructors who wish to supplement this presentation with further examples of global metaethics, normative ethics, applied ethics, and casuistry, there is an accompanying reader of original essays that was commissioned especially to accompany this book.

Acknowledgments: I thank the anonymous reviewers of an early draft of the manuscript for their comments and suggestions. I would also like to thank the authors of the companion reader (*The Morality and Global Justice Reader*) for supporting this two-book project. I gratefully acknowledge Sandra Beris, Erica Lawrence, Michelle Asakawa, and the entire Westview team for producing and promoting this book. Finally, I'd like to thank Karl Yambert, my editor at Westview. His careful reading of the manuscript and his suggestions have improved the book.

PART ONE

GLOBAL METAETHICAL JUSTIFICATION

PART ONE
INTRODUCTION

Part One consists of two chapters devoted to exploring certain foundational points—or metaethical principles—that support our inquiry into global morality and justice. There are many candidates for metaethical principles depending upon which moral standpoint one takes. Chapter 1 sets out two such positions: *realism* and *antirealism*. Realism accepts that there are real moral facts that exist in the world: The task of ethics is to discover what they are and how they are to be applied. Antirealism posits that ethics is to be discovered by language usage within a cultural context or created by the agreement of two or more parties.

Both realism and antirealism are expressed through several moral theories: realism by deontology and utilitarianism, and antirealism by noncognitivism and contractarianism. Two other moral theories—ethical intuitionism and virtue ethics—can also express either realist or antirealist worldview orientations, depending on the presuppositions underlying them.

Chapter 2 discusses the particular metaethical principles that I assume in my presentation: the personal worldview imperative, the shared-community worldview imperative, and the extended-community worldview imperative. The reader's understanding of these three imperatives will assist him or her in the exposition of normative problems in Part Two.

CHAPTER I

The Way People Think About Ethics and Social/Political Philosophy

Stop right now! No, I'm not telling you to stop reading the text, I'm exhorting you to put down all your preconceptions of what is right and wrong in the world and then to reconstruct them according to a logical plan that makes sense to you personally. Sounds intriguing, doesn't it? What's the catch? Simply this: that you'll have to take on this project with total earnestness (*sincerity*) and use the best possible machinery to generate your result (*authenticity*). The price tag is steep, but the rewards are great. Are you ready?

Good. Let's begin. What do we mean by *ethics* and *social/political philosophy*? Various answers are given to this question. Let's start with a few fundamental worldview positions that you need to assume or accept before we can go forward.

Ethics

I define ethics as the science of the right and wrong in human action. This is often called the naturalistic or *realistic* position. This means that the maxims of ethics—such as the prohibition against murder—are actually true in the world, based upon facts about who we are as humans existing as we do. If this is correct, then all people at all times are prohibited from committing murder (here defined as the taking of an innocent human life at will). This would apply around the world and across all time periods (from the origins of rational and feeling *Homo sapiens*).

Others define ethics in terms of satisfying cultural expectations that exist within distinct robust cultural milieus. For example, I was once told by Raja Nasr

5

(who used to be head of school at a college in Beirut) that in Lebanese culture, interpersonal loyalty is more important than doing one's own work on tests. This was a real problem at the school because it led to widespread cheating—at least as "cheating" is defined by some people outside that culture. In contrast, the honor codes at several U.S. colleges require that if you know another student is cheating (even if it is your friend) you have to confront him or her with the demand, "If you don't turn yourself in, I will." Now, I am sure that this is an extreme example. But there are other such examples, among them concerning a woman's place in society or the role of religion in political life. When ethics is about meeting social expectations, the resulting ethical maxims are a matter of agreed-upon conventions and not "real." Those who hold this position are non-naturalists or *antirealists*.

How do you determine which side you support? Here are a few hints. If you practice one of the major religions of the world, then chances are the realist position is most appealing to you. This is because belief in a monotheistic God that is the source of Truth and Goodness would incline you to accept the real existence of ethical norms.

If you believe strongly in the social autonomy of various cultures and their right to make their own rules about everything, then antirealism will be most appealing to you. This is because you hold that assent and commendation are pivotal in ethical judgments. Viewed in this way, "assent" and "commendation" are *attitudes* that are not cognitively grounded. Instead they derive their action-guiding force from cultural expressions that are mutable across time and space.

As a test, ask yourself how you react when you read international news stories. Do you say that other cultures are sometimes wrong even when they are following their traditional customs? Or do you say, "I'm glad I don't live there, but they have every right to do what they do." What do you think of controversial groups around the world such as the Taliban, Hamas, or the Tamil Tigers? The answers to these questions should help you begin to formulate your thoughts on this.

Theories of Ethics

Theories of ethics may be parsed in various ways. I will follow the aforementioned realist and antirealist distinction to highlight six theories.

Realist Theories

Utilitarianism is a theory that suggests that an action is morally right when the consequences of that action produce more total utility for the group than any other alternative action. Sometimes this has been shortened to the slogan, "The greatest good for the greatest number." This emphasis upon calculating quantitatively the general population's projected consequential utility among competing alternatives appeals to many of the same principles that underlie democracy and capitalism (which is why this theory has always been very popular in the United States and other Western capitalistic democracies). Because the measurement device is natural (people's expected pleasures as outcomes of some decision or policy), it is a realist theory. The normative (or value claim) connection with aggregate happiness and the good is a factual claim. It is factual because happiness or pleasure (or at least self-assessments of the same) can be measured using social science techniques of statistical sampling. Utilitarianism's advocates point to the definite outcomes it can produce by an external and transparent mechanism (the statistical sampling). Critics cite the fact that the interests of minorities may be overridden.

Deontology is a moral theory that emphasizes one's duty to do a particular action just because the action, itself, is inherently right and not through any other sorts of calculations—such as the consequences of the action. Because of this nonconsequentialist bent, deontology is often contrasted with utilitarianism. In contradistinction to utilitarianism, deontology will recommend an action based upon principle. "Principle" is justified through an understanding of the structure of action, the nature of reason, and the operation of the will. Because its measures deal with the nature of human reason or the externalist measures of the possibility of human agency, the theory is realist. The result is a moral command to act that does not justify itself by calculating consequences. Advocates of deontology like the emphasis upon acting on principle or duty alone. One's duty is usually discovered via careful rational analysis of the nature of reason or human action. Critics cite the fact that there is too much emphasis on reason and not enough on emotion and our social selves situated in the world.

To help you understand the differences between deontology and utilitarianism, consider the following case study.

Case: Murder in Northern Ireland

You are a constable of a small, remote rural town in Northern Ireland. The town consists of Irish Catholics (20 percent minority) and Irish Protestants (80 percent majority). All 1,000 Catholics live in one section of town, which sits on a peninsula that juts into the river just east of the main section of town.

(continues)

Case: Murder in Northern Ireland *(continued)*

One morning a young Protestant girl is found raped and murdered next to the town green. By general consensus it is concluded that a Catholic must have committed the crime. The Protestants form a citizens committee that makes the following demand upon the constable: "We believe you to be a Catholic sympathizer. Therefore, we do not think you will press fast enough for this killer to be brought to justice. We know a Catholic did the crime. We have therefore sealed off the Catholic section of town. No one can go in or out. If you do not hand over the criminal by sundown, we will torch the entire Catholic section of town, killing all 1,000 people. Don't try to call for help. We have disabled all communication devices."

The constable worked hard all day in an effort to find out who committed the crime. It was now one hour before sundown, and he had no leads in identifying the criminal. He didn't know what to do. His deputy said, "Why don't we just pick a random Catholic and tell them he did it? At least we'd be saving 999 lives."

"But then I'd be responsible for killing an innocent man," replied the constable.

"Better one innocent dies and 999 be saved. After all, there's no way the two of us can stop the mob. You have to give them a scapegoat."

There are several key issues in this case: (1) Would the constable be guilty of murder if he randomly chose an innocent scapegoat? If so, would either utilitarianism or deontology ever allow such an outcome? And (2), isn't killing 1,000 people a worse outcome than killing merely one? What would utilitarianism and deontology say about this?

Swing Theories

This case leads us to consider "swing theories," which may be either realist or antirealist, depending on the presumed source of the ethical suppositions.

Ethical intuitionism can be described as a theory of justification about the immediate grasping of self-evident ethical truths. Ethical intuitionism can operate on the level of general principles or on the level of daily decision-making. In this latter mode many of us have experienced a form of ethical intuitionism through the teaching of timeless adages such as "Look before you leap" and "Faint heart never won fair maiden." The truth of these sayings is justified through intuition.

Many adages or maxims contradict each other (such as the two above), so that the ability to apply these maxims properly is also understood through intuition. When the source of the intuition is either God or Truth itself as independently existing, then the theory is realist—the idea being that everyone who has a proper understanding of God or Truth will have the same revelation. When the source of the intuition is the person herself, living as a biological being in a social environment, then the theory is antirealist because many different people in different social environments will have varying intuitions, and none can take precedence over another.

Virtue ethics is also sometimes called agent-based or character ethics. It takes the viewpoint that in living your life you should try to cultivate excellence in all that you do and all that others do. These excellences or virtues are both moral and nonmoral. Through conscious training, for example, an athlete can achieve excellence in a sport (a nonmoral example). In the same way, a person can achieve moral excellence as well. The way these habits are developed and the sort of community that nurtures them are all under the umbrella of virtue ethics. When the source of these community values is Truth or God, the theory is realist. When the source is the random creation of a culture based on geography or other accidental features, the theory is antirealist. Proponents of the theory cite the real effect that cultures have in influencing our behavior. We are social animals, and this theory often ties itself with communitarianism (a theory that puts community interests on par with individual interests—called weak communitarianism—or a theory that puts community interest above those of the individual—called strong communitarianism). Detractors often point to the fact that virtue ethics does not give specific directives on particular actions. For example, a good action is said to be one that a person of character would make. To detractors this sounds like begging the question.

To assist you in assessing the worldview claims made by these two normative theories, consider the following case.

Case: Loyalty Versus Honesty in the NYPD

You have been the partner of Sarah Silverman for fifteen years. Sarah is a good cop who occasionally lets her emotions get the better of her. On one case in January the two of you drove the cruiser to an incident in the East Village in Manhattan. A man was beating up a woman in their apartment. You had been called by neighbors who feared for her safety. Sarah went

(continues)

Case: Loyalty v. Honesty in the NYPD *(continued)*

overboard in her reaction (according to Police Regulations). She took the offensive and used her Taser to take down the male without warning him to stop or identifying herself as a policewoman. The electric charge disabled the man, who has filed suit against the New York Police Department. You know in your gut that Sarah "lost it" during the domestic dispute.

You also know that Sarah would be judged to be wrong in what she did according to the professional standards set out in the Police Regulations, which delineate the professional requirements of being a police officer. You have been called in by the district attorney to give a deposition, wherein you must swear under the penalty of perjury that what you say is the truth. If you tell the truth, Sarah will be fired and will lose the fifteen years she has accrued toward her pension (which kicks in at twenty years). If you lie, then you will have allowed a case of police brutality to go unresolved.

Your intuition tells you that even though Sarah lost control of her emotions, somehow what she did was proper (though a bit excessive) given the particulars of this circumstance (after all, the male was severely beating the woman—who happened to be his wife). And Sarah would not have been able to wrestle the wife-beating lout to the ground. What choice did she have except the Taser or her service revolver?

What you have to figure out is whether to think about this quandary via *virtue ethics* (measuring the relative weights of loyalty and honesty) or using *ethical intuitionism*. Would it make a difference if there *really were* a correct answer; that is, if the objects of ethical inquiry really existed?

Antirealist Theories

Ethical noncognitivism is a theory that suggests that the descriptive analysis of language and culture tells us all we need to know about developing an appropriate attitude in ethical situations. Ethical propositions are neither true nor false but can be analyzed via linguistic/media devices to tell us what action-guiding meanings are hidden there. An example of a linguistic/media device can be found in the depiction of young African American males who have been accused of a crime. In a study of the local news in Chicago, black criminals were disproportionally portrayed as scowling in mug shots or in video clips walking with handcuffs led by white police officers.[1] The same study found that African American criminals were shown in very negative images 2.4 times more often than their European-descent criminal counterparts. This shows how social attitudes with embedded racist messages are passed on via the media. The same is true in print journalism. Examine the words your local newspapers used to describe "terrorist suspects," Muslims, Jews, Palestinians, and so on. If you compile a list of what you find, it will likely be composed of words with negative connotations.

We all live in particular and diverse societies. Discerning what each society commends and admonishes is the task for any person living in a society. Individually, we strive to fit in and follow the particular social program described by our language, media, and culture. Because these imperatives are relative to the values of the society or social group being queried, the maxims generated hold no natural truth-value and as such are antirealist. Advocates of this theory point to its methodological similarity to deeply felt worldview inclinations of linguistics, sociology, and anthropology. If one is an admirer of these disciplines as seminal directions of thought, then ethical noncognitivism looks pretty good. Detractors point to corrupt societies and the inability of ethical noncognitivism to criticize these from within (because the social milieu is accepted at face value).

Ethical contractarians assert that freely made personal assent gives credence to ethical and social philosophical principles. These advocates point to the advantage of the participants being content with a given outcome. The assumption is that within a context of competing personal interests in a free and fair interchange of values, those principles that are intersubjectively agreed upon are sufficient for creating a moral "ought." This "ought" comes from the contract and extends from two people to a social group. Others universalize this, by thought experiments, to anyone entering such contracts. Because the theory does not assert that the basis of the contract is a proposition that has natural existence as such, the theory is antirealist. Proponents of ethical contractarianism tout its connection to notions of personal autonomy that most people support. Detractors cite the fact that the theory rests upon the supposition that the keeping of contracts is a good thing, but why is this so? Doesn't the theory presuppose a metamoral theory validating the primacy of contracts? If not, then the question remains, "What is it about making a contract with another that creates normative value?"

In order to assist readers in thinking about ethical noncognitivism and contractarianism, I present the following case.

Case: A Contract in the Black Forest[2]

Wolf Sullowald, a former butcher, was watching a television program in southwest Germany about changing social attitudes on suicide. The television reporter said that most European Union countries would join the

(continues)

> **Case: A Contract in the Black Forest** *(continued)*
>
> Netherlands soon in legalizing euthanasia due to social attitudes changing about the right of people to take their own lives, at will. It was then that Wolf concocted his plan. Having always wanted to make use of his technology expertise on the Internet to do something different, he decided to solicit someone to kill himself during a live Internet feed, after which Wolf would butcher, cook, and consume the body. The entire episode would surely attract a wide audience. Wolf posted his request on Friedhoff's Space, a free Internet site (similar to Craig's List) that posts a variety of requests and opportunities. Within two weeks, an Austrian named Trieste e-mailed that he was interested. The two drew up a contract and had it witnessed by their friends in front of a Web camera. Two months later the terms of the contract were read on camera by two people (a friend of Wolf and a friend of Trieste). Then Trieste killed himself on camera, and Wolf proceeded to butcher Trieste and prepare his body according to a famous recipe. Wolf then ate Trieste and ended the Internet event with these words: "This event could only happen under the new social sentiment about the right of all people to commit suicide and the freedom of all people to make contracts that govern their lives. How great it is to live in these times."

Which is the dominant theory in this case—social attitudes (ethical noncognitivism) or ethical contractarianism? Which has the stronger claim on ruling conduct? Can they work together? What do you think of these sorts of approaches?

For the purposes of this text, we will assume these six theories to be exhaustive of philosophically based theories of ethics or morality.[3] In our discussions in subsequent chapters you should be prepared to apply these terms to situations and compare the sorts of outcomes that different theories would promote.

Social/Political Philosophy

A second key set of concepts necessary to explore global ethics is one's disposition and action response concerning those that are different from one's own worldview and the shared community worldview in which one lives.

Social/political philosophy is an amalgam of concerns that raises the level of ethical focus from the individual level to that of the group. In social philosophy, customs within existing communities are examined to see whether they might be normatively commended or not (according to some extension of a theory of ethics and understanding of the role of culture). *To commend* is to give one's positive approval to some action or state of affairs. *Norms* are standards by which we give our assent or dissent. They can be based on realist or antirealist criteria. In political philosophy, the creation of governing institutions and the justifications for their operation are the points of concern. As we enter into our discussion of the international sphere, three key question areas will be introduced: *confronting the "other,"* the nature of states and institutions, and the *legitimacy of political change.*

Confronting the "Other"

I believe that in the context of global ethics there are three stances that can be assumed when confronted with those different from one's self (that is, states and regions of the world in which the values and way of life differ from one's own). It is important here to distinguish between a judgment of whether the other culture is different due to nonmoral differences (such as eating with the right hand only or wearing a head scarf) and moral differences (such as female genital mutilation). For the purposes of this section, let us assume that the "other" is differentiated only by nonmoral differences. These are the most common, dealing with racial/ethnic issues, dress, and general behaviors that depict a community's way of life. "Different" (in this way) is often troubling to many individuals. Thus, it often provokes some sort of action response.

The first sort of response is *competition.* When a country or region differs from your own, one response is to compete with it in order to become the more powerful. This is the response of *kraterism* (rule of the strongest). In cases like this, one country or region will seek to overcome the other and to try to change the other so that it is less "other." A prime example of this is the European colonization of much of the world during the sixteenth to nineteenth centuries. Because of Europeans' superior war technology, they could go where they liked (for the most part), plunder other countries, and change many of their customs and, thus, their culture. The idea behind the competitive response to otherness is that: (a) the other is different, (b) the difference is not pleasing to the more powerful country,[4] and (c) the more powerful country responds by finding ways to change the weaker country with all tools at its disposal, including armed regime change.

The second sort of response to otherness is *toleration*, one advocated by John Rawls.[5] Toleration begins in much the same way as competition: (a) the other is different, (b) the difference is not pleasing to the more powerful—but tolerant— country, but (c) the more powerful country allows the other country to continue as it has, despite grave reservations. Behind this tolerance is a disposition toward largesse on the part of the more powerful country to allow unpleasing behavior within a certain range in the name of global cooperation. Though Rawls is avidly not utilitarian, this move smacks of such.[6] Thus, within the international realm some liberal nations (meaning republics that recognize democracy and liberty and that respect the plight of the poor) will put up with at least some hierarchical nations in the spirit of toleration—but this has limits when one confronts burdened and benevolent absolutist societies. In those cases, assistance is required so that they become liberal societies. Certain "rogue" or "outlaw" societies may exceed the limits of toleration and may be targeted for regime change.[7]

The third sort of response is *acceptance*. When one accepts the "other," the following dynamic occurs: (a) the other is different, (b) the difference is not pleasing to the more powerful country, and so (c) the more powerful country parses its displeasure into two categories—(i) aesthetic issues, such as the choices a country makes in culture and religion, and (ii) ethical lapses, such as human rights abuses and genocide. Displeasure over aesthetic issues will require more than toleration. Rather, the more powerful country will strive toward accepting the other while also seeking to effect more or less gradual change in the other that will bring it into the extended shared-community worldview as a legitimate member.

In the cases of ethical lapses, some sort of action response is necessary. Whether this action response is violent or nonviolent will depend upon the sort of violation and possibility of various reactions to it. My approach will be that violence is the very last resort that should be undertaken. But this does not mean that nations should wait and do nothing. Various nonviolent approaches have been effective in international change, such as the embargo of South Africa to end apartheid.

The Nature of States and Institutions

States and institutions are social constructions founded on some mix of social justice and common agreement based upon cultural constructions. If we are to consider the propriety of how nations ought to behave, it is important that we have some idea about just what a nation is. Various people have written about this issue, often referring back to the seventeenth-century social contract philosophers John Locke and Thomas Hobbes and their two competing theories, statism and cosmopolitanism.[8]

The *statist theory* has two forms—the strong and the weak. In the *strong-statist* theory, one's state represents the highest form of community membership that one enjoys: citizen of a state. This membership can be described via a social contract (generally implicit) that says that your state has nurtured you and given you various sorts of advantages. In return the state expects virtually blind loyalty:

my country right or wrong. Socrates seems to accept this in his famous argument from the *Crito* (pp. 49–51)[9] on civil disobedience:

1. Man ought never act unjustly—Assertion [A]/ 49a4
2. To repay injustice with injustice is unjust—1 [inference from premise #1]/ b10
3. To repay injustice with injustice ought not be done—1, 2/ b10
4. [To do harm is the same thing as doing evil][10]—A
5. To do evil is unjust—A/ c2
6. To repay evil with evil is unjust—5/ c4–5
7. To repay evil with evil ought not to be done—1, 3, 6/ c10
8. [Suffering is an evil and/or an injustice]—A
9. Suffering does not permit us to do evil or to act unjustly—3, 7, 8/ c11
10. A man must carry out just agreements—A/ e5
11. A state to survive requires that laws have force and apply in all cases—A/ 50b 3
12. Individual exceptions to the laws mean that the laws do not apply in all cases—Fact [F]/ b5
13. Individual exceptions to the laws undermine and harm the state—11, 12/ b5
14. Each individual makes an agreement with the state to abide by its judgments—A/ c4
15. This agreement is a just mutual transaction with give and take—A/ d–e
16. To retaliate against the state is to harm the state—F/ 51a
17. To retaliate against the state is to do evil to the state—4, 16
18. To do evil to the state even when the state does evil to you ought not to be done—7, 9, 17/ 51a2
19. Retaliating against the state should not be done—17, 18/ a3-6
20. To seek individual exceptions to the law should not be done—4, 13, 18
21. To not abide by the judgments of the state is to break a just agreement—14, 15/ c6-f5a7
22. Man ought not fail to abide by the judgments of the state—14, 15, 21

---

23. Man has an obligation to abide by the judgments of the state and not to seek individual exceptions to the law—20–22/ 53a8-e3

In this text, Socrates seems to be taking the strong-statist view that an individual in State X takes on special obligations because of that membership.[11] This would seem to imply favoring the state over other states and favoring citizens of your state over citizens of other states. This is a rather partisan view of the world. The state takes on a strong legal and legitimating role for all the communities in that state.

The *weak-statist* view drops the partisan view of personal allegiance in all events. In its stead it merely sets out a legalistic model in which the state has a legitimate legalistic role in the affairs of the world. Legitimate states possess sovereignty over some given area of land and may act in the interests of its citizens within that region. Implicit within this approach is the idea that there is a standard of legitimacy that involves some interactive connection between the citizens, their respective micro and macro communities, and the government that is formally the state's voice to the world. If this interaction does not exist, then the state is not legitimate and should not be recognized by other sovereign states.

The alternative view to statist theory is often termed *cosmopolitanism.* It holds that nations and their ensuing national interests are morally irrelevant in determining or executing obligations to the people of the world. In this context it will refer to the position that, contrary to weak statism, all national designations (be they national boundaries or any ensuing duties therein) are conventional and do not imply any real moral obligations at all. We are all equal. What passes as a state is merely a conventional parsing based upon past wars and conquests. It has no real moral character and should be ignored when evaluating global ethical "oughts." States and international organizations are legitimate when they recognize this dynamic and illegitimate when they do not.

The choice among these positions is critical for anyone engaging in global ethics. Further argumentation from my own point of view will be set out in Chapter 6.

The Legitimacy of Political Change

The final question in this chapter affects one's standpoint on the other questions. It seeks to understand how political change happens and which instances are to be morally approved and which are to be morally disapproved.

For our purposes here let us define *political change* as either (1) the substantial change of an existing government and its resulting policies, or (2) the creation of an entirely new government that starts all over again to solve the issues of governing a country. Both can occur either peacefully or via force. Is the mode of political change important? Does peaceful change possess an advantaged position? If so, then how much is it worth? For example, the thirteen American colonies (that later became the United States) and Canada were ruled by the same colonial power, Britain. They both objected to certain colonial policies. However, the American colonies decided to revolt and won independence through the barrel of the gun[12] whereas the Canadians chose a peaceful route but had to wait until 1867 for their independence—eighty-three years later. Is peace worth eighty-four years? This is a question that readers should ask themselves.

Then there is the tension between (1) and (2) via gradual change and radical change. Are some regimes so ill-suited to representing the communities within a region that they cannot be modified but must start anew? What principles justify this? May other countries intervene to help the change move forward? Why or why not? Does it matter if the country in question is engaged in internal outrages against its own citizens, such as massacres or forced relocation? What about its behavior to its neighboring states? These many questions are covered in more detail in Chapters 6 and 14.

Key Terms

ethics, theories of ethics, social/political philosophy, confronting the "other," statism, cosmopolitanism, authenticity, sincerity

Critical Applied Reasoning Exercise

Select one of the rich countries in the world and write down the name of the country on a piece of paper. Next, select a poor country in the world that is currently in a severe crisis and write down the name of that country on a piece of paper. Now, write a 1.5-page policy-position paper on what the response of the rich country to the poor country should be, given the conditions in both countries today. Be sure to back up your suggestions by using appropriate distinctions raised in Chapter 1.

Notes

1. R. M. Entman, "Modern Racism and the Images of Blacks in Local Television News," *Critical Studies in Mass Communication* 7 (1990): 332–345.

2. This case is very loosely based on the Armin Meiwes case in Germany that occurred in March 2001.

3. For the purposes of this book the words *ethics* and *morality* will be taken to be exact synonyms.

4. The reason that the focus is upon the more powerful country is that only the more powerful country has a response that would effect change to another country that did not see a need to change itself.

5. John Rawls, *A Theory of Justice* (Cambridge, MA: Harvard University Press, 1971): 211–220.

6. Under my examination of the personal worldview imperative under completeness understood as the affective good will, this sort of inequality is not allowed (see Chapter 2).

7. John Rawls, *The Law of Peoples* (Cambridge, MA: Harvard University Press, 1999): parts 2–3.

8. For more here, see David Luban, "Just War and Human Rights," *Philosophy and Public Affairs* 9, 2 (1980): 160–181; and Michael Walzer, *Just and Unjust Wars* (New York: Basic Books, 1977).

9. Page numbers refer to the Greek text edited by John Burnet, *Platonis Opera* (Oxford: Clarendon Press, 1900); the translations are my own.

10. Bracketed premises denote suppressed premises or enthymemes that are necessary to generate a tight inference but are not found in the text itself.

11. Please be aware that Plutarch cites a saying of Socrates that he is not a citizen of Athens or a Greek but rather is a citizen of the world.

12. It should be noted that Mao Tse-Tung in his red book declared that political independence could only be achieved via the barrel of a gun; see *Quotations from Mao Tse-Tung* (Peking: Foreign Language Press, 1966), "Problems of War and Strategy" II: 225.

CHAPTER 2

The Personal, Shared-Community, and Extended-Community Worldview Imperatives

One's personal *worldview* constitutes the sum total of one's factual and normative understandings about the world. Each of us is enjoined to take ownership of our worldview via sincere and authentic questioning. Sincere questioning will be understood to be a commitment by each individual to utilize his or her highest capacities in this search—no half-hearted investigations allowed! This is serious business. In addition to sincerity, we all need some sort of process that will effectively focus and structure these foundational investigations. I call this process authenticity. Before we can authentically answer the questions posed in Chapter 1, it is necessary to introduce some theoretical devices that will provide a structure for the overall normative exercise.

The Personal Worldview Imperative

An imperative is a command. These metaethical principles are presented as fundamental requirements for all *Homo sapiens*. These commands require personal reflection about one's own conception of what is good as well as how one should fit into geographical and international communities. The structure of the command mode means that these exercises are not optional. We all are enjoined to enter into this sort of reflection in order to be sincere and authentic people living on earth.

The first of these theoretical devices is the *personal worldview imperative:*

> All people must develop a single comprehensive and internally coherent world-view that is good and that we strive to act out in our daily lives.

One's personal worldview is a very basic concept containing all that he or she holds as good, true, and beautiful about existence in the world. There are four parts to the personal worldview imperative: completeness, coherence, connection to a theory of ethics, and practicality. Let's briefly look at each in turn.

First is *completeness.* Completeness refers to the ability of a theory or ethical system to handle all cases put before it and to determine an answer based upon the system's recommendations. This is functionally achieved via the good will. The good will is a mechanism by which we decide how to act in the world, and it provides completeness to everyone who develops one. There are two senses of the good will. The first is the *rational good will*, which means that each agent will develop an understanding about what reason requires of us as we go about our business in the world. Completeness means that reason (governed by the personal worldview and its operational ethical standpoint) should always be able to come up with an answer to a difficult life decision. In the case of ethics, the rational good will requires engaging in a rationally based philosophical ethics and abiding by what reason demands. Often this plays out practically in examining and justifying various moral maxims—such as maxim alpha: "One has a moral responsibility to follow through on one's commitments, ceteris paribus (all other things being equal)." This maxim is about promise-making. One could imagine someone, call him Luke, going through the process of sincerely and authentically trying to define and justify moral maxims via reason and a chosen ethical theory. Imagine that Luke has accepted maxim alpha. Imagine also that Luke has asked Jennifer out to a big social event at his college. Jennifer accepted, but then one week before the event, Monique (a student whom Luke greatly prefers to Jennifer but never approached because Luke had thought she was out of his league) calls up Luke and asks *him* to the school event. Luke had made a prior promise to Jennifer. But Luke really would prefer going with Monique. What should Luke do? The rational good will (as Luke, himself, had developed it via maxim alpha) says that Luke should carry through with his promise to Jennifer since there is no conflicting moral issue that would invoke the ceteris paribus clause in the maxim. For Luke to act otherwise would be an instance of denying completeness based upon the rational good will. Luke should keep his promise to Jennifer.

Another sort of good will is the *affective good will*. We are more than just rational machines. We have an affective nature, too. Our feelings are important, but just as was the case with reason, some guidelines are in order. For ethics we begin with sympathy. Sympathy will be taken to be the emotional connection that one forms with other humans. This emotional connection must be one in which the parties are considered to be on a level basis. The sort of emotional connection I am talking about is open and between equals. It is not that of a superior "feeling sorry" for an inferior. Those who engage in interactive human sympathy that is open and level will respond to another with care. Care is an action-guiding response that gives moral motivation to acting properly. Together sympathy, openness, and care constitute love.

In the above case on promise-making, Luke wouldn't be concerned with making and justifying moral maxims such as maxim alpha. Instead, he would be developing his capacity to connect sympathetically with other people. If Luke sympathetically connected with Jennifer, his caring response would guide him toward maintaining his promise to Jennifer because to do otherwise would sever the sympathetic connection. Luke would not be acting like a loving person if he were to do otherwise. Likewise, he would respond to Monique's offer by acknowledging how happy it made him and how he would very much enjoy seeing her in the future in another venue. This sort of affective good will comes from one-on-one personal connections that elicit caring responses. The affective good will is every bit as comprehensive as the rational good will.

When confronted with any novel situation one should utilize the two dimensions of the good will to generate a response. Because these two orientations act differently it is possible that they may contradict each other. When this is the case, I would allot the tiebreaker to reason. Others demur.[1] Each reader should take care to think about his or her own response to such an occurrence.

A second part of the personal worldview imperative is *coherence*. People should have coherent worldviews. This also has two varieties: deductive and inductive. Deductive coherence speaks to our not having overt contradictions in our worldview. An example of an overt contradiction in one's worldview would be for Sasha to tell her friend Sharad that she has no prejudice against Muslims and yet in another context she tells anti-Muslim jokes. The coherence provision of the personal worldview imperative says that you shouldn't change who you are and what you stand for depending upon the context in which you happen to be.

Inductive coherence is different. It is about adopting different life strategies that work against each other. In inductive logic this is called a sure-loss contract.[2] For example, if a person wanted to be a devoted husband and family man and yet also engaged in extramarital affairs, he would involve himself in inductive incoherence. The very traits that make him a good family man—loyalty, keeping one's word, sincere interest in the well-being of others—would hurt one in being a philanderer, which requires selfish manipulation of others for one's own pleasure. The good family man will be a bad philanderer, and vice versa. To try to do both well involves a sure-loss contract. Such an individual will fail at both. This is what inductive incoherence means.

Third is *connection to a theory of being good*—that is, ethics. The personal worldview imperative enjoins that we consider and adopt an ethical theory (see Chapter 1). It does not give us direction, as such, to which theory to choose except that the chosen theory must not violate any of the other three conditions (completeness, coherence, and practicality). What is demanded is that we connect to a theory of ethics and use it to guide our actions.

The final criterion is *practicality*. It is important that the demands of ethics and social/political philosophy be doable and its goals be attainable. A *utopian* command may have logically valid arguments behind it but also be existentially unsound—meaning that some of the premises in the action-guiding argument are untrue by virtue of their being unrealizable in practical terms. If, in a theory of global ethics, for example, we required that everyone in a rich country give up three-quarters of their income so that they might support the legitimate plight of the poor, this would be a utopian vision. Philosophers are all too often attracted to tidy, if perhaps radical, utopian visions. However, unless philosophers want to be marginalized, we must situate our prescriptions in terms that can actually be used by policymakers. Philosophers involved in ethics and social/political theory must remember that these theories are to apply to real people living in the world. In taxation policy, for example, at some point—let's say at the point of a 50 percent income-tax rate—even the very wealthy among us will feel unjustly burdened and will refuse to comply with the policy. Thus it is utopian to base a policy upon the expectation that the rich will submit to giving up 75 percent of their income. An *aspirational* goal, by contrast, is one that may be hard to reach but is at least possible to achieve. For the purposes of this book, the aspirational perspective will be chosen over the utopian.

The purview of the personal worldview imperative is the individual as he or she interacts with other individuals in the world. Each of us has to do as much as possible to take stock of who we are and what we think we should be. Our consciousness is in our power to change. Though factors of environment and genetics are not to be dismissed, in the end it is the free operation of our will that allows us to confront the personal worldview imperative as a challenge for personal renewal.

The way that our worldviews change is via a process whereby we *confront novel normative theories*. There are three stages in the process: (1) Overview and justification, in which one considers the theory and its justification. (2) Dialectical understanding, in which one first reflects upon one's own worldview and then upon the novel worldview change that is being suggested. As a result of this process a person will have three possible reactions—(a) coinciding and amplification (the new worldview supports the existing worldview); (b) dissonance and rejection (the new worldview is so abhorrent that it is rejected out of hand; and (c) overlap and modification (the new worldview is intriguing and warrants further consideration). (3) Dialectical interaction. Once the overlap and modification level has been achieved, the agent "conceptually tries out" the new worldview to see whether it accounts for facts in the world and his or her most deeply held values (though some of these may change at this stage). This can be considered to be a "test drive" of the new way of viewing some novel normative vision of life. If the test drive seems to warrant a change, then the agent has purchased a new worldview perspective.

The Shared-Community Worldview Imperative

The second theoretical construct concerns our membership in communities. The first community that most of us know is the family. In the family we are bound by filial ties of love and shared sacrifice for common goals.[3] This is the smallest and often the most effective of all communities. Other communities substitute friendship and mutual understanding built through one-on-one interpersonal activity. These communities may center on where one lives (the neighborhood), where one works (the business), where one worships (the church, temple, mosque, etc.), and so on. There is often a political institutional structure at this level. In some villages it is the town government. In larger cities it is often the precinct. Generally this intimate committee of the whole can exist up to around 500 people. Let's call these the *micro communities*.

Larger groups we will call *macro communities*. When there is some proximate connection to the larger groups due to locale or another mark of similarity, the individuals in the macro community identify as being members of that community and cite it as a part of their personal identity. The largest macro community would be the nation itself. From the macro community various institutional structures are created so that the business of the community gets done.

The essential unit in either sort of community is the people who make up the community. The people act as the sovereign. In the case of a micro community the governmental structure is often carried on by designated representatives along with the advice and consent of the micro community as a whole. This is what gave rise to the town-meeting style of New England polity. In the case of the macro community, the government structure is carried on by surrogates (elected in a democracy) who are charged with representing the people. If they don't, then (in a democracy) they will be discharged from office.

Though most countries in the world are not effective democracies, this does not mean that other forms of government cannot engage in a social dialogue so that the wishes of the people are represented to their leaders in some way and that affords some real interchange. This may occur in various settings, but the accountability factor in these nondemocratic nations is certainly lower (see Chapters 10 and 11).

Both micro and macro communities develop social and cultural attitudes that affect life in those communities. These attitudes or worldviews have normative character so that they also need some structural guidance through an imperative aimed at the community, the *shared-community worldview imperative*:

> Each agent must contribute to a common body of knowledge that supports the creation of a shared-community worldview (that is itself complete, coherent, and good) through which social institutions and their resulting policies might flourish within the constraints of the essential core commonly held values (ethics, aesthetics, and religion).

There are five important parts of this imperative that deserve attention. The first criterion is *agent contribution*. This means that members of a community have responsibilities to be active members. One cannot ethically shift this responsibility completely to others. Even in communities in which there are elected officials, each person in the community has an obligation to periodically check to see whether he or she thinks the community is doing what it says it's doing and whether what it says it's doing is proper policy. When either of those conditions is not being met, members of the community have an obligation to engage whatever institutional mechanisms of protest and change that are open to them.

The second criterion is the reference to the *common body of knowledge*, which represents what is culturally accepted to be good, true, and beautiful about the world. Many communities (especially most macro communities) are diverse. In order to create acceptance within some community, it is necessary to recognize the nonmoral character of these differences. Sometimes the moral and the nonmoral become confused. In these situations one must refer back to the personal worldview and the relevant theory of ethics that have been embraced in order to separate an ethical from a nonethical practice.[4] It is easy to be prejudicial against what is new or unfamiliar, but when the unfamiliar is merely different and nonethical, the common body of knowledge must expand to accommodate it. However, when the unfamiliar is immoral, the common body of knowledge should give direction for the proper way to exclude such an input to the community (for example, Charles Manson's killing cult).

The third criterion of the shared-community imperative describes common traits shared by the personal worldview imperative: *complete, coherent*, and *con-*

nected to a theory of good. As per our discussion of the common body of knowledge, these pivotal criteria allow the members of the community to evaluate new members of the community so that they might be accepted or not. New doesn't necessarily mean bad (as per the fifth criterion below).

The fourth criterion enjoins that the *creation of social institutions* occurs within the guidelines set out by the imperative. The way communities act is via the creation of institutions that represent the worldview of the micro or macro group. It is important that the institutions that are so created actually represent the sense of the shared worldviews of the group's members. It is certainly possible for an institution to be created that loses its original mission and strays in the way that it operates. When this occurs, it is the community's responsibility to put the institution back on course (revise it) or to eliminate it.

Finally, the last part of the imperative is an acceptance of the *diversity of the community in terms of core values;* ethics, aesthetics, and religion. The acceptance of diversity is very important. People are different. Embracing these differences and allowing institutional space for them is morally and practically important. Though there is a limit to this acceptance, the default position in the shared-community worldview imperative is that diversity is a prima facie good and a healthy state of affairs for the micro or macro community. The burden of proof to the contrary is upon those who believe that such behavior is unethical.

In my view, these five aspects of the shared-community worldview imperative lay the groundwork for ethical communities that operate effectively for all their members.

The Extended-Community Worldview Imperative

The final theoretical construct is an imaginative construction that extends community membership to those beyond the conventional boundaries of our micro and macro groups. To intellectually grasp this aspect of community membership we need to import a new concept: the *extended community*. The extended community is one in which the agent is remotely connected. For example, I live in suburban Maryland just outside Washington, D.C. I am a member of various micro communities (such as my college and my son's school's parents group) and macro communities (such as my city, county, state, and nation). In each of these I have some direct or indirect contact that is proximate and tangible: I can write my representative or senator, and I can get into my car or travel via public transit directly to the physical domains of the state or national capital. Each of these is connected proximately to me through a tangible, operational, institutional structure that operates (in theory) under the principle of sovereignty set out above.

The extended community is a little different. Even though I can travel to the extended community by rail, sea, or air, I do not have immediate access. I must present a passport, and I can be denied entrance. I have many fewer tangible in-stitutional rights in a foreign country than I do at home. The foreign culture is different than my national culture. In some cases I may be completely ignorant about its customs, government, and social circumstances. The media often make it more difficult for me to find out facts on many foreign nations—particularly those that are poor and don't seem to fit our perceived national interest. Because of these aspects of remoteness there may be a famine occurring in Mali or severe storm damage on one of the islands of Indonesia that many people in the United States (for example) don't even know about.

International ignorance is a large cause of international apathy. To address a background condition necessary for morality and global justice, we must em-brace a third sort of worldview imperative: the *extended-community worldview imperative*:

> Each agent must educate himself and others as much as he is able about the peoples of the world—their access to the basic goods of agency, their essential commonly held cultural values, and their governmental and institutional structures—in order that he might create a worldview that includes those of other nations so that indi-vidually and collectively the agent might accept the duties that ensue from those peoples' legitimate rights claims and act accordingly within what is aspirationally possible.

The extended-community worldview imperative has three principal parts. The first has to do with *self and micro community education*[5] about the peoples of the world. This educational exercise should include important facts like geo-graphical situation, political and institutional structures, culture, and how the people fare with respect to the basic goods of agency (see Chapter 3). This edu-cation process should be ongoing. The point is to allocate space in one's con-sciousness and in the consciousness of those in your micro community to the existence and lives of others remote from you. Because this is an imperative, obe-dience is not optional.

The second feature has to do with the way you incorporate others into your worldview. Fulfilling this has to do with the operation of one's *imagination*. The imagination is the power of the mind that makes real and integrates what is ab-stract into lived experience and vice versa. When one educates himself about the lives of others, the imagination steps in and makes possible rational and emo-tional applications of the good will in assessing one's duties in response to others' valid rights claims, and in creating an extended style of sympathy. Normally, sympathy requires two people in direct contact. In the extended variety of sympa-thy, the knowledge gained through self and micro community education is put to work by the imagination to construct an image of some typical person living in another country, such that the vividness of their imagined situation sparks an approximation of direct person-to-person sympathy. In this way, the rational and affective good will act together to exhort one to action on behalf of another.

The third feature refers to an *action response*. Those in other countries who have legitimate rights claims are entitled to our response via our correlative duties. Ignorance of their plight does not absolve us from our responsibility. What often gets in the way is that we view those in the extended community as having their own society (which is viewed as the proximate provider of goods and services). Because our world is set up on the model of individual, sovereign states, many people believe that each country should take care of its own. The community model offers some support to this analysis. However, in the end this sort of parochialism fails because the boundaries of states are not natural facts but socially constructed conventions. Where one country ends and another begins is an artifact of history and military conquest. The boundaries of states are artificial and do not indicate natural divisions (even when the boundary between states is a mountain range or a river).

Thinking in this way is important because it shows that the way we parse ourselves (via geography, language, or culture) is rather arbitrary. There is a much stronger sense (based on human biology) that our existence as *Homo sapiens* is the only real robust boundary that counts among our species.[6] However, there is much truth in the old adage "out of sight, out of mind." When we are ignorant of the plight of others and when we haven't undergone the imaginative connection of the other to ourselves, then it is certainly the case that we will be less likely to be moved to action.

The extended-community worldview imperative exhorts us all to educate ourselves about the plight of others in the world and then to respond with individual and corporate action according to our abilities to act effectively. It must become a top priority issue to us all.

Key Terms

worldview, personal worldview imperative, shared-community worldview imperative, extended-community worldview imperative, completeness, coherence, utopian, aspirational, imagination, action response, good will, confronting novel normative theories

Critical Applied Reasoning Exercise

Write three short (one page each) essays.

Essay One: The Personal Worldview Imperative. Think about your own worldview and identify one deductive contradiction you'd like to change; or, concerning the category of completeness, whether you think your personal good will is stronger in its rational perspective or in its affective perspective (give an example).

Essay Two: The Shared-Community Worldview Imperative. Identify one micro community of which you are a part but which you believe is sagging in its collective worldview. How could you make a positive difference for the better?

Essay Three: The Extended-Community Worldview Imperative. Search the Internet for a map of a continent about which you are less familiar. Locate one country and find out about its people, their customs, institutions, and government. What legitimate needs does this country have right now?

Notes

1. This is particularly true of some feminist ethicists. See Rosemarie Tong, "A Feminist Personal Worldview Imperative," in *Morality and Justice: Reading Boylan's A Just Society*, ed. John-Stewart Gordon (Lanham, MD: Lexington/Rowman and Littlefield, 2009): 29–38.

2. The phrase "sure-loss contract" comes from the notion of betting houses. Say you were betting on the finals of the World Cup: Brazil v. Germany. If you gave 5–1 positive odds for each team, then your betting house would go out of business. A positive assessment of one team requires a complementary negative assessment of the other: Failure to observe this results in a sure-loss contract.

3. Obviously, there are many families that fall short of this goal, but the description I present is at least aspirational as defined above.

4. It is important to distinguish a nonethical (nonmoral) practice from an unethical (immoral) practice. The former does not concern ethics whereas the latter is judged to be wrong by some theory of ethics.

5. Of course, if one is in the position to influence the macro community via the media or public lectures, this would be helpful, too. However, this is a position only open to a few. To impose this duty generally upon all would be utopian.

6. Of course, the existence of other species poses other problems. For an example of this sort of analysis see Thomas White, *In Defense of Dolphins* (Oxford: Blackwell, 2008).

PART TWO

NORMATIVE ETHICS IN A GLOBAL CONTEXT

PART TWO
INTRODUCTION

In Part Two we examine key normative issues that are necessary in order to address applied ethical problems in a critical fashion. Chapter 3 explores the origin of obligation to others—particularly in a global context. Various answers to the obligation question come from the respective ethical theories of ethical intuitionism, contractarianism, utilitarianism, capability theory, and agency, and with the Table of Embeddedness.

Chapter 4 sets out three foundational arguments to support human rights: legal, interest-based, and agency-based.

Chapter 5 explores cultural relativism, moral relativism, world religions, and the East-West divide in order to accurately depict a landscape that presents some real challenges.

Finally, Chapter 6 considers the nature of the state and national identity in the light of the goals of cosmopolitanism. This discussion segues into an exploration of distributive justice theories (the principal focus of the book) and retributive justice as a challenge to global cooperation.

CHAPTER 3

The Foundation of Global Justice

This chapter will explore various ways of grounding a theory of global justice and will end with my preferred approach. Let's begin with examining a few key concepts. These areas of concern help form the environment by which we can think about theories and their justifications. Remember that justifying a moral theory that one can personally accept is one of the features of the personal worldview imperative. Our brief examination of normative theory will be intended to stimulate personal reflection rather than hammer home one and only one artifact.

Key Concepts

Relationships Within Extended Communities

The first key concept is the nature of the relationship of people within extended communities (we'll call the term *extended community relations*). As noted in Chapter 2, our normal understanding of communities begins at the lowest level of micro communities: the family. In the family we form intense personal relationships that are lifelong. As the micro community grows larger, these intense relationships increasingly give way to friendships, then to acquaintanceships, and then to superficial interactions. At some point the personal connectedness ends. We then enter the macro community, in which the features of connection are robust institutional arrangements centered on legal and political connectedness.

The extended community is similar to the macro community except that (1) it lacks the robust institutional arrangements, and (2) the legal and political connections are rather remote. In their place, I have suggested that individuals should

33

educate themselves and those around them so that they might imaginatively bring others into their personal worldview. This process can create a form of constructed sympathy for the plight of those in other countries. It is important to note that this sort of relationship may occur from one side only. Mr. X can form an imaginative understanding about the peoples of various parts of Kenya even though those in Kenya do not know who Mr. X is. This marks the difference in constructed sympathy from the direct sympathy found in micro communities and person-to-person interactions. In the two latter cases the relationship must be reciprocal. If it isn't, then it isn't authentic. Constructed cases of sympathy and applications of the rational good will work differently, requiring only the effort of one side of the equation. Thus, to be in Mr. X's personal worldview and part of his extended community, one merely needs to be imagined by Mr. X and have an interest shown in his or her plight with an understanding that Mr. X commits himself (and those about him whom he can muster in his micro and macro communities) to providing some assistance within Mr. X's ability and means.

Institutions

The second key concept is the role of operational institutions in understanding duties and obligations. *Institutions* are recognized sets of rules that govern social or political conduct. *Robust institutions* are those whose recognition and power (legally or via culture) are great enough to be able to positively reward (or punish) those who follow (or disregard) their prescriptions for behavior. *Virtual institutions* are those that are recognized within some community but that lack the power to positively reward (or punish) those who follow (or disregard) their prescriptions for behavior. In virtual institutions observance of the rules is voluntary and is observed via some form of the honor system. For example, within almost every country on earth the criminal code is a robust institution that can identify, capture, and punish miscreants. In contrast, the institution of polite manners (in most cases) is voluntary, with only a harsh look or statement by the offended party as penalty.

Institutions originate *formally* via laws that are debated and discussed in legislative bodies—the laws themselves can create the institutions, as in the case of governmental institutions, or the laws can prescribe the creation of private institutions, as in the case of corporations and nonprofits—and *informally* via cultural understandings that arise from the shared-community worldview.

When living within a micro or macro community, one needs to understand the relevant robust and virtual institutions within his or her sphere of life in order to be an effective actor within the community. When it comes to the extended community, things are rather different. This is because most of us do not live within an extended community: if we did, it wouldn't be *extended*.[1] For the most part, the interactions are imaginary and therefore constructed. In the same way, the institutions are constructed virtual institutions. Even in cases in which there is a quasi-legal structure (such as the United Nations), the ability to effectively reward and punish is severely limited. Thus, the real impact on human social/political action is limited. Some visions of the future include measures that would strengthen world government so that the extended community might dissolve into another level of the macro community. This would require that individuals be able to view themselves as connected via robust institutions with all the nations of the world. Whether this is possible (and thus aspirational) or merely a whimsical dream (utopian) remains to be seen.

Goods of Agency

The third key concept is an overview of what peoples in the extended community might want, which we'll term *goods of agency*. World wealth totals about US$50 trillion[2] (with $14 trillion coming from the United States alone). If we were to propose spreading this wealth evenly among the people of the world, we might be able to give each individual $7,000. This would go very far in some subsistence societies, though it would mean little to the richest 1 percent of the U.S. population (whose mean income is $5 million and who own 20 percent of the wealth in the country, or about 7 percent of the wealth of the whole world). However, such a proposal to spread the wealth around the world is certainly utopian.

Instead, let's think in terms that real people can connect with: the necessities of life. These are the goods that allow a person to live. Living means being able to act in the world. I believe that human agency—acting in the world to achieve our vision of the good—is the most fundamental value that each of us holds for ourselves, and it applies to us all generically. But acting requires a few prerequisites. If we don't have the biological necessities of life, we die. If we die, then we cannot act. So at the very minimum we need the biological necessities of life. These can be debated, but I suggest they are food, clean water, sanitation, clothing, shelter, and protection from unwarranted bodily harm, understood also as including basic health care (whether preventive, palliative, or curative). These necessities keep people alive—and yet in the world today they are elusive to millions. Let us call these necessities of life the *level-one basic goods of agency* (see Table 3.1).

Justice

The fourth key concept is that of *justice*. There are various senses of this term stemming (in the Western tradition) from Plato's expansion of the term *dike* (just) to *dikaiosune* (justice). Thus, justice can be both an emphasis upon right actions by individuals as well as a broad social term commending the way the state treats its citizens. This treatment includes primarily distribution of goods among its citizens (*distributive justice*) but also the way the state treats its miscreants (*retributive justice*). In this context we will emphasize the former function; the latter will be discussed in Chapter 6.

Justifications

Intuitionism

Most texts on international justice and ethics create scenarios that appeal to the reader's intuitive response. Thought experiments are presented that are meant to commonly appeal to these intuitions. For example, take the famous Shallow Pond thought experiment of Peter Singer.[3] In the thought experiment Singer says, "If I am walking past a shallow pond and see a child drowning in it, I ought to wade in and pull the child out. This will mean getting my clothes muddy, but this is insignificant, while the death of the child would presumably be a very bad thing." The example is one that virtually all readers would agree with. Because no other normative calculation is given to command helping the drowning child, ethical intuition is the default support. Singer then applies this to our relationship to those in need—especially (in this case) to the people dying in east Bengal in 1971. Just as we all should save the child, we should also contribute money to save these people and others in a similar situation.

However, there is disagreement over how close Singer's analogy really is to helping people in a distant land. Is the application exact to the dynamics that exist when we think about helping others in distant lands? Building on Singer's Shallow Pond, Peter Unger has constructed thought experiments that capture more specifics—for example, the *remoteness* of other peoples and the *extent* of the obligation.[4] The advantage of basing one's obligations on intuitionism is that intuitionism is an easy moral theory to grasp and apply. The disadvantage is that the methods used to increase public awareness—thought experiments, television and Internet advertisements, and so on—are susceptible to various interpretations and possibly place the audience in the position of being convinced by emotional scenes and situations—not unlike being manipulated by the tools of advertising. For detractors of intuitionism, this is a substantial drawback because the tools of advertising can be employed to sell anything. Perhaps it is important to have logical arguments that aren't so conveniently pliable.

Contractarianism

Many political theorists have postulated a social contract between citizens and the state to which they belong. Though this form of justification for social/political theory seems to be strongest within a nation rather than in the international sphere, one modern practitioner of contractarianism, John Rawls, has extended contract theory (the original position) to the international sphere.[5] Rawls claims that the making of national law requires an original position imposing five essential features: (1) the original position models the parties as representing citizens fairly; (2) it models them as rational; (3) it models them as selecting from among available principles of justice those to apply to the appropriate subject, in this case the basic structure; (4) the parties are modeled as making these selections for appropriate reasons; and (5) the parties select reasons related to the fundamental interests of citizens as reasonable and rational.[6] The making of international law requires an original position imposing three additional points: (6) parties are situated symmetrically and thus fairly; (7) parties are rational and guided by fundamental interests of democratic society; and (8) parties are subject to a veil of ignorance properly adjusted for international terms.[7] Rawls contends that the process that liberal peoples engage in when making international law should contain the two original positions, which along with the character of liberal peoples imply the traditional principles of international justice:

1. Peoples are free and independent, and their freedom and independence are to be respected by other peoples.
2. Peoples are to observe treaties and undertakings.
3. Peoples are equal and are parties to the agreements that bind them.
4. Peoples are to observe a duty of nonintervention.
5. Peoples have a right of self-defense but no right to instigate war for reasons other than self-defense.
6. Peoples are to honor human rights.
7. Peoples are to observe certain specified restrictions in the conduct of war.
8. Peoples have a duty to assist other peoples living under unfavorable conditions that prevent their having a just or decent political and social regime.

Certainly these results that Rawls claims from his second original position are fine principles. Proponents will point to these progressive points as signposts for measuring future progress on the planet. Detractors will point to the great reliance upon institutional structures in justifying and administrating Rawls's moral order. Because institutional structures in the world today are weak, at best, this may be a drawback to his account. Rawls seems to require a robust United Nations with sovereign authority to overcome such objections.

Utilitarianism

Another key contender for justifying principles that would support progressive policies for international social and political justice comes from utilitarianism.

The most ardent proponents of this approach are those who view the problem economically. Utilitarianism is easily adaptable to free-market and socialist-based capitalism. Thus, the proponents of economic globalization as the mechanism to lift the many out of poverty and link the nations of the world in self-interested interdependence point to utilitarianism as their model of choice. The arguments for and against globalization are many and various. Proponents point to metaphors that extend Bernard Mandeville's beehive into the world itself![8] If every nation works toward its own economic self-interest and the result (like the bees) is a thriving hive (an international economy for all), then what could be better? The idea has captured the imagination of many political and economic theorists, such as Thomas Friedman in *The World Is Flat*.[9] Friedman develops a sense of connectedness that goes beyond economic globalization as it incorporates the new media for communication and connection. All of these features make many hopeful about a justification for global justice. However, detractors will point to periodic global recessions as a danger to justice. In good times people might be friends, but bad times often bring out the worst in us all, especially if our motivation for doing good or right depends on economic self-interest. There also are detractors who point to those who aren't sharing in the economic good times as a destabilizing economic input into the social order: Such a scenario might create potential terrorists who will disrupt the world (due to dissatisfaction with the fact that they have been left out of the opulence). Finally, there are other detractors who maintain that governments rather than businesses should be leading the way in global justice because businesses have profit as their raison d'être.

Capability

Amartya Sen has been advocating another sort of justification for global justice.[10] The following argument demonstrates the essence of this claim from Sen's exposition:

1. Measuring poverty consists in two exercises: (a) identification of the poor and (b) aggregation of the statistics regarding those identified as poor—Assertion [A] (p. 102)
2. The most common aggregation exercise (1-b) is a head count based upon income levels (1-a)—A (p. 102)
3. The common approach does not differentiate levels of being poor—A (p. 103)
4. The strata of poor people is important: (a) it allows for the ordinal approach (useful in distributing resources), (b) it follows the Gini Index (acknowledged as the most reliable econometric device for poverty),

and (c) it allows for more complex models of social choice (more complex is more accurate than less complex)—A (pp. 103–105)

5. The common approach is deficient in accounting for poverty—1–4 [inference] (p. 106)
6. Personal differences (such as disability) skew the need for income and complicate the capability of the individuals involved—Fact [F] (p. 107)
7. Poverty is (a) an acknowledgment of deprivation and (b) a matter of identifying the focus for public action (the first is more descriptive while the latter is primarily normative)—A (p. 107)
8. Diagnosis should precede prescription—A (p. 107)
9. [We should determine 7-a before moving to 7-b]—6–8
10. There are variations in social accounts of poverty (vis-à-vis basic needs), but there is general agreement upon diminished capability—A (pp. 108–109)
11. [General agreement offers a better basis for description and reaction] —A
12. The capability approach is superior to the "basic need" approach for describing and solving social inequality—10–11 (p. 109)
13. Poverty is having minimally adequate capabilities—A (p. 111)
14. Utility and low-income analysis do not account for the man who squanders his money (p. 110) or the man who voluntarily fasts (p. 111) whereas the capability approach can handle these—A (pp. 110–111)
15. Capability analysis is superior to utility and low-income analysis— 13–14 (p. 112)
16. Specific deprivations can significantly affect capability—A (p. 113)
17. Hunger (especially in a rich nation) is a multifaceted outcome that is not adequately described by the common approach of income alone— A (p. 114)
18. Some of the multifacets in #17 may include inadequate health care, violent modes of inner city living, social care, etc.—A (p. 115)
19. The capability approach involves multifacets—A (p. 115)
20. The capability approach uniquely treats hunger and specific deprivations—16–19 (pp. 115–116)

---

21. Capability analysis is superior to income analysis in accounting for social inequity—5, 9, 12, 15, 20 (p. 116)

This argument may be a little difficult to those who do not think per economic social choice theory. Sen's own version of this when applied to welfare economics won him a Nobel Prize. A few key points will simplify this approach. First, capability is all about freedom. By freedom, it is meant freedom of opportunity. Opportunity may not track exactly according to resources. For example, if one is hungry because of the fast of Ramadan, this is *different from* someone being hungry because he or she is desperately poor and cannot get anything to eat. Both are poor. Under the resource-based theory they should be treated alike (according to Sen). But under capability theory only the person who has no opportunity to eat is really in distress. On the flip side, if a person is wealthy and has a severe disability, then she has limited capability even though she is rich. The net result from this is that capability analysis is resource independent. It looks at freedom of opportunity as the primary source of analysis.[11]

Proponents of this approach point to its redefinition of the goal of the process: from providing a market basket of goods to enable human freedom via opportunity. Detractors say that it really begs the question. They say that everyone wants the same end product, but the question is *how do you get there?* The answer that Sen gives (education, food, clothing, equal rights for women, etc.) hearkens back to the market basket approach.

Moral Agency and the Table of Embeddedness

We now arrive at a natural transition to the final justification in this presentation. This justification, which I personally endorse, begins with the individual wherever she may live in the world. What can she justifiably claim for herself such that everyone else incurs an obligation to provide it to her?

The Moral Status of Basic Goods

Consider now this argument:[12]

1. All people, by nature, desire to be good—Fundamental Assertion
2. In order to become good, one must be able to act—Fact
3. All people, by nature, desire to act—1, 2
4. People value what is natural to them—Assertion
5. What people value they wish to protect—Assertion
6. All people wish to protect their ability to act—3–5
7. Fundamental interpersonal "oughts" are expressed via our highest value systems: morality, aesthetics, and religion—Assertion
8. All people must agree, upon pain of logical contradiction, that what is natural and desirable to them individually is natural and desirable to everyone collectively and individually—Assertion
9. Everyone must seek personal protection for his or her own ability to act via morality, aesthetics, and religion—6, 7

10. Everyone, upon pain of logical contradiction, must admit that all other humans will seek personal protection of their ability to act via morality, aesthetics, and religion—8, 9
11. All people must agree, upon pain of logical contradiction, that because the attribution of the basic goods of agency are predicated generally, it is inconsistent to assert idiosyncratic preference—Fact
12. Goods that are claimed through generic predication apply equally to each agent, and everyone has a stake in their protection—10, 11
13. *Rights and duties are correlative*—A

---

14. Everyone has at least a moral right to the basic goods of agency, and others in the society have a duty to provide those goods to all—12, 13

The most controversial premises in this argument are #1, #8, #11, and #13. It is here that proponents and objectors will focus. In premise #1 some might contend that the assertion of "interest" may disadvantage children and the disabled. They may also think that there are those who are nefarious. The reply is that when we talk about human nature we are speaking in the vernacular of "for the most part." Those who fall outside this range can be viewed in the context of the norm and regarded as protected people. The reply to nefarious people is that their evil comes about via ignorance and not because they see themselves as the agents of evil (this is also subject to "for the most part" caveat to account for pathological criminals).

In premise #8 the rather scientific induction about the relation of goods to action and the fact that this might be viewed equally at the level of the individual or at the level of the group requires an acceptance of moral realism based upon the nature of human action. Objectors would be the antirealists who would deny that human action has a normative character. The reply would be that the antirealists are wrong based upon the scientific perspective on the goods necessary to permit purposive action toward the good (see the Table of Embeddedness).

Premise #11 is somewhat less controversial because it purports to be about the nature of subsumption in axiomatic systems. For example, if a general law said that no citizens in Society X may commit murder, then it would be illogical for Juan (a citizen of Society X) to assert that he had permission to murder. Objectors would be those who don't believe that ethics or social/political philosophy can ever be formulated in nested axiomatic systems. Again, the reply would be that these antirealists are wrong based upon the scientific perspective on the goods necessary to permit purposive action toward the good.

Premise #13 is the least controversial of all. It asserts merely the well-accepted relation to valid rights claims against some group of people such that the aforesaid group of people incur a duty to justified right claim holder (be it an individual or another group). Detractors would be those who disagree with any but legal rights claims—that is, those who disagree that there are any valid moral rights (there is some overlap here with objectors to premise #8). The same sort of reply would be given as per #11 and #8.

The obvious question that the previous argument on the moral status of basic goods raises is: What are these so-called goods of agency? This question is really about creating a scale of goods that are instrumental to action. If it is the case that human nature is all about acting so that we can try to move toward our vision of what we perceive to be good, then what is necessary to get there? Earlier in this chapter I suggested several level-one basic goods of agency—biological principles necessary for life itself. If we are dead, we cannot act. If we are dead, we cannot move toward our vision of the good.

But the bare minimum is not enough. If we are ultimately concerned with public policy and how we will enable the people of the world to achieve their natural human design (to act in order to achieve their own vision of the good), then it is important to make some gradations in the goods (resources) put forward. For ease in discussion, let us agree to call the basic goods necessary for human action the most deeply *embedded*.[13] Other goods/resources are also important but may be rated in hierarchal order according to their functional relation to their instrumental value of furthering human action. Table 3.1 shows one possible hierarchy of such goods.

TABLE 3.1. Table of Embeddedness

Basic Goods

Level One: *Most Deeply Embedded* (that which is absolutely necessary for human action):

- Food, clean water, sanitation, clothing, shelter, protection from unwarranted bodily harm (including basic health care)

Level Two: *Deeply Embedded* (that which is necessary for effective basic action within any given society):

- Literacy in the language of the country
- Basic mathematical skills
- Other fundamental skills necessary to be an effective agent in that country (in the United States, some computer literacy is necessary)
- Some familiarity with the culture and history of the country in which one lives

(continues)

TABLE 3.1. Table of Embeddedness *(continued)*

- The assurance that those one interacts with are not lying to promote their own interests
- The assurance that those one interacts with will recognize one's human dignity (as per above) and not exploit one as a means only
- Basic human rights such as those listed in the U.S. Bill of Rights and the United Nations Universal Declaration of Human Rights

Secondary Goods

Level One: *Life Enhancing*: Medium to High-Medium on Embeddedness

- Basic societal respect
- Equal opportunity to compete for the prudential goods of society
- Ability to pursue a life plan according to the personal worldview imperative

Level Two: *Useful*: Medium to Low-Medium Embeddedness

- Ability to utilize one's real and portable property in the manner she chooses
- Ability to gain from and exploit the consequences of one's labor regardless of starting point
- Ability to pursue goods that are generally owned by most citizens (in the United States today, a telephone, television, and automobile would fit into this class)

Level Three: *Luxurious*: Low Embeddedness

- Ability to pursue goods that are pleasant even though they are far removed from action and from the expectations of most citizens within a given country (in the United States today, a European vacation would fit into this class)
- Ability to exert one's will so that she might extract a disproportionate share of society's resources for her own use

---

NOTE: *Embedded* in this context means the relative fundamental nature of the good for action. A more deeply embedded good is one that is more primary to action.

The import of the Table of Embeddedness is that it identifies the strength of agents' claims to various sorts of goods according to their degree of indispensability to human agency—here called *embeddedness*. In cases of conflict between claims for different goods, the agent's (or group's) claim to more-embedded goods trumps the claim that logically can be made on behalf of those who desire less-embedded goods. This would cause a realignment of income in most societies and between societies when applied to the whole world. Advocates of this position are those who think that there should not be such a large gap between the "haves" and "have-nots." Detractors would be those who think that whatever one acquires according to rules of his society are his to use as he wants to, regardless of what others have.

Key Terms

extended community relations, institutions, goods of agency, justice, Table of Embeddedness

Critical Applied Reasoning Exercise

You are the speechwriter for the director of the United Nations Children's Fund (UNICEF). The director will be making a high-profile speech to the General Assembly that will be on worldwide television next week. Choose one of the justifying theories discussed in this chapter and use that point of view to argue for greater funding for your program to combat starvation among the very poor children of the world. Be sure to frame your appeal within logical arguments.

Notes

1. Those individuals in the government, international business, or other enterprises that have global exposure and are required to travel extensively in these areas would be exceptions to the general maxim that we do not live in our extended community. Casual tourists often encounter an ersatz version of the extended community.

2. *Wall Street Journal,* April 1, 2008. Of course, these figures have taken a great reduction in the recession of 2008 on forward. The net actual amount is often calculated at 20–30 percent lower as of the writing of this book.

3. Peter Singer, "Famine, Affluence, and Morality," *Philosophy and Public Affairs* 1, 3 (1972): 229–243.

4. Peter Unger, *Living High and Letting Die* (New York: Oxford University Press, 1996): chs. 1–2.

5. John Rawls, *The Law of Peoples* (Cambridge, MA: Harvard University Press, 1999).

6. Ibid., 30–31.

7. Ibid., 32.

8. Bernard Mandeville, *The Fable of the Bees,* ed. F. B. Kaye (London: Liberty Fund, 1924).

9. Thomas Friedman, *The World Is Flat* (New York: Picador, 2007).

10. Amartya Sen, *Inequality Reexamined* (Cambridge, MA: Harvard University Press, 1992) and Martha Nussbaum, *Women and Human Development: The Capabilities Approach* (Cambridge: Cambridge University Press, 2000).

11. Amartya Sen, *The Idea of Justice* (Cambridge, MA: Harvard University Press, 2009).

12. This is set out in more detail in Michael Boylan, *A Just Society* (Lanham, MD, and Oxford: Rowman and Littlefield, 2004): ch. 3.

CHAPTER 4

Human Rights

Imagine that you open a magazine or encounter on your Web browser a pop-up image of a child somewhere in the world who is in severe need, such as that caused by famine or disease. Whoever it is who has taken the trouble to disseminate that image may well have taken the extended-community worldview imperative into his own hands: He wants to educate as many people as possible about a reality that they might not otherwise be aware of.

A visual image is very evocative in creating a space in which you, as a comparatively affluent agent (yes, compared to the distressed child, you are presumably affluent), come into contact with the person living elsewhere—the other. The image is intended to stimulate the imaginative sympathy toward the other as described in the extended-community worldview imperative (Chapter 3). If you are confronted by the image and if you care to let the image into your consciousness, then the sympathetic process that leads to care has begun. But what is this process about?

One possible response is motivated by *charity*, in which you, the affluent agent, are moved by extended sympathy to connect to the plight of the people of whom you have just become aware. You decide whether that connection moves you enough to forgo the new shoes (or iPhone, or the extra textbook assigned as optional reading in your Philosophy class) and instead send (say) $100 to the cause represented by the image before you. What makes the charity process distinct is that it is up to you, yourself, whether you will give to charity or not. The choice is yours. If you say *yes*, there will be those who pat you on the back as having done a good thing. If you say *no*, no one will have a word to say against you.

Another kind of response is rooted in the moral interest in the extended-community worldview perspective that is created by the concept of *human rights*. The human-rights approach operates rather differently from the charity approach.

47

The person depicted in the image represents various individuals who lack level-one goods of agency on the Table of Embeddedness (see Table 3.1). If Chapter 3's argument on the moral status of basic goods is correct, then the child in the image and others like him have an absolute moral right—a *human right*—to those fundamental basic goods.[1] This isn't optional. From the human-rights approach, if you say *yes* to helping the child, people will only say you've done your duty. There will be no pats on the back. If you say *no*, people will say that you have failed in your basic moral duty to others.

There is a stark difference in these two approaches. The charity approach views the human condition as rather like an egg carton. We all exist on our own, separately. If you choose to look outside your own comfortable position in the egg carton, then you are doing more than you are required to do. Under this approach, all that you are required to do is to look after yourself and to clean up after the messes you make.

The human-rights approach makes claims that entail correlative duties. When you fulfill your duty, you are doing just what you are required to do. This is a normal part of life: You should fulfill your legitimate moral duties. The underlying assumption is that we live both as individuals and within communities.[2] In a complete account of morality and global justice, the individual narrative dominates in morality and the community perspective dominates when one examines micro, macro, and extended communities.

Every reader of this book should pause a moment and ponder where you stand on this issue. Do you have a moral duty to help starving and sick people, and refugees and victims of war, for example; that is, do those people in need have a legitimate claim for your help? Or is anything that you might do to help them an optional act of charity? Much rides on this.

Justifications for Human Rights

There are three principal justifications for human rights: legal, interest-based, and agency-based. Let us address these in order.

Legal Justifications

First, there are legal-based justifications for human rights. What is a legal justification? The term *legal* is relative to an institutional setting. Institutions make up their own rules of operation. Those who live under the domain of these institutions must comply or face the consequences (which vary according to the punitive authority of those institutions).

The grounding for institutions and the legal systems that support them is antirealist, based as those systems are on combinations of cultural consensus and the rule of power, as distinct from appeals to natural rights and moral realism. Take, for example, universal voting privileges' in the United States. When my mother was born, in 1917, women in the United States couldn't vote. According to the legal-justification perspective, there was no *right* for a woman in the United States to vote. Under this approach, a right is not a right unless it becomes operative through institutional acceptance,[3] and because there was no *law* allowing female suffrage, there was therefore no *right* of female suffrage. The basis for this perspective is antirealist because laws (rather than natural rights) are cultural constructs that vary from place to place and from time to time (ethical intuitionism). It is vain to seek some sort of underlying justification aside from prudential or other worldview interests that are recognized.

So how is legally justified change effected? The principal antirealist theory to justify change is contractarianism, according to which the mechanisms for reinterpreting the social contract are based upon political will. The American Declaration of Independence makes this view explicit in its claim that governments derive "their just powers from the *consent of the governed*" and that it is the "right of the people to alter" (or even abolish) the government as necessary. If enough women and men ("the governed") decide that they want women to have the right to vote, then they will engage in the political process to try to change the terms of the contract: the laws governing the land. This is indeed what happened with women's suffrage, when the Nineteenth Amendment to the U.S. Constitution was ratified in 1920 through the institutional process of approval by three-quarters of the states. According to this view, a right is not a right unless it becomes operative through institutional acceptance.[4]

Legal justifications for particular operative human rights may change over time, but they may also remain *un*changed over time, even though the times themselves change significantly. Such rights may then become historical artifacts, no longer operative in the new era. Consider, for example, the foundation of the American "right to keep and bear arms," the Second Amendment to the U.S. Constitution, adopted in 1791 as part of the newly independent country's Bill of Rights: "A well-regulated Militia, being necessary to the security of a free State, the right of the people to keep and bear Arms, shall not be infringed."

But what does this mean in contemporary America? The rule, codified in the very foundation of American law, seems to be particularly grounded in the colonial and early republican experience of the United States in which people had no police force or standing army to protect them and so had to rely on mustering local militias of private citizens to protect themselves. But how does this translate to the United States today, in which most people enjoy police protection against unwarranted bodily harm as well as the protection by the several branches of the armed forces against threats of insurrection or invasion?[5] And if the Second Amendment contemplated the use of muzzle-loading muskets for defense, are modern automatic weapons, such as military assault rifles, also "arms" of the kind protected by the Second Amendment? The parameters of the contemporary right of American citizens to "keep and bear arms" in the light of the two-century-old justification of that right remains a contentious issue and the source of lawsuits that reach even to the U.S. Supreme Court.

The philosophical point is this: Legal grounding of human rights requires a considerable measure of specificity tailored to particular institutional settings in particular times and places. For that reason, legal groundings shy away from appeals to foundational or universal principles. This means that a legal statute cannot by itself resolve the ambiguity that is found in most human affairs. Instead, it takes a group of judges to determine how a law is to be applied by reference to precedent (legal positivism), or by sensibility to consensus within the shared-community worldview of "the governed" (legal realism), or—in rare instances—by appeals to natural law.

Natural law is the position that asserts a synonymy between legal and moral law. Under this approach legislators are obliged not to violate the moral law when they create statutory law. Now most statutory law does not address moral issues. For example, the traffic laws on how fast one may drive are functionally determined with a view to public safety but, as such, do not possess a moral dimension. Thus, morality views these as permissions. Legislators can do what they want given the functional safety standards. But other laws may have moral import. Immigration laws and laws concerning equal opportunity and the like are not permissions. From the moral realist's perspective they interact with real ethical principles that exist universally. Because these principles are higher than any statutory law, they constitute the ultimate standard for judicial review.

When one enters the international sphere, the force of the legalistic approach is compromised even more because the various nation-states that sign some particular agreement (contractarianism) often represent a particular constituency at a particular moment in history. When a new head of state comes into power, he or she does not necessarily feel bound personally by the individual acts of a predecessor, and because there is no world government with executive or judicial power of enforcement, the signatories to international treaties are really subject to an honor system.[6] In practice this often means that weak countries must comply whereas rich and powerful countries comply at their pleasure.[7] When there is no one with the power to enforce contracts, the only reason any nation might be expected to comply would be its own self-interest, the particulars of which can be quite changeable as circumstances alter.

✳ Interest-Based Justification

A second perspective on human rights seeks a moral justification via an interest-based approach—that is, an interest in protecting one's *well-being*. Jonathan

Mann suggests, "The implicit question of the modern human rights movement is: 'what are the societal (and particularly governmental) roles and responsibilities to help promote individual and collective well-being?'"[8] People have an interest in—and right to—maintain and promote their well-being. If human rights is fundamentally concerned with well-being, then, following Joseph Raz, "'X has a right' if and only if X can have rights, and, other things being equal, an aspect of X's well-being (his interest) is a sufficient reason for holding some other person(s) to be under a duty."[9] The key issues here are how to assess a given individual's current or potential well-being, and how to balance individual well-being with the collective well-being. Is it in tune with the Table of Embeddedness? How do health care and public health figure in?[10] These are difficult questions. But the point of view is to take the worldview positions of typical individuals within a society and try to determine what is minimally necessary for them in order to achieve well-being. Much like the capabilities approach discussed in Chapter 3, the focus is on some end state. In whatever way that well-being is defined, then whatever it takes to achieve well-being within a society constitutes a ground for a legitimate rights claim. Because well-being is an abstract, subjective property, the means to the end product will also be more conceptual and subject to a variety of strategies to achieve a reasonable state of well-being in as many people as possible.

Advocates for this approach say that, compared to the legalistic approach (that is, oriented to particular cases), the interest-based grounding of human rights in well-being provides a more theoretical foundation (because it is grounded in achieving well-being), so that difficult ethical cases will be solved by theoretical principles and not by particular-to-the-moment legal decisions. Detractors assert that well-being is the responsibility of the agent. What *can* legitimately be claimed are the goods necessary for human agency, but after that the pursuit and achievement of well-being are up to the individual. This latter criticism in fact defines the third of our justifications for human rights: agency-based arguments.

✳ Agency-Based Justification

Agency-based justifications of human rights assert that policies to promote well-being are best served by identifying those specific goods most conducive to the pursuit of well-being. Some of those goods will be the biologically based, level-one basic goods listed in the Table of Embeddedness (Table 3.1), and some will be culturally based, level-two basic goods, such as the basic educational requirements within a society and the way one understands particular political liberties—such as the right to bear arms. Once one knows what these goods are, the issue becomes how to provide the goods to the people.[11]

The force of the agency basis of human rights rests upon the conditions necessary for humans to commit purposive action. From an agency-based perspective, the desire to commit purposive action—and especially to attain ends that the agent believes to be good—amounts to something close to human nature. Now, any of us can be mistaken about what truly constitutes the good. One person might think that having athletic prowess is to achieve the good. That person might sacrifice all to achieve it. But when the body ages or when injury occurs, this goal will be seen to be fleeting. Another might choose money or power. But the essential point is that the way you use your agency goods in your quest for the good is up to you. Within an agency-based perspective, then, it is the duty of others to facilitate your access to what you need to be at least a minimally effective actor in the world. The rest is up to you.

Interest-based and agency-based justifications certainly overlap, but they each approach the world with different foundational aims. The interest-based perspective looks at an end product—well-being—and tries to figure out what is needed to get there. The agency-based perspective looks to provide what is necessary to allow voluntary, purposive action to take place so that one might pursue his or her vision of the good. In the agency view, a state of well-being may well be a laudable goal, but the aim is to facilitate action, not to ensure a given outcome of that action.

Each theory describes a primitive level that would stand as a justificatory basis of public policy.

Applying Human Rights to the World

Human rights is one of the most controversial concepts in global ethics and justice today. Many countries (such as China, Burma, Saudi Arabia, Iran, Iraq, and Afghanistan) declare that talk of human rights is a cultural artifact of a specific time (i.e., the eighteenth-century Age of Enlightenment) and place (Europe) and thus is not a natural right at all but a constructed social institution. In that view, the promotion of human rights agendas constitutes cultural imperialism when applied to different countries around the world today. Such a controversy often pits the moral realists (who often support a single international standard) against the moral antirealists (who are skeptical of such a standard).

Thus, when countries (such as the People's Republic of China) assert that Western concepts of human rights should not be applied to them, they might be confronted by the universalist arguments of the moral realists while finding some support among the antirealists. What are we to do?

If we choose to justify human rights via the legalistic option, then the approach of legal realism would be one of the preferred choices of moral antirealists[12] as it assumes an interest in social norms, as they presently exist. Another moral antirealist approach would be legal positivism. In legal positivism, it is precedent that is decisive. The theoretical justification is that like cases should be treated in a like manner. Thus, one looks to the case law history in one's own tradition first and then in older historical traditions when one's own tradition does not give a clear outcome (that is, is incomplete). In the United States, for example, U.S. case law is examined first, then British case law. (Some practitioners even suggest going back to Roman law if the former two are indecisive.) Legal positivism does not work so well between cultural traditions because it is concerned with staying the course. Thus, in the international realm, a multiplicity of traditions that do not overlap eviscerate the effectiveness of this approach. Natural law would find supporters from the moral realism camp.

Between the interest-based or agency-based human rights, the former is more plastic to various cultural settings. This is because the reasonable preconditions for minimal well-being differ from society to society. What constitutes living a good life can have a strong cultural bent to it. If living the good life is synonymous with well-being, then the interest approach would be more culturally variable. However, the result will tend to support a statist approach (because states and individual cultures are taken to be the natural unit). Under the interest-based approach there is some flexibility in level-two basic goods and all secondary goods.

In contrast, the agency-based model begins with the biological conditions necessary for agency. These apply to any organism that is a member of *Homo sapiens.* The agency approach thus has a universalist (moral realist) bias to it. For proponents of moral realism this is a plus. All level-one basic goods may legitimately be claimed by everyone regardless of his or her membership in any particular society on earth because they are biologically based. The agency approach has some cultural variability in level-two basic goods (e.g., education and liberty rights) and level-one secondary goods (equal opportunity in the personal and community realms).

Each of these theories has arguments to support it. I recommend you take stock of your personal worldview in order to determine which of these justifications of human rights is persuasive.

If the cosmopolitan (who considers oneself first and foremost to be a citizen of the world above being a citizen of some particular country) wishes maximum flexibility in setting out the rule of law that gives the context for human rights, then the legalistic justification for human rights is the choice. If one wishes to move gently toward a "soft" universalism, then interest-based theories are preferable. Finally, if one wants some "hard" universalism (namely, level-one and level-two basic goods from the Table of Embeddedness), then the choice should be agency-based theories. Legalistic theories are inherently statist. Interest-based approaches can move either way, but the agency approach is firmly cosmopolitan. This is because it is rooted in a biological view of the essential conditions that permit purposive agency to pursue the good.

However, more needs to be said about the various cultural components of global ethics and justice. These will be taken up in the next chapter.

Key Terms

charity, human rights, legal justification of human rights, interest-based justification of human rights, agency-based justification of human rights

Critical Applied Reasoning Exercise

You must write a two-page memo to your boss at the World Bank to justify the loan to support a project to improve literacy among women of Country Z, which does not have a cultural tradition supporting the status of women. You need to first decide whether this initiative involves charity or a human right, and, if the latter, what sort of justification you will bring forth to support your case. Be specific.

Notes

1. Of course, several of the other justifications mentioned in Chapter 3 could also generate these stark human rights claims.

2. It should be clear by these remarks that I seek to strike a balance between the individual and community perspective; see Michael Boylan, *A Just Society* (Lanham, MD, and Oxford: Rowman and Littlefield, 2004): 130, 135 n 34.

3. Beth Singer makes this argument in *Operative Rights* (Albany, NY: SUNY Press, 1995).

4. Ibid.

5. My views on gun control are set out in Michael Boylan, "Gun Control in the USA: Ethical Perspectives for the 21st Century," *Clinical Orthopedics* 408, 1 (February 2003): 17–27.

6. The United Nations is a forum for discussion among many of the nations of the world. However, there is little strong power to punish big donor states who pay the fees that allow the UN to continue.

7. Several contemporary examples of the U.S. noncompliance with World Trade Organization rulings and regulations can be found at http://trade.ec.europa.eu.

8. Jonathan Mann, "Health and Human Rights," *British Medical Journal* 312 (1996): 924–925.

9. Joseph Raz, *The Morality of Freedom* (Oxford: Clarendon Press, 1986): 166.

10. For a discussion of this problem from the interest-based account, see Kristen Hessler, "Exploring the Philosophical Foundations of Human Rights" in *International Public Health Policy and Ethics,* ed. Michael Boylan (Dordrecht: Springer, 2008): 31–44.

11. For a more formal presentation of this, see Boylan, *A Just Society,* ch. 3; and Alan Gewirth, *Reason and Morality* (Chicago: University of Chicago Press, 1978): 135–145.

12. This terminology can be confusing. The term *realist* in legal realism refers to the empirical realism of cultural positions that exist in a country at any given time. Under this theory of law it is the duty of the judiciary to interpret the law according to current cultural preferences. For example, sodomy laws were upheld by the U.S. Supreme Court until cultural acceptance of the rights of homosexuals gained ascendancy. After this, the Court changed its rulings. By contrast, "realist" in moral realism refers to the real ontological existence of moral objects such as "good." The moral realists would consider the legal realists as being moral antirealists.

CHAPTER 5

Culture and Religion

The role played by different cultures and religions is one of the most important problems to confront when assessing the proper state of global ethics and justice. Many people consider religion to be a part of culture. I separate the two because of the unique role that religion plays in the lives of most people of the world in their understanding about what is true, which I take to be different from what is conventional—that is, culture. Accordingly, this chapter looks first at the issue of cultural and ethical relativism as it relates to morality and justice. It then turns to the claims of religion and how they, too, bear on morality and justice. The chapter ends with a brief examination of a clear clash of Eastern and Western cultures on the issue of human rights.

Cultural Relativism

Do you take sugar in your tea? Would it offend you if someone ate his hot dog with his left hand? Should married men grow beards? What do you think about veils and headscarves? These are just a few examples of customs that have real meaning to various societies on earth. The tendency to allow such difference in behavior flows from the freedom of human action (supported in Chapter 2 when the behaviors are in accord with the personal worldview imperative). Basic freedoms are a level-two basic good in the Table of Embeddedness (Table 3.1). Some flexibility in dealing with others within the context of their social traditions is therefore a good thing. To trump such level-two freedoms—such as prima facie rights to individual autonomy—one would have to appeal to even more embedded rights—that is, to the rights of access to level-one basic goods. Barring such a level-one appeal, all people whose actions do not violate the personal or community worldview imperatives should be allowed to do what they desire. Let us call this legitimate cultural relativism. Under this form of *cultural relativism* the practices in question are either moral obligations (that which we are ethically obliged to do), or moral permissions (that which we are permitted to do or not to do, according to our whim).

Two features are often brought forward to legitimate cultural practices:

1. The voluntary nature of the act and the compliance of the parties: Do all of the parties participate in the practice of their own volition, without coercion or deception?
2. The historical heritage of the practice: Has the practice been an integral part of that culture for some time?

But often there is confusion on just what a practice actually consists of and whether it really falls within the bounds of morality. Some of this confusion may be linguistic and thus involve misunderstanding. The Islamic term *jihad* is an example of linguistic ambiguity. Among Islamic believers, jihad has traditionally been concerned with concentrated attention and renewal at the personal and social level. It has often been a part of one's personal observation of fasting during the month of Ramadan or going on pilgrimage to the holy city of Mecca. However, because of our war-torn world today, jihad is often associated with high-pitched declarations of violence against non-Muslims. This latter usage is atypical when viewed in the larger historical context, but it is easy to see how a term or phrase adopted from one language to another can evoke reactions that may not be entirely accurate.

At other times, a culturally accepted practice is nonetheless an ethical prohibition, or what I would call illegitimate cultural relativism. For example, the practice of female genital mutilation (sometimes mistakenly called female circumcision) has a deep cultural past in some North African societies. Performed by older women on the younger women, the practice is intended to make sexual intercourse painful for women so that when they become wives, they are not inclined to cheat on their husbands (though there is no analogous practice that is performed upon men).[1] Female genital mutilation (1) is done with the apparent consent of the young women and (2) has a long cultural history. Does this mean it's an instance of legitimate cultural relativism?

Moral Relativism

In order to be clearer about these issues, we need to define the moral realm. I argued in Chapter 1 for a "hard" definition of *ethics* as the science of the right and wrong of human action. Other accounts soften this claim to something like the *perceived* or *recognized* right and wrong of human action. This latter, "softer" claim really accepts *moral relativism*, which believes that ethics is about codifying what it is that particular social and cultural practices praise and condemn, while also noting that such practices vary according to place and time. Moral relativism is often a feature of the normative theories depicted as *moral antirealism.*[2] The antirealist is committed to some variety of moral relativism (at least between cultures).[3] This approach basically appeals to what *seems right*—or is perceived or recognized as right—within a society. The imperative is to ascertain the cultural landscape via language and perceived practices and then to adapt practices to that landscape.

In contrast, the claim that ethics is the science of right or wrong is a stronger claim based on moral realism. It is here that the word *science* comes to play. If the groundwork of moral imperatives has a factual basis, then its discovery is a science—rather than a guess or intuition, or the social study that is the province of the antirealists.

Let's briefly look at the attraction that each theory has, for the acceptance of one or the other of these approaches will affect one's approach to the problems discussed in Part Three. Antirealists believe that we cannot get beyond the normative givens in our culture. These cultural trappings include language and established practices. The task of the individual is to discern what a given culture approves of, and then to do it. Ethics, in this context, is a rather descriptive exercise. The ethicist is on par with the cultural anthropologist. The normative function comes from the givens of the society and is not really subject to change (unless there are contradictory imperatives existing side by side incoherently).[4]

Realists, in comparison, think that we can supersede our particular culture, historical era, or other social descriptions. For example, in the United States from around 1830 onward there was a growing popular movement against human slavery. Abolitionists—those who sought to abolish slavery—fought against what had been for more than 220 years an accepted state of affairs in the United States and which had existed for even longer in Europe. (Most of the decision-makers in the United States during this time period came from Europe or were European descendants.)

How was it that abolitionists rose up to be a major social force? The advocates of slavery pointed to religious documents such as the Bible to justify the practice of slavery. The abolitionists also cited the Bible and other religious documents but interpreted them differently, based upon a community worldview that created a different hierarchy of primary ethical principles than those professed by the advocates of slavery. Each side had their own reading of the passages. Thus, there seemed to be no intersubjective criteria for adjudication. Because of this impasse in argumentation, the fate of slavery became a political problem (that eventually led to the Civil War in the 1860s).[5]

It is a frequent consequence of those who do *not* believe in moral realism that the end result of disputed questions about human action devolves into who has the stronger political hand: Might makes right. If you can control the political climate, then in a descriptive sense *you are right*. "Right" means what is anthropologically accepted due to conditions of social and political power dynamics.

It is important to separate this question from the one that asks, "who controls the rules in the society?" For the antirealists, it's all about power dynamics. When you are in power, whatever you do is right. This is because right is the same thing as having public opinion, the laws, and the police on your side. In the case of slavery—with the 1850 Fugitive Slave Law, which required even citizens of states where slavery was outlawed to return escaped slaves to their masters in slave states, and the Supreme Court's 1856 Dred Scott decision, which ruled that slaves were merely property without the rights of human beings—it was clear that the power was on the side of the slavery advocates. The power structure supported their claims. Did this mean it was *right*? Does the concept of *right* have any meaning apart from what is the status quo?

The abolitionists believed that slavery was not a matter of historical tradition, linguistics, or cultural givens. Rather, it was an issue that could be debated upon the factual merits of the place of liberty in the hierarchy of legitimate claims that people may make against the society in which they live. The abolitionists were passionate that slavery anywhere at any time was *always* evil.

You must decide for yourself whether moral realism or moral antirealism is correct. Ultimately, your belief will determine your answer to the moral relativism question and condition your responses to the problems described in Part Three.

World Religions

Religion is an important part of culture. Religion presents itself to people in two ways:

1. As a source of truth about what is.
2. As a means to instill that truth into the structure of daily life.

For clarity let us call the first sense of religion *theology* and use the second sense to refer to the establishment of social institutions that aspire to translate theological truths into patterns of personal, social, and sometimes political life.

In one important aspect, theology is like philosophy. Both profess to be about what is true. Both set out many foundational posits that cannot be defended by externalist measures. For example, philosophy holds that a proposition and its opposite cannot both be true at the same time. For example, one cannot be at the same time pregnant and not pregnant; either one is or one is not pregnant. But how do we know this? This fundamental law of logic is taken on faith.

The parallel in theology is that there exists something that is true (often called God) that is separate from and higher than us. But how do we know this? The fundamental axiom of theology is taken on faith.

Though in the most abstract form these two are similar, the fleshing out of what follows is often rather different. Theology takes the form of religion, in which the application of the theory begins by regarding sacred texts as the source of truth. But because of the inevitable ambiguities of language and interpretation, someone must come forward to set out an action-guiding version of the texts. However, because these texts are rendered via the critic's internal theory of knowledge, there is not a common moment that all can share; each person must accept a particular interpretation on faith, but without an intersubjective means of agreement, not all people will necessarily accept the *same* interpretation.

A common problem in ethics occurs when one person declares a religious vision that violates the ethical. The book of Genesis, for example, relates that God spoke to Abraham and told him to kill his son, Isaac, as a sacrifice to God—an act that Abraham, following God's command, set out to do, until he was stopped by an angel. The New York serial killer Son of Sam (David Berkowitz) heard what he took to be authoritative voices emanating from a dog that commanded him to shoot and kill people, which he did. Both Abraham and Berkowitz claimed that they were supernaturally commanded to commit murder. How does the community ascertain an authentic vision from a homicidal delusion? Because the intuition is personal, there is no way for the community to comment on its authenticity. The problem in social/political philosophy occurs when religious leaders proclaim their personal interpretation of the religion as applied to ethical or to social/political action. Again, how are we to evaluate their vision whether women should wear burkas or whether adulterers should be stoned to death? Because policy resides in a religious/political leader as a private revelation, there is no way socially to evaluate it.

In the case of philosophy, the application of the theory is externalist—for those of us who espouse a realistic epistemology (theory of knowledge). It thus asserts an externalist tie to real-world sensory experience that is available to other members of the community as well, such that their sensory experiences in common solidify claims to truth. This is the basic approach of natural science. Because most of our sensory experiences seem to be largely similar to others (especially when measured by an agreed-upon device—like a ruler to measure length), we feel very comfortable with this type of presentation. This is precisely the sort of externalist epistemology that makes claims in philosophy trump those of religion in cases of conflict.[6] Thus when religious leaders contradict what philosophical morality dictates, people should, I would contend, follow philosophy over religion.

Thus, religion has a place in culture as both a source of truth and a social means for applying such truth to the community. However, in this second function, it is my contention that religion must act as the follower of philosophy. In cases of conflict, moral philosophy should outweigh the claims of private religious revelation.

East Versus West

Certainly there seems to be a divide of sorts between the way some moral obligations are viewed in the West versus the way they are seen in the East. A key example is human rights. One view purported by Beth Singer suggests that human rights only become *operative* when they are successfully claimed and made into law by their society.[7] Thus, according to Singer, the people of China (who may never have had a robust tradition of recognizing human rights but rather emphasize Confucian virtues of service and duty to others) do not have any human rights as such until people in the society, through publicity and dialogue, obtain general consent for recognizing that right. When it is recognized, the right is possessed. The recognition occurs through formal and informal institutions that prescribe behavior.

Other philosophers (such as myself) support a universalist approach. We believe that though Singer may be correct *descriptively* in the way social/political change occurs, her position begs the question of *why* people feel they are justified in making a rights claim in the first place. I have argued in Chapter 3 that one can construct an argument on the moral status of basic goods and ensuing justified-rights claims.

Despite one's approach to the controversy on whether there is or is not a naturalistic grounding for human rights, there still exists the practical problem of how we can confront a society that has not had a tradition of human rights and somehow help it transition to a state of affairs where such rights are recognized. Using Thailand as an example, Charles Taylor gives one interesting account of how these sorts of social/political transitions might occur.[8]

1. Rawls believes that progress on human rights will only come about when there is overlapping consensus on what human rights are and how they should be applied—Assertion
2. The biggest hurdle to this is the distance between Western and Eastern traditions—Assertion

3. [If a natural bridge on human rights can be found between Western and Eastern traditions, real progress on human rights can be realized][9]—1, 2

4. The Western tradition is established upon the Christian Natural Law tradition that came into fruition in the eighteenth century's affirmation of subjective rights—Assertion

5. The Eastern tradition is established upon Confucianism, which is community oriented, and Islam, which supports harsh punishments—Assertion

6. [To bridge the two traditions some amelioration must occur within the native frameworks of the conflicting societies]—4, 5

7. Human-rights claims are sources of conflict, for they pit groups against each other, thus undermining the community—Assertion

8. In the traditional Thai community the king establishes dharma (the laws of the universe)—Assertion

9. [For there to be accommodation in Thailand, the community and origin of law must be modified]—7, 8

10. Reformed Buddhism supports the individual quest for enlightenment and supports reform from the people for social justice—Assertion

11. Reformed Buddhism offers an avenue of accommodation for Thailand—9, 10

12. The doctrine of *ahimsa* and the movement toward gender equality offer Asian countries individual awareness and nonviolent social change—Assertion

13. The doctrine of *ahimsa* and the movement toward gender equality offer an avenue of accommodation for Asia—9, 12

14. The loving nature of God in the Qur'an can modify the harshness of the prescribed punishments in the shari'a—Assertion

15. The loving nature of God in the Qur'an can offer an avenue of accommodation among Muslims—9, 14

16. The norms, legal forms, and background justifications for a consensus on human rights can come from religious and cultural traditions—6, 9, 11, 13, 15

---

17. Progress on human rights is possible through overlapping consensus that comes from religious and cultural traditions—3, 16

Taylor's argument is important because it moves us away from a "who is right and who is wrong?" perspective to a "how can we ameliorate cultural perspectives?" He draws upon John Rawls's influential book *The Law of Peoples* and believes that when one is envisioning realistic change, one must begin with points in common.[10] If we look at Taylor's prescription as a series of tactics (regardless of whether one is a realist or an antirealist), then we have an insight into how we might bring about community recognition of human rights where it hadn't existed before.

Why is this important? The answer is that we must do more than merely debate these topics. Philosophers must be on the vanguard of progressive social change. In my short stay in a policy think tank at the Center for American Progress in Washington, D.C., I learned a lot about the practical way policy is formed in the U.S. Congress. The center sponsors the writing of policy papers and then selectively lobbies for some of them to bring about actual change. This is the way policy and laws are made in the United States. It was my passion there to introduce philosophical theory into the mix. I sought to base my policy forays on principles inherent in *A Just Society.* I had limited success. Taylor's argument is an exercise in this sort of policy creation.

So often in philosophy we write for an academic journal that has a circulation just beyond our range of friends and acquaintances. But what if the policies we are debating in these pages actually comes to be? This should be our goal in ethics (a field of practical philosophy). In the tradition of Socrates, Zola, Sartre, Gandhi, and King, I am advocating that my readers aspire to more! We must reclaim a forum for public dialogue amidst the self-interested lobbyists. The way to understand and to confront these issues is to seriously examine one's understanding of his or her personal worldview and then to situate oneself into his or her micro, macro, and extended communities. Where do you find yourself? What are your duties?

Turn to Chapter 6.

Key Terms

cultural relativism, moral relativism, religion and ethics

Critical Applied Reasoning Exercise

You are an employee of Google and are stationed in China. The Chinese government wants to bring your company into the largest Internet market in the world. However, its administrators have some particular demands. They want you to offer e-mail service and to allow the government to be able to data mine the e-mail communications of private citizens for key terms such as "Tiananmen Square." You know that these various terms might be found in e-mails of human rights activists. Your company wants to be the first on the ground in China. But you also don't want to be the agent of brutal police state policies. What do you do? Use some of the language of cultural analysis found in this chapter.

Notes

1. Notice the linguistic spin. Describing the procedure as "female circumcision" brings it into a familiar context to male circumcision (a Jewish custom that many Christians also observe). The difference is that in male circumcision only the foreskin of the penis is removed; no function is impaired. This is an example of linguistic confusion in cultural relativity.

2. For a brief introduction to some of the issues in the moral realism v. antirealism debate, see these publications by antirealists: Simon Blackburn, *Essays in Quasi-Realism* (Oxford: Oxford University Press, 1993); Gilbert Harman, "Moral Relativism Defended," *Philosophical Review* (1975): 3–22; and R. M. Hare, *The Language of Morals* (Oxford: Oxford University Press, 1952). Compare them with the works of moral realists: Christine Korsgaard, *The Sources of Normativity* (New York: Cambridge University Press, 1996); Alan Gewirth, *Reason and Morality* (Chicago: University of Chicago Press, 1978); Christian Illies, *The Grounds of Ethical Judgement* (Oxford: Clarendon Press, 2003); and Michael Boylan, *A Just Society* (Lanham, MD: Rowman and Littlefield, 2004).

3. There is, of course, the response that the moral antirealist does *not* deny that there may be universal moral principles across time and space, but merely that it would be impossible to *know* that these exist. It would not be unfair (based upon their own terms of discourse) to move to the conclusion that such universals do not exist unless there is some empirical base to which said claim could be verified.

4. Of course, even if one were to discover that incoherent premises existed side by side, it would not solve the problem of which one to choose.

5. Whether the Civil War in the United States was fought over slavery is a disputed question. For an overview of some of these issues, see Philip Van Doren Stern, *Life and Writings of Abraham Lincoln* (New York: Modern Library, 1999); and Chandra Manning, *What This Cruel War Was Over: Soldiers, Slavery, and the Civil War* (New York: Vintage, 2008).

6. Boylan, *A Just Society,* 71–77.

7. Beth Singer, *Operative Rights* (Albany, NY: SUNY Press, 1993).

8. Charles Taylor, "Conditions of an Unforced Consensus on Human Rights," in *The East Asian Challenge for Human Rights,* ed. Joanne R. Bauer and Daniel A. Bell (Cambridge: Cambridge University Press, 1999): 124–144.

9. Bracketed premises denote suppressed premises or enthymemes that are necessary to generate a tight inference but are not found in the text itself.

10. I make a similar point in describing how social/political change occurs in *A Just Society,* ch. 1, where I set out a multistep process that has as its focus an *overlap and modification* dynamic.

CHAPTER 6

Justice, the State, and the World

Justice primarily concerns *distributive justice,* in which we consider how goods and services ought to be distributed to the peoples of the world. The secondary concern of justice concerns *retributive justice,* in which states or other groups seek redress for real or perceived harms. This chapter addresses these two aspects of justice within the context of how we are to understand what the world looks like. Of particular interest will be the question of whether arguments for the moral status of basic goods (see Chapter 3) rely on membership within states, or not.

The Nature of States

The world parses itself into sovereign entities called states or nations. What are states? For our purposes,

> States will be considered to be cultural/social sovereign macro communities that have established, recognized, robust geographical boundaries for the sake of commerce and common purpose.

The ideal state recognizes and advances the cultural traditions and values of the society, and represents its people in a truly responsive way. The Preamble to the U.S. Constitution, for example, defines succinctly what the founders intended the new government to accomplish responsively for its citizens: "establish justice, ensure domestic tranquility, provide for the common defense, promote the general welfare, and secure the blessings of liberty to ourselves and our posterity."

The modifier *recognized* in the definition of the state is important, then. Some claimants to the title of state violate the internationally recognized codes of civic conduct (such as by violating human rights[1] or engaging in aggressive military behavior against their own people) and are thus considered by other nations of the world to be outlaw states. These states may exhibit other features of statehood—such as having robust geographical boundaries for the purposes of commerce—but there is no common purpose because the government of the state does not responsively represent its people and may, in fact, be actively engaged in repressing the people in order to maintain power.

By *represent* I mean that the cultural traditions and values of that society (including religion) should be truly considered by the country's rulers. Ironically, perhaps, it is often true that theocracies—even though claiming to represent a divine moral force within government—nonetheless fail to represent their people. After the fall of the Soviet-supported government in Afghanistan, for example, the Taliban—a fundamentalist Islamic movement—filled the power vacuum to create an Islamist theocracy. However, the manner of the government's management of the country's affairs did not seem to represent the society and culture of Afghanistan.[2] For example, since the 1960s Afghanistan had significant representation of women in government. Women had some discretion in public dress and educational opportunities (primary and some secondary). When the Taliban took over, women were removed from government and public life. Their public dress was dictated and educational opportunities were restricted.[3] Another example of changing the culture is in the Taliban's attitude toward art. Afghanistan has a rich tradition of artistic expression in music, painting, and sculpture. But the Taliban took the Decalogue's prohibition "you shall not make an idol" to refer generally to art. They even dynamited an old and venerated statue of Buddha on this very principle.[4] These are just two examples of how the Taliban sought to transform the society to meet the rulers' ideological beliefs. Just because a theocracy takes power does not mean that such a government is responsive to the culture and social/political wishes of the citizens of that country. Often, it is the case that such aspiring nations are not recognized by other states. This lack of recognition illustrates that they are not fully actualized states.

The *nation-state* is a rather modern invention. Smaller political units such as tribes and chiefdoms dominated much of human history.[5] Populations in these micro communities often traveled about in search of game to hunt, whereas other micro communities established agricultural patterns that required them to stay in a place until crops were harvested. Such micro communities differed from states because they generally did not possess robust geographical boundaries. Membership in tribes and chiefdoms is based primarily on kinship among the members rather than on allegiance to a geographical entity, as is the case in states.

In earlier times when communications were carried on by foot or horse, most states were small. The famous polities of ancient Greece, such as Athens and Sparta, were in fact city-states, as were Venice, Florence, and Genoa in Italy of the Middle Ages and Renaissance.

The rise of the macro nation-state began with military conquest and empires. In the Western tradition the empire of Alexander the Great and the Roman Empire were the model. In the Middle East the Turkish, Persian, Babylonian, and Islamic empires also fit the bill. In Africa some prominent examples were from Nubia (Egypt), Mali, Songhai, Aksum, and Zimbabwe. In the Americas prominent empires included Mayan, Aztec, and Inca. In Asia two prominent empires were the Mongol and Tang.

Ancient empires, such as those of Alexander the Great and the Roman Empire, were comprised of smaller states, kingdoms, and other territories that were dominated by a ruling central entity that was ethnically and culturally distinct from its subjects. The control exerted by the ruling authority of an empire was often indirect and slight, commonly consisting of reliance on local governors in the distant dominions to exact tribute and forward it to the central authority. However, and especially as means of travel and communication improved, the level of control also increased. The largest empire in history, the British Empire of the eighteenth through twentieth centuries, maintained control of colonies and other territories all around the world.

The modern nation-state is arguably a product of eighteenth- and nineteenth-century European nationalist movements that argued that each "people" or "nation" deserved its own country or state. The concept thus combines geography with culture and ethnicity, such that Italy is the nation formed from the unification of hitherto independent Italian-speaking kingdoms and city-states in the second half of the nineteenth century and Germany is the nation formed from the unification of numerous German-speaking states about the same time.

The nation-state claims absolute sovereignty over the people within its borders and defends those borders against the claims of other states. In many instances these nationalistic claims were advanced as movements (and wars) of independence against dominant powers such as the Austro-Hungarian, Russian, or Ottoman empires. Thus the origins of the modern nation-state are steeped in blood, both to win independence and to annex disputed territories to the state.

Some individuals believe that the landscape provides a sort of natural justification for state boundaries. These natural boundaries, which include rivers, mountain ranges, and oceans, may be pleasing to the geologically inclined among us, but they are problematic. Why is this so? Well, for one thing, there are no tags from God on whether one river or another constitutes a natural boundary. Why one mountain range or another? The Mississippi River once was the western boundary of the

United States. Then Manifest Destiny—another name for legitimated conquest—came into play, and the U.S. western boundary came to be the Pacific Ocean (and ultimately, beyond).

In his *Second Treatise of Government* (1690), John Locke argues that, by virtue of the work they perform to extract and transform the resources of the natural world, people make that portion of the world their own property:

> Though the earth and all inferior creatures be common to all men, yet every man has a "property" in his own "person." This nobody has any right to but himself. The "labour" of his body and the "work" of his hands, we may say, are properly his. Whatsoever, then, he removes out of the state that Nature hath provided and left it in, he hath mixed his labour with it, and joined to it something that is his own, and thereby makes it his property.

Furthermore, because the property belongs to the worker who created it, no one else can rightfully claim it:

> It being by him removed from the common state Nature placed it in, it hath by this labour something annexed to it that excludes the common right of other men. For this "labour" being the unquestionable property of the labourer, no man but he can have a right to what that is once joined to.[6]

In the light of a Lockean interpretation of property claims, what are we to make of the extensive historical record of military conquest in the formation and expansion of states? Can one community secede from another, declaring itself a new state and removing with it a portion of the territories formerly belonging to that larger state? Under what conditions, if any, can a state legitimately claim and seize for itself some or all of the territory claimed by other people, whether those others are organized within a state or not?

In the case of the United States of America, the country's western boundary was extended by the Louisiana Purchase of 1803. Soon, the concept of Manifest Destiny came to express the informal doctrine that the expanding nation had a God-given right—even a duty—to acquire the remaining lands even farther to the west, extending to the Pacific Coast. In part, Manifest Destiny was invoked to ensure that the western regions did not fall irretrievably into the hands of the European powers, Britain and Spain (and then Mexico, after its independence from Spain), which might pose a military threat to the young nation. But Manifest Destiny also implied a policy of armed aggression to displace the native peoples who lived on the land and "owned" it in Locke's sense of making active use of the land and its resources.

As Locke purported, the forceful seizure of another's property is unjustified. It is a violation of a commonly held principle of distributive justice: protection from unwarranted bodily harm (a level-one basic good). This miscarriage of distributive justice in turn calls for a response entailing some form of retributive justice (that is, giving back what was unjustly taken).[7]

So why is there so much unjustified taking in the history of the world, and what are we to do about it? This is an important question. It involves some of the root concepts in distributive and retributive justice. In the first case, what is a just distribution of land and resources? For the most part this question is asked of groups of people (micro or—more generally—macro communities). To ask such a question of a group through its social/political means of communication generally involves thinking of the group's interest or (in the case of a dictator) thinking of the dictator's personal interest. In the former case, some instance of due diligence will require a consideration of the interests of the entire community. In the latter case, it will be only a factor in the decision-making process of the often pathologically narcissistic ruler.

In either case an unjustified taking (following Locke's assumptions) is a violation of a commonly held principle of distributive justice: protection from unwarranted bodily harm (a level-one basic good). This miscarriage of distributive justice obviously entails a response in retributive justice (the giving back of what was unjustly taken).

What do people think of this kind of injustice? In my experience, people generally accept the brute reality of military conquest as representing an accomplished fact. But why is this? I assume it follows the principle that "might is right." Those who can snatch things for themselves earn the right to those things. I have called this justification *kraterism,* after the ancient Greek word for the exercise of power, *kratos/krattein.* One could call a country ruled by kraterism a *kratocracy* (in contrast to a democracy, which is the rule by the people).

In abstract theory, the solution is simple: If the United States unjustly took land from native nations, it should give the lands back to those peoples. But we all know that will never happen, for that would involve wrongly taking land away from the people who have since owned and used it. Right?

I suppose in this case that the *wrong* is, in fact, a *right.* So let us say that Country A invades Country B and rules over it. What should the position of Country B be? The ethical issues involved depend upon the ethical theory that is used to evaluate the situation. For example, if one were an antirealist ethical intuitionist, then the answer would be whatever the decisionmaker felt about the situation. If one were an antirealist ethical noncognitivist or antirealist virtue ethics advocate, then the answer would rely upon the culture of the winning side. If one were an antirealist contractarian, then it might be assumed that some sort of peace treaty would be the basis of the ongoing status. But if one were an ethical realist utilitarian, then a utility calculation would be taken among all people involved (both the victor and the vanquished) considering both short- and long-term consequences (long-term consequences might include how the victor might feel if it were on the other side). The ethical realist deontologist would try to discern which moral principles are at stake and which duties ensue.

Regardless of the moral theory lens applied, in most cases the people in Country B dislike the takeover. We can ignore cases in which the conquered people are happy over their lot. But what about the discontents? Let's look at some historical examples.

The Celtic people of Cornwall warred often with the English Saxons, and by the late tenth century Cornwall had been made a part of England. There were popular uprisings in 1497 and 1549, but by the time of the English Civil War (1624–1651) the Cornish largely thought of themselves as English. When Prime Minister Tony Blair offered limited devolution of power to Cornwall in the late 1990s, the Cornish representatives turned him down, explaining that they had been assimilated into English culture and society.[8]

In another example, the Celtic people of Ireland were subjugated by Henry II of England in the late twelfth century, and Edward I extended English rule over Celtic Wales and Scotland a century later. However, English rule was tenuous and was challenged frequently by nationalist uprisings. Ireland eventually gained partial independence in 1922 (though the status of Northern Ireland continues to be an issue of some dispute). Scotland fought regularly against the English and still sports a Scottish Independence Party. Though Ireland, Scotland, and Wales participate with England in the United Kingdom, in important respects these Celtic peoples have never been fully assimilated into English culture or the English polity. Many within Ireland, Scotland, and Wales have maintained separate cultural traditions (including language) as well as a considerable degree of formal political autonomy. They were not assimilated.

Some nations exist in exile, divorced from the exercise of power and sometimes even from the territory that is a defining criterion of the state. For example, Sein Fein (the political arm of the Irish nationalism movement) was a shadow government in domestic exile. It claimed to be the legitimate government of Ireland but was not recognized and was not in power. Still, Sein Fein kept itself separate from the Irish Republican Army. Another example was the exiled government of Charles II of England. Charles left for France after his father (Charles I) was beheaded in 1649 during the English civil war, in which the antiroyalists took power. From exile, Charles maintained his claim that he was England's legitimate ruler and waited for an opportunity to return and reclaim power—which he eventually did in 1660. His is an example of a government that had neither international recognition nor sovereignty within the country but yet continued to claim legitimacy for itself.

In the wake of the communist conquest of China, Tibet was also conquered. Its people's spiritual leader, the Fourteenth Dalai Lama, was forced into exile, and many political leaders fled to Nepal. In 2010 the Nobel Prize Committee gave its peace prize to Liu Xiaobo, an imprisoned advocate of democracy in the People's Republic of China and an advocate for a free Tibet.

Also of interest are the conditions of promoting commerce and common purpose within the context of the social macro community. The measure of this is the interest in the good of the nation's citizens. This means that any legitimate state must establish some mechanism whereby an interactive relationship can occur between the government and the people such that the sovereign power exists for the sake of the people and not vice versa. Instances in which the sovereign asserts power in such a way that the legitimacy of the ruling authority is indistinguishable from that of the state itself are taken to be *dictatorships.* Unless the dictator creates interactive relationships with the people such that the well-being of the people and not the dictator is primary, the state will be classified as an outlaw government—one in which the legitimate purposes of ruling via the interests of the people through open and interactive means are not maintained. Many of the countries in Africa, Asia, and South America fall under this category, representing a sizeable portion of the world's population.[9]

These various cases illustrate some of the complexities involved in understanding nationhood. What follows from this? First, that the status of nationhood is not all that simple. The communities and their institutions that make up the state exist within a milieu that provides its members more or less of the basic goods of agency, but no society in the world provides its citizens with the ideal: level-one and level-two basic goods of agency and level-one secondary goods. The question then becomes, "against whom should rights-claims for basic goods of agency be made?" Should it be against the citizens of a given society? Or against all those in the world who are able to be of assistance? In the first case we have a purely statist model of the kind we have been discussing whereas in the latter instance we have a cosmopolitan conception.

Cosmopolitanism

The word *cosmopolitanism* implies that one's *polis* (or state) is the *cosmos* (for our purposes here, the world). The cosmopolitan considers himself to be a citizen of the world. But what does this mean, and how does it affect legitimate rights claims?

On the one hand, the argument for the moral status of basic goods in Chapter 3 seems not to be oriented toward membership in any given state. There is no mention of particular national citizenship in any of the premises. This would suggest that the rights-claim is against all people on the earth subject to their ability to contribute (the "ought implies can" caveat). Let us accept this.

The moral status of basic goods argument is generally interpreted as an argument for *positive duties* in response to legitimate rights-claims. That is, the state has a moral obligation to provide basic goods and services to those making legitimate claims for them. However, it need not stop there. *Negative duties* are also involved: People must compensate victims for the deleterious consequences of their actions. This is generally interpreted as recompense for loss of life, limb, or money.[10] If Community A harms Community B, then Community A must recompense Community B for its losses. (More on this in the last section of this chapter.)

Thus, it seems that a cosmopolitan interpretation of the argument on the moral status of basic goods requires that positive and negative duties be fulfilled. But how will this take place? What is the mechanism of enforcement? At the moment there is no world government. The United Nations and its subsidiary bodies can make judgments, but as we have seen earlier, the enforcement of its judgments upon the richer countries—such as the United States—amounts to a voluntary action on their part. If, for example, the United States doesn't want to comply with a World Trade Association ruling, there is no authority to compel it to do so. The same is true regarding other wealthy and powerful members. Though the organization aspires to more, at present the only authority the United Nations has over its wealthier members is voluntary. Poorer nations are subject more to economic and political pressures to comply with the will of the wealthier countries.

Barring a universal world government, the next best bet would be regional organizations and treaties. But these fare no better. So what is the solution? At present there are two sorts of solutions: governmental (tax financed) and nongovernmental (voluntarily financed) provision of basic goods to those who require them. The first is largely entrenched in the nation model whereas the latter can be cosmopolitan because it draws upon contributions internationally.

But the garnering of funds is really only half the battle. The other half is getting the goods to the people. This is trickier than it might at first seem. Distribution must be accomplished through the model of nations, which means the presiding government will have jurisdiction over the distribution of any aid to its people, no matter whether the aid arrives via the UN (and its various arms), individual governments, nongovernmental organizations (NGOs), or individual actions on behalf of a limited number of other individuals. This has been problematic in the past. Medicine, food, clothing, and other forms of aid must often pass through agencies of the local government on their way to be distributed to the people. This would be fine if the aid actually reached the people. Too many times, though, these goods are diverted and sold on the open or black markets to line the pockets of corrupt officials.

Also, many nations are sensitive about receiving aid. They wish to conceal from their own people that the aid came from the outside, because the acceptance of outside aid can be seen as an implicit acknowledgment that the resident state is deficient. Even (or especially) in impoverished nations, the cloak of nationhood is very important—even if the cloak is threadbare—which means that unreceptive governments sometimes block even desperately needed aid to their people. Often local nations block the four forms of delivering aid: via the UN (and its various arms), individual governments, NGOs, and individual action on behalf of a limited number of other individuals. Unreceptive governments can block this aid. They can also try to steal it or otherwise divert its purpose. Because of this, the specter of nationhood has a practical importance in the world today—especially as it applies to the interests of those in power within the states, whether they be political or economic minions.

Cosmopolitanism, in practice, is thus a tag that variously applies to those who have nothing left to lose and to those (in the four categories of aid givers) who consider themselves moved to realize the aims of the argument on the moral status of basic goods.[11]

Distributive Justice

I consider five prominent theories of international distributive justice: *kraterism, unfettered capitalism, aristocracy, socialism,* and *egalitarianism*.[12]

Kraterism

Kraterism comes from the ancient Greek word *kratos* (n.), *krattein* (v.), meaning power or the powerful snatching of something for one's own use. I use the term to refer to a system of distributive justice, "to each according to his ability to snatch it for his own use." This is the most common system of distributive justice in the world. The powerful find ways of taking a very large share for themselves on the basis of their ability to do so and get away with it. Laws are no object. The true kraterist can get away with anything. If he's caught and punished, then he never was a real kraterist.

Unfettered Capitalism

Laissez-faire capitalism is similar to kraterism with the added suggestion that the invisible hand of the market will solve the excesses of bald kraterism because market competitors will keep each other in check out of self-interest. Unfettered capitalism operates according to this distribution formula: "to each according to his valued work." This maxim is often misinterpreted as "to each according to his work." The adjective *valued* is key because there are many excellent hardworking practitioners who earn less money than mediocre slackers who are employed in socially valued areas—such as professional sports, entertainment, or some sinecures in finance, business, or law. Black market drug dealers are among the most highly compensated sales force in the United States. Rather than due to excellence and hard work, their financial success is the result of fitting into market demands. The upside to capitalism is its efficiency; its downside is its lack of social responsibility.

Aristocracy

Aristocratic theory suggests that goods and services in society should be allocated according to one's birth into either money or social status, or (commonly) both. Throughout the world, one's parents and their social and political influence are important factors in one's ability to succeed. With low inheritance taxes in most countries, great sums of wealth can be passed on to children who have done nothing to deserve it but were simply fortunate to be born to that family.[13] Thus the distribution formula is, "to each according to his inherited station or bank account." Advocates say that this system instills continuity and the shared history of success.

Socialism

Socialist theory advocates distributing goods according to need. In order to eliminate the subjective aspect of need, some specification of needs is required concerning what constitutes categories that will be publicly recognized—such as the Table of Embeddedness presented in Chapter 3. For example, Society X might make it a national goal to give all citizens level-one basic goods. In the international arena, a similar calculation can be made—such as the UN's Millennium Goals for development: ending poverty and hunger, combating HIV/AIDS, and promoting universal education, gender equality, child health, maternal health, environmental sustainability, and global partnerships. The distribution formula is "to each according to his or her needs." Advocates of this approach focus on some sort of rights-based argument or ethical intuitionism. Detractors say that the problem is intranational and not international.

Egalitarianism

Egalitarian distributive justice is often misunderstood as taking all goods and dividing them by the number of claimants. However, such a procedure would make this system of justice very impractical. A better rendering of the theory is to give equal consideration to everyone's need in a way that would be beneficial to them. Take health care, for example. Let's assume John and Mary are sick. To cure John we need to give him ampicillin that costs $4 per dose. To cure Mary we need a special antiviral drug that costs $2,500. If we treated each equally according to their needs, then each would receive the appropriate drug. In this form, egalitarianism is a subset of socialism. However, when dealing with less tangible goods— such as gender equality—the case is a little more difficult. To treat John with the same respect and consideration as Mary, it is possible that we will have to take away some perks that John has enjoyed as a privileged male even as we give other social goods to Mary. The distribution formula is "to each according to a principle of equal respect and appropriate need." Advocates say that this addition to socialism makes it fairer. Detractors say that everyone should fend for himself and that it is impractical to go through these sorts of calculations.

You might clearly support one of these theories of distributive justice over the others. Or, you may choose cozily compatible duos such as kraterism and capitalism, or socialism and egalitarianism. I have taken the controversial stance of supporting a mixture of all five.[14] Why is this? The answer goes back to the utopian versus aspirational distinction discussed in Chapter 2. Sure, it might be nice to go with the socialism and egalitarianism combo, but is this really a viable choice in the world? It seems to me that we cannot ignore the reality of kraterism as a force in the world, and I believe that we will never be able to eliminate it. Therefore, let's try to harness its energy for the good. The energy comes from its emphasis on the individual and his reward in an arena that exalts power. This creates strong motivation for individuals who feel they will be successful according to such ground rules. Motivation is an important element to get things done. Kraterism allows a clear and definite resolution to problems by creating scenarios in which there is a clear winner and loser.

The downside is that "might" does not make "right." In its logical extension, anarchy would result. The extreme emphasis on the individual can undermine the shared-community worldview imperatives. However, when kraterism is combined with other theories, its downsides can be moderated.

Likewise, capitalism is one of the most productive economic theories in the history of humankind. It is an efficient system that creates wealth faster than any other system—except when there are "market corrections." Our goal, then, should be to harness the efficiency of production that results from capitalism's reward-for-work formulae. It is also a strength that the theory rewards valued work and is very good to the individual who wins in this arena.

However, without a partner, unfettered capitalism quickly devolves to kraterism, because it relies upon a model of selfish choice. Bernard Mandeville believed that unfettered capitalism was like a beehive in which all the worker bees were acting selfishly and magically a common good appeared.[15] However, this seems like a religious tenet, at best.

Another problem with unfettered capitalism is that it promotes an overly simplified model of desert and the value of human work that is often to the disadvantage of the "other" in society (the poor, minorities, and the dispossessed). Unfettered capitalism desperately needs a socially conscious partner to strengthen its weaknesses and temper its excesses. In this way capitalism transforms to "fettered" capitalism.

Socialism and egalitarianism are both socially cooperative partners to capital-ism. Detractors to these two theories say that they encourage free riders because they are not selfishly based. They are less efficient than the competitive theories of kraterism and unfettered capitalism and may create an unduly large space be-tween work and reward (because of higher taxes for social welfare).

On the positive side, both systems can be a morally humanizing element in the mosaic of distributive justice. Both are strongly compatible with arguments for the moral status of basic goods and the foundation of morally based public policy according to the Table of Embeddedness. These two theories are most sup-portive of my argument about providing the basic goods to all, or in any case to the degree that that is possible—even when such policies might require higher taxes for those who are more wealthy. This will result in spreading the pains and rewards more evenly in society. Thus, these two theories can constitute a moral beacon for public policy.

There is something troublesome about a theory of justice that is not based on deserts but on preferment, as aristocratic theory is.[16] But aristocracy (whether based on nobility or economic station) gives a sense of institutional history and stability to the community. Stability is important, but it can also be a roadblock to change. Thus, to harness what aristocracy can give, one must look to the historical continuity that is necessary for any meaningful change to continue forward.

Another plus to aristocracy is that sometimes these intergenerational bastions of wealth use their power and resources cooperatively for the betterment of those less fortunate. For example, in the United States, the Kennedy and Rockefeller families have donated much to charity, and some family members have given themselves over to public service.

Of course, intergenerational wealth can also be a tool to become a bully. These "old families" can decide that they are above the rules that bind the rest of us and opt for a version of kraterism.

Critics of my mosaic approach have said that we should accept the best theory (theories) of distributive justice and move on from there.[17] They lean to the utopian side of political theory. But what good is an unattainable theory? For ef-fective public policy, we must recognize that all forms of distributive justice will be present to some extent in all societies (free or oppressed). The extent of their pres-ence and how they are publicly expressed is a matter of cultural/political diversity. To offer the reader a quick view of how one might create such a mixture, Table 6.1 summarizes some of the features of each theory. All are applicable as instances of global justice (though aristocracy has a statist flavor to it because most intergenera-tional families of wealth and power exist within a national context). But this need not be the case. Bill and Melinda Gates, for example, have given an international focus to their foundation.

TABLE 6.1. Strengths and Weaknesses of Theories of Distributive Justice

Theory	Strength	Weakness
Competitive Theories		
Kraterism	1. Clear and definite resolution to problems (winners and losers) 2. Good if you win so that it invites new players into the arena 3. Exalts the individual so that it stimulates individual participation (the energy factor)	1. Fails to reward the achievements or meet the needs of the unpowerful 2. "Might" doesn't make "right" 3. Undermines community worldview imperatives because of its individual focus
Unfettered capitalism	1. Highly efficient wealth-creating system 2. Good if you win so that it invites new players into the arena 3. Valued work is rewarded	1. Rewards market demand rather than excellence or hard work 2. Promotes exploitation 3. No social responsibility built in
Swing Theory		
Aristocracy	1. Sense of continuity and stability 2. If cooperative, then the intergenerational wealthy families can be a positive force for change	1. Rewards accidents of birth rather than rewarding individual achievement or meeting needs 2. Can express itself through using intergenerational kraterism to effect undue influence
Cooperative Theories		
Socialism	1. Distributes according to needs that may be contrary to the self-interest of the well-off 2. Spreads pain and prosperity over the entire society 3. Is consistent with the Table of Embeddedness and the moral right for basic goods	1. Prioritizes need over reward of individual effort or achievement 2. Encourages free riders who are selfish 3. May unduly separate work from reward
Egalitarianism	1. Distributes according to appropriate need 2. Promotes equal respect 3. Reduces the distance between the advantaged and the very poor	1. Prioritizes need over reward of individual effort or achievement 2. Penalizes those who think that respect should follow from competitive deserts 3. May jolt the advantaged because the level of their preferment will be lessened

Retributive Justice

Retribution means "giving or paying back." International retributive justice is the theory and mechanism that addresses the giving back to aggrieved peoples and nations in the face of wrongs that have been done to them.

The basic concept of retributive justice can be illustrated by a domestic analogy: Marsha steals Julie's math book because she has lost her own. Julie has to buy another math book, which costs her $100. When it is discovered that Marsha purloined the book, she returns it to Julie. Julie now has two math books, though she needs only one. She sells one of her copies back to the bookstore for $40. Thus Marsha's actions cost Julie $60 plus the inconvenience of having to find and buy a replacement math book, and then resell a duplicate copy. In a perfect system of retributive justice one might decide to charge Marsha $100 for her adventure. If she had spent this amount at the beginning, then there would be no problem. But she chose another way: the way of theft. It would seem logically right to compensate Julie $100 in addition to the return of the textbook. Julie would then have her book back, plus the $60 she lost by reselling the duplicate copy she had to buy, plus another $40 for her trouble. When the numbers are low, the $40 for Julie's "trouble" might seem appropriate. However, when we begin to talk about real money, there need to be some general guidelines as to what is appropriate.

First, let us distinguish between actual loss and other associated harms. In actual loss, Marsha should pay Julie only the money that Julie lost in the transaction, that is, $60. This seems to be unassailable based on the principle that each individual should be secure in the possession of his or her own property. Theft is unacceptable because it undermines society. Theft might involve the loss of a level-one basic good (such as food) or a level-two secondary good that is useful for life (such as a car). If there is physical violence in the theft, then there may be multiple goods at stake: a level-one basic good concerning protection from unwarranted bodily harm for the assault and a level-two secondary good concerning a good useful to attaining one's personal life plan. In these situations, the more embedded good should be the focus of retribution, and that retribution should involve a penalty beyond mere repayment, as a further disincentive to theft.

Retribution, then, is about crime against individuals within a state and about the state's responsibility to make whole its own citizens who have been wronged. Both aspects of retributive justice should be grounded in the Table of Embeddedness (Table 3.1) and the argument for the moral right to basic goods.

Let's now transition to the international sphere. What sorts of goods are at stake here? For one, we need to create a translation formula between the moral claims to goods in the Table of Embeddedness and the social and political group dynamics that exist in larger spheres. Most people would recognize that there should be some sort of isometric transformation between the two: Large numbers of individual claimants within a society will determine the group characterization of that description.

Can there be a seamless transition between the claims of morality and those of justice, as I contend? Some theorists would contend that the argumentative justifications are different *in kind*, such that social/political philosophy operates on entirely different principles than does moral philosophy.[18] Generally, the two-theory advocates consider social contracts as the basis of the social/political bent.[19] There is something very appealing about contracts that everyone endorses. We'll examine the strength of this approach in the following situations:

- Situation one: A husband and wife agree that anything that goes on within their bedroom is okay. The man likes beating up his wife. She agrees to be beaten. Is this ethically correct?
- Situation two: The women in a community perform genital mutilation upon the teenaged girls. It happened to them so they continue the practice. It seems that everyone agrees to the practice, including the young girls themselves. Is this practice justifiable just because people agree to it?
- Situation three: A nation creates a constitution under which only male landholders can vote, and also appoints members of one house of the national assembly who have the power to block the peoples' elected choices to the other legislative house. Just because everyone agrees to this arrangement, does this make it right?

I would contend that more than a mere contract is needed to make something ethical. Contracts exist within another context: The larger moral context is based on another independent theory. I define this using one of the major realist moral theories: virtue ethics, utilitarianism, and deontology. The underlying principles of ethics are applicable to social/political problems as well. In my view, contracts (like all institutions) cannot prescribe morality. They depend upon ethical background conditions that validate individual assent to the contracts. Immoral contracts have no legitimate action-guiding force. Thus, I would say that contractarianism is not a full-fledged justification for a moral theory and as such is incomplete to justify a social/political theory.

A second follow-up question is whether social/political philosophy operates differently in nationally based theories of social/political philosophy than in globally based theories of social/political philosophy. This is a methodological question that needs to be answered *before* we engage the issue of international retributive justice.

The only way to properly answer this question is to return to the justification of national borders question. What is there about being in a state that makes theories of social/political justice different? If the boundaries of states are largely conventional, then there is no real robust boundary. If there is no real robust boundary, then shouldn't the dictates of ethics lead to social/political philosophical principles within the *state* that equate with social/political philosophical principles within the *world*? My own position (which need not be yours) is that the key arguments concerning the moral status of basic goods and the Table of Embeddedness suggest that there is no compelling argument for nationalism over cosmopolitanism.

If this is correct, then we can conceive—at least in principle—of a world in which the earth is the essential unit and nations are to be viewed as subunits within the general whole. However, there is a secondary question of sovereign political units defined as nations that others recognize as legitimate. In a practical sense of being able to levy taxes, regulate commerce, and administer justice, for example, the national unit has power and a presence that makes it the primary gatekeeper to its own citizens. A *national gatekeeper* is the legitimate ruling authority within a state. But what if there is some dispute about who is the gatekeeper? Let's examine three examples: slavery of African Americans in the United States, military conquest of Native Americans, and disputed sovereignty in Palestine.

Slavery of African Americans

The ancestors of most African Americans were forced to come to the United States (i.e., the American colonies) and work as chattel. This occurred for about two and a half centuries, from shortly after the founding of Jamestown to the official end to slavery as mandated by the ratification of the Thirteenth Amendment to the Constitution at the end of the Civil War. Yet, for more than another century, punitive laws kept African Americans in an underclass status, especially in the South. What sort of retributive justice should be instigated in this case?

You might note that legal redress has already been accomplished—almost all apartheid laws in the United States are off the books—and you might assert as well that this social problem has therefore been solved and that no other measures need to be taken. Or you could opine that further compensation is in order—such as reparations for the cruel treatment of ancestors and for the incomplete empowerment policies still in effect for those living today. How should we respond to these two positions?

Military Conquest of Native Americans

Native Americans in the United States have experienced a history of expulsion from their lands as White Americans settled the continent. At the conclusion of the French and Indian War in 1763, when the British and their Indian allies had defeated the French and their Indian allies, King George III of England decreed that all the newly won lands west of the crest of the Appalachian Mountains would be reserved for Indian nations whereas the English settlers would occupy the colonies on the Atlantic seaboard. However, despite the decrees and many treaties ostensibly meant to protect the natives and their lands, they were relentlessly pushed west by the sheer numbers of westward-migrating English settlers, either in defiance of official settlement policies or with the active support of the U.S. government, which included military action. Under the Indian Removal Act of 1831, for example, President Andrew Jackson oversaw the forced relocation of Cherokee, Creek, Choctaw, and Seminole peoples from their homelands in the South across the Mississippi River to present-day Oklahoma. Thousands died along the so-called Trail of Tears. But even the territory west of the Mississippi was not safe for them. As we discussed earlier, the notion of Manifest Destiny justified continued displacement of Native Americans as the White settlement of the West continued throughout the nineteenth century. The U.S. Army "pacified" Indian insurgents led, for example, by Geronimo and Cochise of the Apaches, and forcibly removed whole tribes to reservations. Even the reservations were not a haven, however, as these lands came under pressure from White Americans when valuable mineral deposits were found within reservation boundaries.

The second sort of situation is military conquest. This is a tortured question. Conventions for war have existed for all of recorded history, in both the West and East. But these are often toothless unless someone with power is prepared to enforce them. Most of us agree that *might does not make right*, and yet the practical fact of conquest (barring a world government with power to enforce its will) is one that will probably win the day. Thus, for example, the British in their initial conquest of native peoples in what is now the United States paid no heed to the fact that they were engaged in aggressive war (universally barred in all traditional theories of rules of war) but deluded themselves into believing that their actions were justified on some principle of charity: They were Christianizing these savages so that they might attain eternal salvation (or at least that was the cover story). Probably, they were really like most conquest-oriented regimes that are really intent on economic gain with a public relations move that covers up the figure of bare kraterism.

When the United States gained sovereignty, the doctrine of Manifest Destiny was hyped so that God was invoked in some sort of historical design. The savages should be caged in reservations, and if there was a mistake on the size of the prison, it could be changed according to interest in mineral rights: gold, copper, and oil.

Should today's Native Americans be compensated for their ancestors' losses? You might believe that immoral seizures of land and other property are not legitimate and that anything improperly taken should be returned to the aggrieved party. Or you might note the impracticality—to say the least—of returning Manhattan, for example, to the Indians for the equivalent of the $24 that Peter Minuit reputedly paid for it in 1626—or for any other price, for that matter.

Sovereignty in Palestine

The Middle East is the seat of the three Abrahamic religions: Judaism, Christianity, and Islam. Each feels a special calling to protect its various interests in the region. The Jews lived in the area commonly called Palestine—between the Jordan River and the Mediterranean Sea—long before Christianity or Islam began. By Biblical tradition, Jews first occupied the "Promised Land" (so-called because Jews considered the land promised to them by God) some 3,500 years ago, conquering the Canaanites native to that region. Jews were forcibly expelled from the region by the Babylonians in the sixth century BCE and again by the Romans in the second century CE. Beginning in the seventh century, Muslim Arabs swept across much of the Middle East and North Africa, including the land of Palestine and the city of Jerusalem, which is holy to Jews and Christians (as well as to the Muslims themselves). In the twelfth and thirteenth centuries, European Christians launched a series of wars—the Crusades—to remove Jerusalem and the Holy Land from Muslim control, though they ultimately garnered little success. In modern times, the breakup of the Ottoman Empire (which had ruled much of the Middle East) at the end of World War I, the rise of nationalist independence movements among its many subject peoples, and the systematic murder of Jews in the Holocaust of World War II all contributed to the establishment of the Jewish state of Israel in Palestine in 1948, with the support of European powers and the newly founded United Nations. However, Arab Palestinians resisted what they saw as the illegitimate seizure of their land, and hundreds of thousands fled or were expelled from the land in the ensuing fighting between Israelis and Arabs. Hundreds of thousands of Palestinians left the land again in another Arab-Israeli war in 1967.

The Palestinians want the right to return to where they lived before with their property, either in a state of their own or within a multiethnic state they share with the Jews. The Israelis want recognition from Arab nations and the stateless Palestinians that Israel has a right to exist. What is to be done? Which claim is the more legitimate, that of the Jews who lived in the area first—and who won the territory by military victories millennia apart against the Canaanites and the Arabs—or that of the Palestinians, who have occupied the territory since the Arab conquest of it in the seventh century? Is there a workable way to recognize both claims as legitimate?

It is clear that there needs to be some generally agreed-upon protocol for international restoration of property and rights under a broad banner of retributive justice. Because we have no sovereign international agency with the power to enforce its will, the only way this can occur is by the consensus of the more powerful nations of the world that they will accept various general rules and the decisions of international agencies—even when such decisions go against them.

Key Terms

states, kraterism, unfettered capitalism, aristocracy, socialism, egalitarianism, distributive justice, retributive justice

Critical Applied Reasoning Exercise

You are an undersecretary of commerce for the United States. The World Trade Organization (WTO, a subunit of the United Nations) has ruled against the United States in a trade dispute with Nicaragua on textile dumping (a practice in which the government subsidizes private industry so that the latter can gain market share and eventually raise prices in some foreign market—a practice prohibited by the WTO).

You personally believe the WTO is correct in its ruling, but U.S. business and labor interests want to protect American jobs and are lobbying to ignore the ruling. Because the United States ignores most rulings against it, there is precedent for you to do the same. However, you believe the ruling to be morally sound. You must write a report to your superior advocating your country's response to the ruling. What do you say? Write a 1.5-page response backing your policy proposals with philosophical reasons.

Notes

1. Allen Buchanan, *Justice, Legitimacy, and Self-Determination* (Oxford: Oxford University Press, 2004), makes much of the requirement of recognizing human rights in order to assert the status of a proper state.

2. One popular novel by a writer who lived under the Taliban captured many of these dynamics: Khaled Housseini, *The Kite Runner* (New York: Riverhead, 2007).

3. Rosemarie Skaine, *Women of Afghanistan in the Post-Taliban Era* (Jefferson, NC: McFarland, 2008); and Marjorie Agosin, ed., *Women, Gender, and Human Rights: A Global Perspective* (New Brunswick, NJ: Rutgers University Press, 2001).

4. An example of this was the destruction of a 1,600-year-old Buddhist statue: see the *USA Today* article at www.usatoday.com/news/science/archaeology/2001-03 -22-afghan-buddhas.htm.

5. The modern system of nation-states is often at odds with tribal micro communities. Some discussion of this can be found in Curtis Keim, *Mistaking Africa: Curiosities and Inventions of the American Mind*, 2nd ed. (Boulder, CO: Westview Press,

2009); N. Bruce Duthu, *American Indians and the Law* (New York: Viking, 2008); and Patricia Crone, *From Arabian Tribes to Islamic Empire: Army, State, and Society in the Near East c. 600–850* (Aldershot, UK: Ashgate, 2008).

6. John Locke, *The Second Treatise of Government: An Essay Concerning the True Original Extent and End of Civil Government* (London: Macmillan, rpt. 1956): ch. 5, §26.

7. Locke argues that productive use of property is necessary in order to maintain a valid property claim, see ibid., ch. 7.

8. Michael LeRoy, "Paving the Way for Peace in the United Kingdom," *Christianity Today* 44 (2000).

9. This is not too far from Rawls's characterization of the same in *The Law of Peoples*—though he goes through a more intricate classification scheme. A calculation of outlaw states under this formula would include China, North Korea, Russia, much of the Middle East, Burma, Thailand, Cambodia, Indonesia, much of Africa, and a few countries in Latin America. Estimated population: 4 billion people (total world population 6.5 billion people).

10. In the law, "harm" has legal status for recompense whereas a "nuisance" or "unpleasantness" does not. The line between the two can sometimes be gray. This is why I have finessed the question by merely broadening the traditional three categories of harm. In the forthcoming book *Marxian Liberalism* Jeffrey Reiman makes this argument that negative duties can be very important in addressing resources to world problems.

11. It is my conjecture that among individual people living in the world, the poor give more proportional charity than do the rich. This is sometimes called the "charity paradox." How this affects this analysis in terms of nation-states and the international picture must be a subject of a future project.

12. For a more complete description of these, see Michael Boylan, *A Just Society* (Lanham, MD, and Oxford: Rowman and Littlefield, 2004): ch. 7.

13. In Hinduism the caste system does assume that people are born where they are on the basis of previous behavior in earlier lives. Except for these advocates, let us assume that birth into one family or the other is random and undeserved. For more discussion on this see Boylan, *A Just Society,* 138–145.

14. Ibid., 172–181.

15. The most tangible rendition of the invisible hand that regulates selfish behavior for the good of all can be found in Bernard Mandeville, *The Fable of the Bees,* ed. F. B. Kaye (London: Liberty Fund, rpt. 1924). However, at the writing of this book the global credit crisis shows that the magic doesn't necessarily happen—especially when the krateristic cheating begins (e.g., Bernie Madoff et al.).

16. See my argument based upon the puzzle-maker model in Boylan, *A Just Society,* 139–140, 144–145.

17. An example of this is found in Christopher Lowry and Udo Schülenk, "Establishing Global Health Obligations and Ethical Diversity: A Commentary on Boylan's 'A Just Society,'" in *Morality and Justice: Reading Boylan's A Just Society*, ed. John-Stewart Gordon (Lanham, MD: Lexington Books, 2009): 161–178.

18. Some believe that the dynamics of ethical analysis are different and take priority over those calculations at the international level. See Garrett Hardin, "Lifeboat Ethics: The Case Against Helping the Poor," *Psychology Today* 8, 4 (1974): 123–126; Alasdair Macintyre, "Is Patriotism a Virtue?" *The Lindley Lecture at the University of Kansas* (Lawrence, KS, 1984); Thomas Hurka, "The Justification of National Partiality," in *The Morality of Nationalism*, ed. Robert McKim and Jeff McMahan (Oxford: Oxford University Press, 1997): 139–157; and Richard W. Miller, "Moral Closeness and World Community," in *The Ethics of Assistance: Morality and the Distant Needy*, ed. Deen K. Chatterjee (Cambridge: Cambridge University Press, 2004): 101–122.

19. There are also some noncognitivists who take a two-theory approach. They contrast popular attitudes as evidenced through language usage as forming a multiplicity of bases by which to approach this problem. For an introduction to some of these issues, see Michael Boylan, *Basic Ethics*, 2nd ed. (Upper Saddle River, NJ: Prentice Hall, 2008): ch. 9.

PART THREE

APPLIED GLOBAL ETHICS

PART THREE
INTRODUCTION

Part Three turns our attention to the types of problems that plague the world today, including poverty; public health; race, gender, and sexual orientation; the lack of political dialogue; globalization; the environment; war and terrorism; and immigration and refugees. There are other problems, of course, but these will strike many as among the most pressing. In each case the following structure is used: a statement of the problem, followed by some analysis of the causes of the problem. Each chapter ends with some possible solutions that are not meant to be definitive but to stimulate the reader especially as he or she confronts the critical applied reasoning exercise that concludes each chapter.

The Chapter 7 discussion of poverty limits itself to: (1) those suffering from the lack of level-one basic goods of agency: food, clean water, sanitation, clothing, shelter, and protection from unwarranted bodily harm, including health care; (2) those lacking level-two basic goods such as basic human liberties and primary/secondary educational opportunities; and (3) those lacking level-one secondary goods, such as an equal opportunity to participate in one's community in such a way that one can live out a personal plan of life in a fair setting.

On public health I have limited my remarks to the traditional understanding of the term as involving the availability of clean water and adequate sanitation, and the prevention of infectious disease. Chapter 8 sketches out the enormity of this problem area.

Race, gender, and sexual orientation are three ways of becoming the "other." Being cast as the other means becoming second-class citizens who do not fully participate in their country's culture and economy. These rampant inequities constitute the focus of Chapter 9.

Democracy and social/political dialogue constitute the subject matter of Chapter 10, which discusses John Rawls's *The Law of Peoples* as well as an outline of the role of social dialogue in autonomy and community autonomy through what I call the *fair government principle*.

The model of economic globalization by which all tariffs are eliminated and companies are no longer tied to nations but serve (or exploit) people around the globe is analyzed in Chapter 11. This is an especially difficult position to evaluate because both supporters and critics have often exaggerated claims on behalf of their positions.

Chapter 12 discusses the environment. This huge area of concern is narrowed to the three problems of air pollution, water pollution, and ground pollution. Though there is much disagreement about environmental problems, the science on these three subissues is quite straightforward.

In the United States and the Middle East during the past decade the issues of war and terrorism have taken a front seat. Because there has been much imprecise discourse on issues that are involved with war and terrorism, Chapter 13 begins by making some essential verbal distinctions among, for example, war, just war, terrorism, and guerrilla warfare. The chapter considers Michael Walzer's arguments about the moral context of war among other arguments about the origins of and justifications for interstate and intrastate violence.

Finally, Chapter 14 contemplates issues concerning immigrants and refugees. The problem of displaced people may result from interstate or intrastate violence or economic or environmental disasters. But when life becomes unbearable, people seek to get up and leave. Issues concerning political and economic reasons for becoming a displaced person are examined in the context of the core principles outlined in Parts One and Two.

CHAPTER 7

Poverty

One of the most vicious problems in the world is poverty. Etymologically, *poverty* comes from the Latin meaning "smallness of resources." As per my presentation of the moral status of basic goods and the Table of Embeddedness (Chapter 3) there are at least three levels of understanding poverty:

1. Those suffering from poverty lack many of the level-one basic goods of agency: food, clean water, sanitation, clothing, shelter, protection from unwarranted bodily harm, and basic health care.
2. Those lacking the basic human liberties, primary/secondary educational opportunities, and level-two basic goods.
3. Those lacking the equal opportunity to participate in one's community in such a way that he or she can live out a personal plan of life in a fair setting—level-one secondary goods.

These three forms of poverty present themselves in a hierarchal order of importance that parallels embeddedness. The end goal is that all people in the world will have both levels of basic goods and the first level of secondary goods. However, we are a long way from that reality. Because this book has advocated aspirational, achievable goals above utopian ones, this chapter will confine itself to addressing disease and the lack of basic food, water, and sanitation requirements from a global perspective.

The emphasis will follow that of the Table of Embeddedness. In subsequent chapters other specific problems will also be identified and discussed against the three imperatives discussed in Chapter 2: personal worldview, shared community worldview, and extended community worldview. The other aspects of poverty (i.e., the lacking of resources necessary for effective agency) will be treated as part of subsequent chapters.

The Problem

Lots of people are dying right now. The two major causes of deaths around the world are famine and disease. The facts about famine are graphic: Almost half the people of the world live on less than $2.50 per day. Using the World Development Bank's dollar purchasing power parity, this means that more than half the world is in poverty.[1] The lack of income generally equates to the lack of the ability to purchase food. In the case of farmers, the coin of the realm must be translated into means to grow and harvest crops. Any way you measure it, the figures about access to food are staggering. According to UNICEF, every day 25,000 children under the age of five die due to poverty. At every moment people all over the world are dying at an alarming rate due to famine. Less than 1 percent of what the world spends every year on weapons would have been enough to put every child in the world into school by the year 2000, but it didn't happen.[2]

Worse yet, deaths from malnutrition are moving in the wrong direction. The number of people who are severely undernourished—that is, on the brink of death by starvation—has increased in the seventy least-developed countries from 775 million in 1997 to 980 million in 2007.[3] One critical factor is the "grain stock" figure (that is, the amount of grain left from the previous harvest when the new harvest begins), which has dropped from 108 days in 1997 to 62 days in 2007. This reduction indicates that the present system has very little "give" to it to accommodate famine and crop failures. The situation is on the brink.

Again, at every moment people are dying of preventable diseases at an alarming rate: 14–17 million die each year.[4] An estimated 40 million people are living with HIV/AIDS (which was accountable for 3 million deaths in 2004 alone). Every year there are 350–500 million cases of malaria, with 1 million fatalities; Africa has 90 percent of the malarial deaths worldwide.[5]

What are we to make of this? Why are so many people dying of famine and disease?

These statistics reflect the most basic cause of human misery: poverty. One way to think about this situation is that poverty limits one's options to procure food, causing famine and death by starvation, and limits one's health care capabilities, causing both increased vulnerability to disease and curtailed treatment opportunities. What are we to do about poverty and its associated consequences?

In the case of famine there are at least two important factors at stake:

- Category I: Supply (a) agricultural production per acre of outputs that are high in calories and nutritional value, and (b) availability of domestic animals such as cattle, sheep, goats, and poultry, and wild animals such as fish and game for supplemental food intake. Together, (a) + (b) can be termed a *regional sustainable food supply.* The supply is deemed to be sustainable if and only if humans take away from the ecosystem an amount that does not diminish the future supply of the agricultural or animal output.

- Category II: Demand (a) maximum population density as a ratio relating to regional sustainable food supply, and (b) population projections as a future ratio relating to sustainable population food supply. Population density and its assumptions about consumption are debits on the supply. Each robust land region in the world can support only a certain population density. When demand exceeds that amount, shortages occur. Future populations can rise or fall. If they rise, shortages might be incurred. If they fall, the people living in that area might enjoy a greater share of the food supply.

In all societies, the bottom line of calorie and nutrition intake is essential for maintaining life and—beyond that—for allowing minimal and then effective functioning. Calorie requirements vary according to size and individual metabolism, but the figures that are commonly used as approximations are: 500 calories per day to stay alive, 1,000 calories a day to minimally function, and 2,000 calories a day to function effectively. In agricultural societies, as distinguished from hunting-and-gathering societies, the ability to control a minimum level of nutritional input is a tremendous step forward. When the crop is more nutritious and caloric than alternatives, more people live, more babies can be brought to term, and more women are able to nurse their children.[6] One key example of this is when in Europe barley was replaced by potatoes as a basic food. Potatoes were easier to grow—subject only to blight[7]—and are more nutritious than barley. Thus, the change to potatoes as Europe's primary crop sparked a population growth.

Animal husbandry and fishing are included at a higher level of development. Cattle, sheep, goats, and fowl require food to live. Sometimes, this food is merely the grassland around the farmer. However, these animals generally require a greater amount of care than do crops because they might wander off or be subject to attacks by predators. Thus, this level of food production may be considered to be a higher-level enterprise (a less-embedded subsection of level-one basic goods). It is higher-level because herding of domestic animals requires more resources than does agriculture. Fishing is in a different category, akin to hunting wild animals.

In each of these cases there is a sustainable level of output relative to the ecosystems and regional biome in question. What makes one geographical area more fecund than another? For agriculture it depends upon the soil quality (measured in nutrients required for the crop in question), water availability and quality (a critical factor),[8] sunlight/temperature and other default conditions, and threats to the output—microbial and insect/animal pests.[9] Thus, given a five-year rolling cycle, one might expect a certain yield on one acre of planted land to be x (measured in a ratio of input to output that includes seeds for the next planting). Generally, it is thought that an agricultural yield of 1:3 is necessary to maintain a minimal 1,000–2,000-calorie diet. Increasing the yield to 1:5 results in a surplus that can be used to feed domestic animals and allows the area's inhabitants to exceed the 2,000-calorie threshold. Unless a new variety of crop is introduced that is beneficial regarding the calorie/nutrition ratio, this acre of land can yield per year (on the five-year average) a given number of edible crops that contain a somewhat reliable number of calories and nutritional value.

There are also limits to consider with animal husbandry. There is only so much grazing land—often considered to be public commons. The land can only support so many domestic cattle or other animals. If one or more farmers exceeds this limit, there will occur a tragedy of the commons in which all suffer from the activity of the few.

With respect to wild animals (including fish) there are similar concerns about sustainable yields. These concern the ongoing number of animals in their natural habitat. If animals are hunted or fished too aggressively, the numbers of that sort of animal will decrease and will thus no longer represent a sustainable figure.

Ideally, population density should be viewed within the sustainability paradigm. This requires thinking both about the number of people in a region and their actual product demand. If we assume the minimum calorie figures mentioned above, then one must factor in these calorie requirements into the food production paradigm. A given tract of land can therefore support a given number of people according to the efficiency of agricultural production, domestic animal herding, and the existence of wild animals that can be fished or hunted. There is a maximum number of people for each of the three levels of calorie levels that support human action at some minimal level. When the population exceeds this figure, either everyone must subsist on less food or there will be intense competition to garner the food necessary to maintain the 2,000-calorie level (at the expense of the losers, who will fall to lower levels—perhaps to starvation). The possibility or indeed the likelihood of competition is exacerbated in situations of increasing population over and above the regional sustainable food supply (that is, by an increase in demand) or shortfalls in food production (that is, by a decrease in supply).

Those who control the means of production—and especially those who own the land—are in positions of particular power in determining the course of competition for food. Take, for example, the case of the nineteenth-century Irish potato crop failure.[10] Due to a blight that markedly reduced the yield of potatoes, the total output was low. Those who controlled the means of production had a choice either to ensure that the Irish field laborers who produced the crop received adequate supplies of potatoes to eat, or to export potatoes to fill foreign orders first so that there might be a return on investment, and give a small remainder of potatoes to the people (even though this would entail massive famine and death). Those who controlled production chose the latter course.

Ironically, considering that it is essential to life, water has strong connections to disease:

1. Water-borne diseases: These diseases occur directly as an individual drinks contaminated water. The principal cause of this contamination is human waste. Untreated waste gives rise to protozoan, bacterial, and viral diseases. These most commonly attack the human intestines. Specific diseases that are water-borne include cholera, typhoid, hepatitis, ameobiasis, giardiasis, *Taenia solium* taeniasis, ascariasis, hookworm, trichuriasis, and strongyloidiasis. These often cause local epidemics that are frequently deadly.

2. Water-washed diseases: These diseases occur when there is not enough water for proper hygiene or cooking sanitation. People cannot rid themselves of contaminants that they might come in contact with and as a result become ill from, for example, trachoma, typhus, and diarrheal diseases.

3. Water-based diseases: These diseases come from hosts that live in water during part or all of their life cycles. When people bathe, swim, or wash their clothing, the contaminated water may come into contact with their skin. In 2000, such diseases as schistosomiasis, dracunculiasis, and lung flukes (caused by carrier snails) affected as many as 200 million people in seventy countries.[11] Elimination of such "black water" would solve this source of disease.

4. Water-related insect vectors: These diseases are spread by insects—such as mosquitoes—that breed in water and infect humans with malaria, onchocerciasis (river blindness), West Nile fevers, yellow fever, and dengue fever.

The role of poor sanitation in breeding life-threatening diseases is especially pronounced in poorer nations of the world. In most of the world, sanitation infrastructure is lacking or incomplete.[12] With almost 60 percent of the world's population at risk for death because of poor sanitation, we are not very far along the road of reaching the United Nations' Millennium Development target to "halve by 2015 the proportion of people without sustainable access to safe drinking water."[13]

The Causes of Poverty

Poverty is a lack of resources that can be interpreted as a paucity of the basic goods of agency. There is a dialectical relationship operating here. When one is poor, she is inclined to miss the basic goods of agency. Also, when one lacks the basic goods of agency, then one is poor. This confusion can be cleared up by saying that our lens of analysis is the Table of Embeddedness. We should ask ourselves what goods of agency we possess or don't possess. Then we can say further that those without any of the level-one basic goods of agency are poor. The lack of those goods makes them poor in an absolute sense. But the *reason why* one lacks those goods might be due to not having enough of the currency of the realm—be it money, goods to be bartered, fertile land, clean water, and so on. The causal account is dialectical. Being bit by a malaria-bearing mosquito is an event of chance that can cause one to be severely impaired in her ability to act. This disability can make her poor. But the reason that she was bit in the first place was that she was bereft of a mosquito net because she didn't have enough money to purchase one. Thus the interaction works both ways. This is what is meant by a dialectical interaction.

Among the primary ways of being poor (via dialectally being cause and effect) are famine and disease. These have multiple causes, which I categorize as national and global. In the first case there are failures of the land within a nation to produce enough to eat (given birth rates and mortality rates). This causes poverty via famine. When the demand exceeds the regional sustainable food supply, shortages will occur. These shortages will be allocated according to the operant theory of distributive justice in effect.

When extreme poverty exhibits itself in famine or disease, the laissez-faire approach could entail Thomas Malthus's pessimistic outcome in which extreme famine or epidemic acts rather like a free market forcing people to die up to a point that would lessen demand so that eventually it would reach the regional sustainable food supply.[14] Things would be in equilibrium until population growth increased again. This type of thinking is like imagining a world in which everyone is merely out for himself. No one assists another. We all get what we can take, which results in a grand display of kraterism and unfettered capitalism. These systems will work—meaning that a subgroup of humanity can go forward. But is it fair? When part of the cause is attributed to internal landlords (as per the Irish potato example) who put profit above human lives, mere progressing into the future by the fortunate is not enough. In my book *A Just Society,* I set out a thought experiment to illustrate a way to think about preferment and individual desert through the activity of a person putting a puzzle together. Assembling a puzzle is not a level linear process; that is, the earlier parts are the hardest and the later parts are the easiest. If a person is given a large completed part of the puzzle of life at the onset, then his or her desert at various completion points (college admission, jobs, government contracts, etc.) are skewed by this fact. If desert means what one does by him or herself, then those with great preferment do not deserve what they have as much as those who have had a longer road to travel. Because most social institutions in the United States and around the world do not look at desert but merely at some end-point designated in time, it is entirely possible that a more deserving person (one who has achieved largely on his or her own) is shut out in favor of another who has done little in his life beyond his initial preferment—much of the assembled puzzle was already given to him at birth. If rewards should be structured upon desert, then our present system of rewards is horribly unfair.[15]

Only in a world in which everyone was treated according to deserts-based criteria using the puzzle-maker model would people be on par in being able to make claims for basic goods (defined as within 5 percent of each other in goods of agency)[16] could someone make a Malthusian sort of claim without being confined to the distributive justice positions of kraterism or unfettered capitalism (aka laissez-faire capitalism). I believe that anything less than a mosaic of all five theories of distributive justice will be unfair and thus unacceptable.

The internal causes of famine are largely due to the regional sustainable food supply along with a more robust theory of distributive justice (containing more than just kraterism and unfettered capitalism).

Global factors that come into play are largely aligned with issues relating to multinational business expansion, aka globalization (see Chapter 12). The dream of globalization is that it will create more money and that, as a result, a little will fall to the poor nations of the world and lift them out of poverty. This is conceptually similar to the "trickle down" theory of economics: Make the lot of the rich better and they will either (1) consume at a higher rate that will mean more jobs for the impoverished, or (2) invest their money in bonds or equities that will strengthen businesses so that they might expand operations and hire more poor people in the process. Either way, proponents say, targeting money at the rich instead of the poor will help everyone. We'll discuss this issue more fully in Chapter 12.

The second major dialectical cause/effect of poverty is the persistence of infectious disease. There are natural conditions that produce disease. As mentioned earlier, many of these are associated with the water and sanitation policies adopted by various countries (either by policy or by default). The lack of attention to creating potable (so-called blue) water for the economic underclass of the world along with sorry sanitation systems creates the conditions for water-borne diseases, water-washed diseases, water-based diseases, and water-related insect vectors. These four scenarios are responsible for a very large share of the world's infectious diseases.

Other major infectious diseases are HIV/AIDS and tuberculosis (TB). In the former case, the major causes are unprotected sexual intercourse between an infected person and a noninfected person and transmission by blood or blood products through medical procedures or by needles that are reused (from an infected agent to a noninfected agent). Tuberculosis has been asserted to be present (in at least a latent form) in almost one-third of the world's population, and 98 percent of the world's TB fatalities come from subsistence societies.[17] People get TB by breathing droplets in the air that contain the bacterium *Mycobacterium tuberculosis*, which is spread by people coughing or sneezing. It then infects the lungs. Tuberculosis is most deadly when the general air quality of a region has a higher amount of these airborne bacteria. Saturation levels are higher among poorer countries than richer ones because there are more infected people to begin with and, by extension, among the poorer areas of these countries. New strains are resistant to traditional antibiotic cures.

In each of these disease cases there are strong correlations between poverty and disease that reflect the dialectical model presented at the beginning of this chapter. These scourges most affect the level-one basic goods of the poor. The correlative duties implied by the Table of Embeddedness and the extended-community worldview imperative require the wealthy nations of the world to take action. This leads us to inquire after the best available solutions.

Possible Solutions

Solutions are never easy. If they were, there would be no existing problems. Earlier the doctrine of aspirational goals was put forth. Aspirational goals are those that may be hard to achieve but are doable. They are distinguished from utopian goals, which may seem true and beautiful in some sense but will be impossible to implement. Striving after utopian goals will inevitably lead to failure and (perhaps) abandonment of the entire project.

This chapter has concentrated on famine and infectious disease as two hallmarks of poverty. (Other features of poverty and global ethics and justice will be dealt with in subsequent chapters.) Let's examine a few ways to think about solutions to famine and to infectious disease.

With regard to famine, we've seen that an important way to think about the problem is as part of a dialectical interaction between the outcome (poverty) and the substantive lack of one or more of the level-one goods of agency. For example, from the point of view of a regionally available and sustainable food supply and the food demand of the population, living in that region would be one measure of meeting legitimate rights claims. So when we think about creating a regional sustainable food supply, how do we get there?

Thought Experiment 7.1: On a sheet of paper, write down factors that would affect: (1) agricultural output, (2) domestic cattle/poultry production, and (3) wild animal hunting/fishing in Bangladesh. Identify five factors for each, and leave some space between items. Now, go to the Internet and do some quick research, then propose one positive policy proposal for each.

It is important to particularize one's search for possible solutions to global famine. The same thought experiment would come out differently if the setting were Mali or Haiti or Nepal. However, each country in need requires careful consideration. According to the extended-community worldview imperative, we must educate ourselves and others about needs in other countries and then marshal up some kind of response (according to the four levels mentioned earlier: individual and micro-community response, nongovernmental organizational response, tax-funded national response, and United Nations–type response).

Some generic inputs here might concern factors that affect crop yield. These might include new seed hybrids and more effective fertilizers. Together, these have been very effective in increasing crop yields, but they also have their drawbacks. Most of the new seed hybrids come from genetic engineering by multinational agribusinesses. The standard procedure for these companies is to obtain wild seed varieties and then to create from them a hybrid that is heartier and outproduces all others under like conditions. On the upside, these new hybrids have markedly higher yields than the wild varies they replace. This means more food and less starvation.

On the down side is the fact that these hybrids tend to take over when planted. For example, when a farmer plants the hybrid seeds, they pollinate with other farmers' crops so that their wild varieties are altered toward the new super-hybrid form. This does two things: (1) It allows the multinational seed company to come in and charge the other farmers for using its patented seeds—even though the pollination of the new seed was not their fault—thus, what was free to these farmers before is now a subject of imposed duty; and (2) it creates a situation in which there is a great uniformity in the germ line of the crops in the area—they all take on the characteristics of the super-hybrid. It is a given in evolutionary theory that diversity is necessary within a species to maintain fitness. When there is too much uniformity, the species is at high risk just in case. Just in case there is a devastating disease or a climate condition that is deleterious to the homogeneous super-hybrid, the fact that there is no diversity means all the crop will fail. The total loss would be much less if there were variants—that is, wild seed—that could withstand the environmental pressures. This is the way evolution works. The super-hybrids work artificially to create a homogeneous strain (necessary for the patent) that put the entire species at risk.

The large multinational companies take the seeds that poor farmers gather at no cost following the harvest and genetically alter them so that the new strain will push out the old strain. The seed companies may at first give these seeds away in a region, all with an eye toward gaining ascendancy, and then sell their new seeds at any price that the market will bear. This is a further hardship on the subsistence farmers. Not only do they have to pay for seeds that they once gathered for free, but the new seeds have the above-mentioned antienvironmental side-effects.

Which outcome should attract our attention: higher crop yields with the genetically altered seeds (along with its drawbacks), or maintenance of wild seeds at the price of lower crop yields but with higher environmental sustainability?

The Table of Embeddedness legitimates the level-one basic goods claim for food in order to act (pro–new seed), but acting counter to environmental sustainability can be seen as an attack on innocents in the future, which also violates a level-one basic good: protection against unwarranted bodily harm. In cases that are equally embedded, some sort of compromise solution must be found.

I would suggest that the international community via the extended-community worldview imperative allow the multinational seed companies to continue creating high-yield hybrid seeds but require that they do so in a manner that causes the least amount of collateral damage. This could be accomplished via the following restrictions: (1) New seeds should not be designed to be predatory over the wild seeds in a region. This will harm the business model of the multinational seed companies but will protect the wild seed genome; (2) seeds should be distributed at a subsidized rate to poor farmers by either the country, an arm of the UN, a collection of wealthy nations, NGOs, or a combination of the above, with the aim being to allow the multinational corporation to make a profit, but not a bonanza monopoly; (3) wild seeds of a region should be stored in a safe place so that they may be reintroduced in case of subspecies extinction. These restrictions are not exhaustive, but they will be the start of a compromise that could help us responsibility provide more food via new hybrid seeds.

Fertilizer is another issue of concern. Most subsistence societies use human and animal feces as fertilizer, which can be less effective than many modern chemical fertilizers. The latter can be custom balanced for the soil, improving yields. This means that more people will eat: Level-one basic goods have been provided.

The down side of these modern chemical fertilizers (besides their additional costs) is that they run off during rainy seasons and pollute the local ground water and surrounding lakes and streams. This pollution can result in cancer and other diseases to humans as well as death to aquatic species.

As in the case with hybrid seeds, the concept of sustainability requires that all these factors be taken into consideration. Sustainability looks at a longer time horizon than the end of a given year's harvest. Unfortunately, short time horizons are often the perspectives of both the poor and those selling to the poor. In the former case it means staying alive another year. In the latter case it means meeting shareholders' projections and perhaps getting a fat bonus in the process.

> Thought Experiment 7.2: You are the leader of Bangladesh. You are holding a meeting with your cabinet ministers to decide policy on allowing hybrid seeds and new potent chemical fertilizer into the country with the government's blessing. Given the trade-offs between genetically altered super-hybrids and lower yield wild subspecies, what should you recommend? The same dynamic holds true with fertilizer. What should you recommend?

Let's now consider the solution area for infectious disease. For simplicity, we will concentrate on malaria, HIV/AIDS, and tuberculosis. Let us also assume that none of these diseases is amenable (in the short term) to a preventative inoculation (vaccine). Thus, the best that can be hoped for is methods of nonbiological prevention and treatment.

Nonbiological prevention focuses on the manner of infection. Because mosquitoes are the cause of malaria, one longstanding method of prevention is to provide people in infected areas with mosquito nets. These nets attend to the fact that mosquitoes are most prevalent in the evening. Draping a net around one's bed significantly lowers the likelihood of being bitten and, hence, infected. In addition, recent research has shown that the mosquitoes can be infected with a virus that will shorten their lifespan to the point before the malaria bacterium becomes toxic. I spoke with individuals at the National Institutes of Health who find this strategy it be one of the most promising in the long run.

Once an individual contracts malaria, he or she must undergo treatment against the active parasite in the blood, which can also attack the liver. Chloroquine, sulfadoxine-pyrimethamine, mefloquine, atovaquone-proguanil, quinine, and doxycycline are intended to slow down and contain the advancing stages of the disease, but they are not cures. In endemic areas of the world, it is recommended that infected patients be seen in the first twenty-four hours, but this is very aspirational in poor countries.

HIV/AIDS presents an even more difficult scenario because the virus is mutating rapidly. The number of viral clades (each clade can be thought of as a subspecies of the pathogen in question) has increased over the past decade so that any attempt at a vaccine seems quixotic. The best nonbiological prevention is the condom (unless we make the utopian assumption that people will just stop having sex). Thus, widespread distribution of condoms is key.

As is the case with malaria, there is currently no known cure for HIV/AIDS. However, the number of drugs that can slow and contain the advancement of the disease has increased dramatically in recent years. Readers are encouraged to go to the website for the National Institutes of Health for the latest list.[18]

In many ways tuberculosis is the worst of the lot because of its ease in spreading and (in the case of several virulent strains) the certain finality of its results. Like the other two infectious diseases mentioned here, there is no vaccine for tuberculosis. A nonbiological control would be to stay away from affected regions. The traditional procedure of quarantine is not a very realistic option in subsistence societies. Thus, in this case treatment strategies are key. Antibiotic treatment of TB can result in a cure; in fact, antibiotics have been so effective that in the early 1970s it was thought that tuberculosis had been eliminated as a world disease. Two drug-resistant strains (multidrug-resistant TB and extensively drug-resistant TB) continue to wreak havoc on subsistence populations, although some possible new treatments are in trials.[19]

Both food and infectious disease pose very formidable challenges. The world's ability to lessen poverty requires serious attention to each. I encourage you to engage the extended-community worldview imperative and seriously consider the problems, causes, and possible solutions that might be implemented.

Key Terms

poverty, water-borne diseases, water-washed diseases, water-based diseases, water-related insect vectors, regional sustainable food supply

Critical Applied Reasoning Exercise

Pick your role: (1) an individual working as an individual, (2) a cabinet secretary working on behalf of your government, (3) the head of a nongovernmental association, (4) the head of some subgroup under the aegis of the United Nations. From one of these perspectives write a 1.5-page action plan that will address both famine and infectious disease in a real country in the world that you have researched.

Notes

1. This statistic is based on the concept of purchasing power parity, which suggests a tie to the prices of basic goods within that country in local currency translated to U.S. currency. Depending upon goods used in the market basket, this means a relative figure between $1.25 and $2.50 per day as indicative of levels of poverty (all within the level-one basic goods but at different measurement points). Shaohua Chen and Martin Ravallion, *The Developing World Is Poorer Than We Thought but No Less Successful in the Fight Against Poverty* (Washington, DC: World Bank, 2008).

2. "The State of the World," *New Internationalist* 287 (1997).

3. U.S. Department of Agriculture, 2008 U.S. Census Bureau, 2008.

4. World Health Organization, www.who.int/healthinfo/bodestimates/en.

5. *The 2007 Human Development Report* (New York: United Nations Development Program, 2007): 25.

6. Ibid., 27.

7. One account of this can be found in Larry Zuckerman, *The Potato: How the Humble Spud Rescued the World* (Boston: Faber and Faber, 1998).

8. See Michael Boylan, "Clean Water," in *International Public Health Policy and Ethics,* ed. Michael Boylan (Dordrecht: Springer, 2008): 273–288.

9. I am ignoring here the properties of the soil itself, which can become depleted when crop rotation is not observed. See D. M. Amatya, et al., eds., *Five Hydrologic Studies* (Asheville, NC: U.S. Department of Agriculture, Forest Service, Southern Research Station, 2005).

10. For a discussion of some of these issues, see Peter Gray, *The Irish Famine* (New York: Abrams, 1995); Peter Gray, *Famine, Land, and Politics: British Government and Irish Society, 1843–1850* (Dublin: Irish Academic Press, 1999); and Cormac Ó Gráda, *Black '47 and Beyond* (Princeton, NJ: Princeton University Press, 1999).

11. World Health Organization, 2000.

12. W. K. Reilly and H. C. Babbitt, "A Silent Tsunami: The Urgent Need for Clean Water and Sanitation" (Washington, DC: Aspen Institute, 2005); World Health Organization, *Global Water Supply and Sanitation Assessment 2000 Report,* www.who.int/water_sanitation_health/monitoring/globalaccess/en/index.html.

13. United Nations Development Programme, *United Nations Development Goals,* www.undp.org/mdg and www.worldbank.org/data.

14. See Thomas Robert Malthus, *Population: Three Essays* (New York: New American Library, rpt. 1960).

15. I have set out a thought experiment centered on a puzzle maker as the best way to think about desert and preferment; see Michael Boylan, *A Just Society* (Lanham, MD, and Oxford: Rowman and Littlefield, 2004): 139–145.

16. I have chosen 5 percent because it is the outside figure used in inductive logic to prove the null set and still generate a valid conclusion. One never has 100 percent concurrence: 97.5 percent and 95 percent are used as two legitimate benchmark standards.

17. Michael J. Selgelid, Paul M. Kelly, and Adrian Sleigh, "TB Matters More," in *International Public Health Policy and Ethics*, ed. Michael Boylan (Dordrecht: Springer, 2008): 233–248.

18. See www.aidsinfo.nih.gov/DrugsNew.

19. The treatments currently in trial are Floroquinolones (phase 3 trials), Nitroimidazoles (phase 2), Diarylquinoline (phase 2), Oxazolidnones (phase 2), and SQ109 (phase 1).

CHAPTER 8

Public Health

Public health often flies under the radar of international observers—especially the casual observer who may not have fulfilled the mandates of the extended-community worldview imperative with enough thoroughness. Public-health issues are commonly less obvious than war, or famine, or outbreaks of infectious disease, and yet they play pivotal roles in each. For our purposes let us distinguish between health care that is delivered in a *clinical* setting, involving individual patients with their doctors, and a *public* setting, involving strategies for dealing with the health care needs of large populations. The first case deals with interpersonal interreactions, and the second concerns macro communities. Strategies for disease prevention will be very different depending upon the perspective of each. For example, in the 1950s significant evidence that smoking was very deleterious to one's health began to appear in the *Journal of the American Medical Association, New England Journal of Medicine, Lancet,* and *British Medical Journal,* as well as in reports from the Surgeon General and the First World Conference on Smoking and Health. These and other medical agencies published articles suggesting to individual medical practitioners that, on a case-by-case basis, they should encourage their patients to stop smoking. The strategy did not work. Smoking did not significantly diminish.[1]

A public-health approach works more broadly. Because the emphasis is on macro community dynamics, public health lends itself very easily to issues of justice and public policy. In the instance of smoking, when the strategy turned to group dynamics and television advertising, the success rate improved. Television shows were encouraged not to show attractive lead characters smoking. Pro-smoking advertisements were banned on television, and even the effects of second-hand smoke came under scrutiny, leading to widespread bans on smoking in offices and public places. This strategy worked much better than the one-by-one clinical approach.[2] It seems that in some situations, the best answer is public health. It becomes important to determine, then, which problems are best situated to clinical settings and which are more appropriately dealt with at the group level. For example, in the United States today obesity is increasingly a serious health problem. Is obesity best addressed at the clinical level or at the public-health level?[3]

Whatever the final range of application turns out to be, public-health ethics is an emerging field with tremendous potential to address important national and international questions. I have edited two books on the subject and barely touched the surface.[4] Needless to say, in one small chapter there will be much selectivity and suggestive compression.

The Problem

Let us consider the following facts. First, the amount of clean water is decreasing even as the population of the world is increasing. Over half the world's people are at risk because of this.[5] As was discussed in Chapter 7, dirty water puts the resident population at risk for disease. Every eight seconds a child dies from drinking unclean water.[6] Infectious diseases—especially malaria, tuberculosis, and HIV/AIDS—take a tremendous toll, especially on subsistence societies. For our purposes let us classify all societies as being either *wealthy* or *subsistence*. In the former case the society can provide level-one and level-two basic goods to all people within the macro-community. In the latter case it cannot.

It should be made clear at this point the distinction between what a society *can* do and what it *actually does*. This is because many societies are able to distribute goods of agency to their citizens (or to other countries) but do not. This is generally because of a deficit in the individual and collective rational or affective good will (see Chapter 2). In these instances the personal worldview imperative, the shared-community worldview imperative, and the extended-community worldview imperative would demand that resources be shared both within one's own country (nationalism) and to those who are in need around the world (cosmopolitanism).

One problem in addressing these issues is that, although the public-health needs are evident in subsistence societies and could be successfully addressed with help from the international community, the wealthiest nations tend to react out of prudential reasons (that is, out of self-interest) rather than moral reasons such as those mandated by the extended-community worldview imperative. Countries with oil and other key natural resources tend to get more aid and attention from the richer nations than do the needier nations such as the Sudan, Mali, Bangladesh, Haiti, and Ecuador.

A second problem is that when the international community does try to intervene, domestic political dynamics often get in the way. For example, in the Sudan recently, the relief operations of NGOs and the United Nations in Darfur were expelled when the president was indicted for crimes against humanity.[7] In this case the president's domestic power base was threatened (in his opinion) by the international community, and he responded by expelling the NGOs and UN agencies that were helping his own people. His action resulted in greater misery and death and, sadly, illustrated how leaders are willing to sacrifice the good of their own population on the altar of political power.

3 A third problem is that there is little consultation and collaboration on critical medical research. The pharmaceutical industry is oriented toward a venture capitalist model, in which big money is gambled on research for the development of blockbuster drugs, most of which will never be brought to market. Accordingly, there is a very strong incentive to work in secrecy, to slant clinical trials toward success, and to fight for intellectual property protection of the drugs that do make it to market. The result is a system oriented toward hugely popular drugs (such as the latest erectile dysfunction cure) in industrialized countries and away from pharmaceuticals that affect the level-one basic goods of marginalized populations around the world through so-called orphan drugs (drugs that are useful to only a small segment of the population and that are thus not very profitable).

These three problems define the task of addressing the current challenge of effective public health intervention within the world's most needy societies.

The Causes

During a cholera outbreak in mid-nineteenth-century London, Dr. John Snow discovered that the outbreak could be traced to water drawn from a common source (the Broad Street pump). Since then, public-health officials have been keen on using the powerful tool of water control for short-term disease control, and sanitation efforts for long-term solutions.[8]

In Dr. Snow's London, the solution was straightforward. There was one country involved and a limited number of polluting sources. In the case of modern water contamination, with many players and interests at stake, matters can be more complicated.[9]

The key issue to be confronted regarding causation is whether public-health policy should be based upon ethical or prudential concerns.[10] The former meets the commands of a normative theory (as per Chapter 1); the latter are dictated by the self-interest of individuals or various groups within the society. For example, why might one wish to rid his area of the factors that cause cholera by improving sanitation and the quality of drinking water? An ethical argument, such as an extended-community worldview imperative, for the improvement of sanitation for the public at large might recognize that the right to protection from unwarranted bodily harm (in this case from lethal bacteria) and the right to clean water and sanitation are both level-one basic goods on the Table of Embeddedness. Because everyone can legitimately claim basic goods simply on the basis of their being human agents in the world, one must take all means to protect against cholera—including cleaning up areas that might lead to an outbreak. This duty is the same no matter if the risk is specific to groups other than those to which the policymaker belongs. After all, this is what the extended-community worldview imperative requires: We have to educate ourselves to what it means to live in the disadvantaged community in question and then educate others and collectively act to bring the basic goods of agency to the extended community. This is a cosmopolitan principle of resource redistribution.

A prudential argument would be that the individual, himself, would support an overhaul of sanitation conditions out of self-interest; that is, if and only if he believes that a given sanitation policy will directly benefit him and those close to him. In the cholera example, someone living outside an infected city might not support a public-health effort for sanitation, or might support it only if he believed he and his family might be at imminent risk of contracting cholera. From his point of view, this is the most efficient allocation of resources. (*Efficient* here means not spending public money on other people apart from the agent.) Thus the adage, "if the program doesn't help me, it's a wasteful program."

Others will support policies that they consider to be in their "enlightened self-interest." These might include preventive measures that may (indirectly) help others whether or not there is an imminent threat or a clear and present danger. These individuals are acting from self-interest but have a longer view of things. They see prevention as the most efficient allocation of resources because reacting in the midst of a crisis is notoriously expensive. These individuals would point to the adage, "an ounce of prevention is worth a pound of cure." In this way the "enlightened self-interest" version of egoism sees public-health measures as an insurance policy that will efficiently address potential problems. (*Efficiency* here means using fewer public dollars to address an issue that may have an impact upon the agent himself. There is some waste involved because the problem might not arise and the solution may help many others apart from the agent—still, the cost savings from acting early offsets this other sense of waste.)

The essence of the problem that public health faces as it tries to address community health problems is the conflict between an ethical approach and a prudential approach (including enlightened self-interest). From a statist or nationalist viewpoint, the prudential case generally wins the day. This is because *prudential* is defined in terms of those in power: the rich and the politically connected (two groups with significant overlap). The key question to ask is "prudential to whom?" My conjecture is that it is the ruling/monied micro minority. They twist the cost-benefit utilitarianism by eliminating the maxim that all count as one. In this case, all count differentially in direct relation to the size of their bank account. Because the rich and powerful within every country have the power to enforce their will in most cases of domestic legislation and public policy, there seems to be an automatic answer to the question of whether prudential or moral reasons should prevail.

Because the structure of government in almost all countries heavily favors the interests of the plutocrats, a state of kraterism ensues. Goods are distributed on one's ability to snatch them for himself, *kraterism.* There are some micro communities (those with fewer than 500 members) that may embrace socialist or egalitarian models of distributive justice. This is because on a smaller scale, communities can nurture the affective good will (see Chapter 2) and react personally to their neighbor. But in national macro communities and in the global community the personal contact is missing. This means that the affective good will becomes dependent upon the rational good will and the imagination. In practice, in these larger realms, kraterism is generally the operational theory (regardless of what the official version of distributive justice is set out to be). The way this is carried out varies. Sometimes the kraterists hide themselves in public propaganda such as the natural rulers of the state deserve more than ordinary citizens (aristocracy and preferment). Or those who have the riches of society (level-three secondary goods) are those who have worked the hardest (meaning at jobs that are valued by that society, regardless of their social worth). Often, there is a combination of sorts. I do not deny that the competitive theories of justice have a place within a well-ordered moral state—but they must be accompanied by the cooperative theories (socialism and egalitarianism—see Chapter 6).

The standoff between the competitive theories and the cooperative theories of justice is at the heart of the justification of the public-health debate. Because of the prominent place that the Table of Embeddedness plays in my theoretical presentation, I would give greater support to the cooperative theories than to the competitive ones in forming public policy. The solution to this sort of dynamic is essential in creating an answer to the pragmatic versus moral grounding for public-health policy.

Possible Solutions

It is my view that public-health policy should be driven by moral imperatives of legitimate rights claims. Each human individually has the exact same claim to level-one basic goods: no more and no less.[11]

The real antidote to the tension between prudential justifications and moral justifications is internationalism. We'll now look in turn at how internationalism can be used on the three problems addressed in this chapter: (1) rich nations don't pay attention to the problems of poor nations unless it is in their national self-interest; (2) political dynamics get in the way of NGOs and the UN agencies effectively intervening within the country; and (3) there is little consultation and collaboration in the area of medical research.

Educating Ourselves to Communities Around the World

First, the rich nations frequently don't pay *intrinsic attention* to the poor nations. This means that other (wealthier) nations consider the poor nation's problems from the viewpoint of that nation from a prudential viewpoint. If we accept that public-health policy should be driven by ethics (via the Table of Embeddedness, the argument for the moral status of basic goods, and the extended-community worldview imperative), then this lack of intrinsic attention is a problem. A quick example can help illustrate the difference between these two viewpoints. Pâté de foie gras is a product generally made from the livers of geese (sometimes ducks). To get a good yield on their investment, goose farmers breed geese for large livers. From a goose's perspective, having a very large liver is not healthy. *Intrinsically*—from the point of view of the affected goose—the breeding methods that promote a large liver are bad. *Extrinsically*, these breeding methods are good for the farmers, who get a better return on their investment. If one were instead to breed these geese for their own well-being, normal-sized livers would be intrinsically good for the geese but extrinsically bad for the farmers' bottom line.

When we apply this analysis to the relationship between rich and poor nations it often works out this way: (1) Rich nations are so keen on self-interest that they do not consider the interests of the country in which they do business—they act extrinsically to the country in which they do business; (2) if they acted according to the intrinsic interests of the country in which they do business it would hurt their profits. In a 1995 interview I did with a World Bank officer in charge of Asian development, I raised this very issue.[12] The officer, S. Janakiram, said that he thought that intervention of foreign multinational countries for any particular resource—be it natural minerals or human capital—required a permanent upgrade in the country's infrastructure. For example, if a company went into the Congo to mine iron ore for steel manufacturing, then that multinational company should do more than just mine the ore and fabricate it elsewhere. Rather, it should set up steel plants in the Congo and also additional factories that make the final products—such as refrigerators, ovens, or dishwashers. In this way the multinational company is not treating the Congo just as the pâté farmers treat their geese. When these mills and factories that fabricate high-skilled finished end products are maintained along with environmentally safe procedures, occupational safeguards, and a relatively robust wage for that country, the multinational company has acted responsibly toward the host country. Multinational businesses that act in an ethically responsible way toward the country in which they are doing business create a positive economic impact on the country, thereby reducing poverty and, a fortiori, improving the country's public health.

National Political Barriers to International Aid

Second is the issue of political discord between NGOs and UN agencies on the one hand and local governments on the other. This difficulty arises from the fact that much of the world lives under some sort of autocratic or oligarch rule—structures that often exist for their own sake and not for the people. (Actually this is a domestic variant of the intrinsic/extrinsic dilemma discussed above.) Plato discusses this exact point in Book One of *The Republic:*

1. Antithesis (the claim of Socrates' opponent): Justice is the rule of the strongest—Assertion (340c)
2. The ruler qua ruler does not err—Assertion (340e)
3. All arts are practiced for the sake of their object's betterment—Fact (341a–342c)
4. Arts hold a relationship of stronger to weaker—Assertion (342c)
5. [Ruling is a craft or art]—Fact
6. [The object of the ruling craft is the people in the state]—3, 5
7. "Ruling" must be practiced for the sake of the people—4–6
8. Rulers act for the best interests of their people (subjects)—2, 7

---

9. Thesis (Socrates' own position): Antithesis is rejected (Justice is not the rule of the strongest)—1, 8

In this argument, Socrates (as Plato's proxy) is arguing against Thrasymachus (an advocate of kraterism) by asserting that a ruler ought to not think extrinsically about furthering his own interest but instead ought to act on the intrinsic interests of his subjects in order to perfect the art of ruling.

Research and "Big Pharma"

Third is the question of research. I have argued elsewhere in more detail for changing our current system of research and development of pharmaceuticals within both the rich and subsistence countries.[13] The reason for the change is that the systems for distributing critical medicines around the world to those who need them do not work effectively. Because the for-profit capitalistic model has not worked to provide the level-one basic goods of health care to all people, my suggestion would be to encourage (via cooperative international tax protocols) the creation of low-profit (or even nonprofit) pharmaceutical companies. The low-profit companies would be managed via public oversight for the common good and in return would be given public protection for consistent (if admittedly low) levels of profit, much as the utility companies in the United States were operated before deregulation in the 1980s. The nonprofit companies will have a mission to produce and distribute orphan drugs (small-market, targeted pharmaceuticals) and meet the needs of those in subsistence societies. These nonprofit companies would work cooperatively with open source research that could not be patented by anyone else. They could team up with university research and form a spirit of cooperation (instead of competition) in drugs that could help subsistence societies (even if the paying market is rather small).

The distribution of pharmaceuticals in the developing world poses a series of problems.[14] For simplicity's sake let us rename the question as distributing drugs to the subsistence societies of the world. Though there are some private distribution schemes such as Médecins sans Frontières (Doctors Without Borders) and One World,[15] the bulk of help in this area is through public-private partnerships. This generally is set out with large competitive model companies such as Merck and GlaxoSmithKline (i.e., "Big Pharma") working on specific problems such as river blindness with *ivermectin* and tackling lymphatic filariasis (a nonremunerative disease target), along with WHO and UNICEF and some HIV programs.[16]

If a license were given to a country to produce a generic version of needed drugs for their own consumption, they could be produced for only a few dollars a dose. In some instances certain pharmaceutical companies have been willing to grant an exception to their patent, though this is controversial.[17] Usually, though, the companies have been reluctant to waive their patents because they fear a black market will import the cheaper versions of their drugs and undercut the commerce of their product in wealthy societies. Under this scenario, their patent will be useless. The companies claim they will not receive their bonanza return on their investment, and this dire outcome will have an effect on the research and development of new drugs. Thus (under this competitive worldview approach), pharmaceutical companies will say that although they are very sorry for the plight of the disadvantaged in subsistence countries (as evidenced, in fact, by their participation in present public-private partnerships), they must first think of their stockholders and maintain the value of their patents.

Under the competitive worldview theories such as unfettered capitalism and kraterism, there is some plausibility to this argument. When one's primary goal is to maximize shareholder stock value, it makes sense to do everything possible to protect it, though this approach inadequately addresses the underlying public-health problems. Thus, from the public-health vantage point the competitive worldview answer is inadequate.[18] This is due to the cost structure of the competitive model.[19]

However, things change under the cooperative worldview model. Under this model of distribution, the new drug companies are a protected industry. They would be either nonprofit or modestly profitable, and in return for eschewing the unpredictable chance for bonanza returns on investment, they would be a protected industry, buffered from the upturns and downturns of the competitive market place. Because of these domestic and international protections, the major drug companies would be able to grant subsistence countries the right to create and distribute more affordable generic substitutes for the more expensive versions of the drugs sold elsewhere. The anxiety of the black market will be lessened because of governmental cooperation on behalf of the companies with public, cooperative missions.

For maximum effectiveness, the major industrial powers (most of whom have already bought into the cooperative model through universal health coverage) might choose to regulate international distribution of pharmaceuticals under the aegis of an international body such as the World Health Organization. In addition, they would work to create a model for establishing incentives for the creation of nonprofit pharmaceutical companies and for transforming traditional pharmaceuticals into protected companies with a cooperative public mission. In this way there might arise a certain international uniformity among most of the wealthy nations of the world. This will serve to protect the companies so that they might better serve the public—both in their own (wealthy) countries and in subsistence countries.

With such international coordination and planning, it might be possible to mount major attacks upon such clearly preventable diseases as malaria, eliminating it from the earth.[20] This would be a boon for public health—not only in the subsistence society but everywhere. With the advent of frequent international travel, there is no such thing as "them" and "us." We are all in this together. We should help the subsistence countries because it is right to do so. People have a valid claim right for the basic goods of agency. However, this is not entirely altruistic because doing so will also make the world a safer place for us all.

Key Terms

public versus clinical health care, moral versus prudential approach, intrinsic versus extrinsic, collaboration on medical research

Critical Applied Reasoning Exercise

Pick one of the problems addressed in this chapter and decide which international entity is best positioned to be most effective in dealing with this problem. Appoint yourself to an executive post in that entity and write a two-page memo describing how your agency will institute a policy to solve the problem you have elucidated.

Notes

1. This is widely documented; see Mary-Jane Schneider, *Introduction to Public Health,* 2nd ed. (Boston: Jones and Bartlett, 2006): 252–255; and Paul I. Ahmed, *Changes in Cigarette Smoking Habits Between 1955–1966* (Rockville, MD: U.S. Department of Health, Education, and Welfare, 1970): 6–14.

2. When the public-health approach was employed, significant progress was obtained: Schneider, 257–266, Allan M. Brandt, *The Cigarette Century: The Rise and Fall of the Product That Defined America* (New York: Basic Books, 2007): ch. 3; John P. Allegrante et al., "A Multi-variate Analysis of Selected Psychosocial Variables on the Development of Subsequent Youth Smoking Behavior," *Public Health Service* (Rockville, MD: Department of Health, Education and Welfare, 1976); Lawrence Garfinkel, "Trends in Cigarette Smoking in the United States," *Preventative Medicine* 26 (1997): 447–450; Jon M. Harkness, "The U.S. Public Health Service and Smoking in the 1950s: The Tale of Two Statements," *Journal of the History of Medicine and Allied Sciences* 62, 2 (2006): 171–212.

3. See Rosemarie Tong, "Taking on the 'Big Fat': The Relative Risks and Benefits of the War Against Obesity," in *Public Health Policy and Ethics,* ed. Michael Boylan (Dordrecht: Kluwer/Springer, 2004): 39–58.

4. The two volumes are *Public Health Policy and Ethics,* ed. Michael Boylan (Dordrecht: Kluwer/Springer, 2004), and *International Public Health Policy and Ethics,* ed. Michael Boylan (Dordrecht: Springer, 2008). The former had an emphasis on United States issues whereas the latter was internationalist in design.

5. A. K. Ahmed, "Serious Environmental and Public Health Impacts of Water-Related Diseases and Lack of Sanitation on Adults and Children," www.cec.org/files/pdf/POLUTANTS/karim_ahmed.pdf.

6. Children's Water Fund, "Did You Know—Facts," www.childrenswaterfund.org.

7. On March 4, 2009, President Omar Hassan al-Bashir of Sudan was indicted for war crimes against the people of the Darfur region of his country: http://news.bbc.co.uk/2/hi/africa/7923102.stm.

8. S. Hempel, *The Strange Case of the Broad Street Pump* (Berkeley: University of California Press, 2007); and S. Johnson, *The Ghost Map* (New York: Riverhead, 2006).

9. B. Stevens, "Assessing the Risks," *Organization for Economic Cooperation and Development Observer* 254 (2006): 26–27; B. C. Barah, Traditional Water Harvesting Systems in India (New Delhi: John Wiley, 1996); P. Börkey, "Safe Water: A Quality Conundrum," *Organization for Economic Cooperation and Development Observer* 254 (2006): 16–18.

10. A fuller version of this argument can be found in Boylan, *Public Health Policy and Ethics,* "The Moral Imperative to Maintain Public Health," pp. xvii–xxxiv.

11. Though, of course, some may have greater needs for particular goods due to natural soma-type or to accident or disease. The general point remains the same.

12. Interview with S. Janakiram in *Ethical Issues in Business,* ed. Michael Boylan (Fort Worth, TX: Harcourt Brace Publishers, 1995): 566–568.

13. Michael Boylan, "Medical Pharmaceuticals and Distributive Justice," *Cambridge Quarterly of Healthcare Ethics* 17, 1 (Winter 2008): 32–46.

14. Richard De George, "Intellectual Property Rights and Pharmaceutical Drugs: An Ethical Analysis," *Business Ethics Quarterly* 15, 4 (2005): 549–575. Klaus M. Leisinger, "The Corporate Social Responsibility of the Pharmaceutical Industry," *Business Ethics Quarterly* 15, 4 (2005): 577–594.

15. Médicins Sans Frontières, "The Campaign: What Is the Campaign?" www.accessmed-msf.org/campaign/campaign.shtm; One World, www.oneworld.net.

16. Merck, "The Story of Mectizan," www.merck.com/about/cr/mectizan/home.html; GlaxoSmithKlein, "Lymphatic Filariasis Programme," www.gsk.com/filariasis/index.htm; Boehringer-Ingeiheim, "Viramune MTCT Donation Programme."

17. John Carey, "What's a Fair Price for Drugs?: Yes, the U.S. Pays Too Much for Its Medicine. But Don't Blame It All on Drugmakers," *Business Week* (April 30, 2001): 105–106; "A Matter of Life and Death," *New Scientist* (February 19, 2005): 44; Donald Berwick, Richard Sykes, and Zackie Achmat, "'We All Have AIDS': Case for Reducing the Cost of HIV Drugs to Zero," *British Medical Journal* (January 26, 2004): 214–218; N. Kumarasamy, "Generic Antiretroviral Drugs—Will They Be the Answer to HIV in the Developing World?" *Lancet* (July 3, 2004): 3–4; Rachel Zimmerman, "Merck Still Draws Fire for HIV Drug for Poor Nations," *Wall Street Journal* (March 3, 2004): D3.

18. S. Nwaka and R. G. Ridley, "Virtual Drug Discovery and Development for Neglected Diseases Through Public-Private Partnerships," *Nature Reviews: Drug Discovery* 2, 11 (2003): 919–928; M. Reich, ed., "Public-Private Partnerships," www.hsph.harvrd.ecy/hcpds/partnerbook/Partnershipsbook.pdf.

19. Centers for Medicare and Medicaid Services, "Health Care Industry Market Update: Pharmaceuticals," www.cms.hhs.gov/reports/hcimu/hcimu_01102003.pdf; Families USA, "Profiting from Pain: Where Prescription Dollars Go," www.familiesusa.org/site/DocSServer/Ppreport.pdf?docID=249.

20. William D. Reisel and Linda M. Sama, "The Distribution of Life-Saving Pharmaceuticals," *Business and Society Review* 108, 3 (2003): 365–387.

CHAPTER 9

Race, Gender, and Sexual Orientation

I will begin this chapter by discussing an article from the *Washington Post*.[1] In the article the reporter talks about new Afghan laws governing Shiite Muslims within Afghanistan that had previously only been applied under Sunni Muslim law. In this "progressive" new statute, women "must seek their husband's permission to leave home, except for 'culturally legitimate' purposes such as work or weddings, and to submit to their [husbands'] sexual demands unless ill or menstruating. . . . Shiite legislators and clerics who drafted and promoted the law have asserted that it protects women."

Most Western readers of this passage would declare that this new Afghan law is written from an androcentric (i.e., male dominant) standpoint. Women are put under the power of their husbands as second-class entities. Why is this? The best explanation is that the males control the culture and the women have to submit or become outcasts. The status of the outcast and the other are the focus of this chapter.

The Problem

This chapter will address three problems of discrimination: (1) by race, (2) by gender, and (3) by sexual orientation.

Discrimination by Race

Discrimination for the purposes of this book will refer to the process of relegating a person or group to the class of *the other*.[2] The designated other is excluded

119

from the community as a fully participating member. According to the Table of Embeddedness, this violates virtually all level-one secondary goods:

Basic societal respect
Equal opportunity to compete for the prudential goods of society
Ability to pursue a life plan according to the personal worldview imperative
Ability to participate equally as an agent in the shared-community worldview imperative

These goods are necessary to lead a fulfilling life according to one's personal worldview. When people or groups are relegated to the status of the other, the level of harm is thus immediate. For the purposes of clarity, let's agree to call the loss of level-one secondary goods being *marginalized*.

Beyond the loss of level-one secondary goods are the possible further harms of the loss of level-one basic goods—food, water, sanitation, clothing, shelter, protection from unwarranted bodily harm, and basic health care—and/or level-two basic goods—loss of liberty or education goods. Again for clarity's sake, we'll call the loss of these basic goods as being *victimized.*

Race will be defined here as referring to any group that is picked out as being *other* on the basis of physical differences other than gender or disability differences. This definition differs from many that contend that there are a fixed number of races that are largely geographical in their origin. This definition is unique in that it considers race not as an objective attribute of the person himself or herself but as an attitude of the observer. If a person has a physical difference that is positively viewed or neutrally viewed, then that person is not of a different race than the audience perceiving him or her. The crucial element is being seen as the *other* due to these (nongender or nondisability) physical differences. This means that race is not a descriptive term but a normative one. To identify someone as being of another race is tantamount to saying that by nature that person is *different* (here, *different* generally means inferior).

Because this process connotes negative audience dispositions, the result is that those so identified are marginalized (at the least) and/or victimized (at the worst). Marginalized individuals face lower expectations by the audience. These are often played out in ersatz psychological screening that seems to support these social attitudes. *Psychological screening* occurs when someone believes some fact to be true. As a result he tends to observe all cases that coincide with his belief as confirming instances and all cases that do not coincide as outlier cases to be ignored—thus reinforcing his beliefs (often stereotypes) even in the face of contrary facts. Being marginalized means that one is not treated as an equal. This can result in subtle or overt discrimination in education, employment, advancement, and social status. In the legal field there is a body of work on what has been termed *critical race theory,* which suggests that within the realm of judicial discretion subtle racist attitudes can steer decisions and appeals in a particular direction that is not advantageous to litigants (whether plaintiffs or defendants) who are perceived as members of a racial minority.[3]

Victimization is often the result of violent racial responses.[4] Some responses might be, for example, extreme and threatening epithets (fighting words) spray-painted on walls to put certain others into fear for their safety. Other responses might be overt hate crimes in which physical injury or death results. During hard economic times and in war these incidences often spike.[5] Overt attitudes of aggression fuel those with latent discriminatory feelings that can create a mob mentality in which people in mass will do things they might never consider doing individually. All around the world, incidents of racial violence occur every day. They are among the many challenges to achieving global justice.

Discrimination by Gender   ✗ India – gang rapes

Gender might seem an easy word to define. We all can tell males from females by their genitalia. But surely this does not tell the whole story. Gender differences (like racial differences) can instigate a categorization of a group of people who are then discriminated against.

Virtually every country in the world has experienced widespread social discrimination by gender (i.e., male against female). As in the case with race, sometimes this discrimination takes the form of lighter burdens of marginalization, such as missing the promotion, not being paid as much as a male colleague, or having certain career paths blocked. On the Table of Embeddedness these are level-one secondary goods.

But there are also the heavier burdens of victimization. These include sexual violence and oppressive living conditions that increase the mortality of women in what is often called the role of drudge wives.[6] Throughout the world, women's access to paid work is severely limited, thus sharply constraining their ability to possess food, clothing, shelter, and other level-one basic goods. Women are also responsible for most unpaid domestic duties. Societies throughout the world value money as the measure of a person, and people are judged by their salary levels. Because women earn less money than men (when they are allowed to pursue paid work) and earn nothing in domestic labor, they are often devalued. As a group they cannot compete on a scale in which level of paycheck is everything. This leads to devaluation in social power, authority, and access to resources. In response to this diminished social position, women are still likely to stick by the family when times get tough: Men are more likely to exit than women.[7] This resonates with the distinction between competitive and cooperative theories of justice. As has been argued earlier, micro communities—such as the family—are the greatest source of cooperative justice theories: socialism and egalitarianism. In most societies—especially in subsistence societies—the general rules of engagement entail the competitive theories: unfettered capitalism and kraterism. The virtues of the cooperative theories are marginalized and considered to be quaint— just the sort of tasks that women are good at. Thus, the virtues of faithfulness to one's children and familial obligations do not rank highly on most social scales. Women attempt to protect the level-one basic goods of their children while many husbands pursue egoistic ends (level-two and-three secondary goods). Perversely, societies around the world reward the latter over the former.

Further, women often are punished by men for suffering as they do in social care. The statistics are stark: Amartya Sen estimated in 1990 that around 100 million women were missing in 1990 in Asia alone as the result of victimization against women.[8] In a recent report, the U.S. Department of State declared that the trafficking of people (largely due to gender) is a growing international problem.[9] Tops on the list in trafficking are Burma, Mauritania, New Guinea, Saudi Arabia, Sudan, and Zimbabwe. In the United States the report cites 14,500– 17,500 people each year who are sold as chattel to work at low-status jobs in society at little to no real pay. Both victimization and trafficking violate rights claims on the Table of Embeddedness. In the former case women are not given adequate education or civic freedom (a level-two basic good) and are not allowed to pursue a life plan consistent with the personal worldview imperative (a level-one secondary good). In the case of trafficking one can add protection from unwarranted bodily harm (a level-one basic good). Wherever they occur, these abuses of the legitimate rights of women require a forceful response. This is a tremendous challenge to global justice that should not be ignored.

Discrimination by Sexual Orientation Jamaica

Discrimination by sexual orientation will be taken to mean discrimination against *homosexual* and/or *transsexual* individuals (those individuals whose gender identity does not match their body's genitalia). Current scientific research conclusively agrees that one's sexuality is biologically given. We don't choose it. It is not a psychological problem requiring therapy. To simplify things, let us consider the fates of two groups: homosexual and transsexual (also known as transgendered) peoples. In the category of discrimination, the result is more often victimization than marginalization. The reactions are not subtle but overt. For example, in the United States, the 1964 Civil Rights law bars discrimination based on race, gender, or religion but does not mention sexual orientation. It is impossible to accurately document the cases of this sort of discrimination because (in the United States by federal law) marginalization is legal and because many feel it is not a problem. Thus, in the United States by federal law, discrimination against gays and transsexuals is perfectly legal (though some states and local jurisdictions have made it illegal). For example, a person can be fired from a job just because it is discovered that she is homosexual or transgendered. No other cause need be given. There is no protection against discrimination in hiring, housing, government contracts, and so on, But it doesn't stop there. Violence against gays in the United States, for example, is often as high as one in four gays reporting having been a victim of violence.[10] Around the world the situation can be worse. In seven countries homosexuals can face the death penalty: Iran, Saudi Arabia, Yemen, United Arab Emirates, Sudan, Nigeria, and Mauritania.

Once again, the *other* is treated violently. This constitutes a violation of the right of protection from unwarranted bodily harm (a level-one basic good) in the case of violence and the equal opportunity to compete for the prudential goods of society and to become a full member of the shared community worldview (a level-one secondary good). Both of these goods are unjustifiably denied to many because of their sexual orientation. This also is a threat to global morality and justice.

The Causes

Discrimination by Race

It is difficult to ascertain just why people discriminate on the basis of race. There may be both biological and social reasons. Kin-selection theory in evolutionary biology postulates that each person is driven by a biological imperative to pursue a "selfish gene" strategy aimed at passing his or her genes to the next generation.[11] In concert with this strategy, a given person seeks to protect and defend, in order: their (1) close relatives (who share large numbers of genes with the person), (2) distant relatives (who share fewer genes with the person), and (3) those who look like the person himself (on the principle that phenotypic traits are genetically based). According to this theory, one would give hierarchal preference to these aforementioned groups of people. If this is correct, then those of a different, minority race (as defined above) would then find that they are always put at the end of the queue by those in the phenotypical majority just in case the minority exhibits different physical features. This is one biological perspective on the origins of racial prejudice.

Many would argue against such apparent biological determinism. An alternate socially based theory would maintain that the shared community worldview of the minority race (as defined earlier) is seen by the majority as being *different* (the other), and, as different, it is bad. When two different worldviews conflict, a common response is for each side to reinforce what it already believes (coinciding and amplification—see Chapter 2), exacerbating the divide between the majority and the minority. When challenges are presented to racial prejudice, dissonance and rejection is the response.

In my opinion, the most probable causes of racial discrimination are biological and social, with the actual mixing point somewhat undetermined at present.

Discrimination by Gender

Gender discrimination also has biological and social origins. Again from the perspective of evolutionary biology, an individual's primary task in life is to pass his or her genes to the next generation. But that goal of "reproductive success" holds different implications for males and females. For males, in this view, reproductive success lies in inseminating as many women as possible, in order to increase the male's number of offspring—a biological imperative that might help explain the apparent prevalence of male promiscuity across cultures.

In contrast, females can have only one child (or a few children) at a time. They must bear the fetus for nine months and then nurture the infant, in most societies breastfeeding it for a period of months or years. Because the these tasks fall biologically upon the woman and because so much is invested in each and every baby, the woman's best reproductive strategy is to find a way to get help raising the child to increase its chances of surviving to pass on its own genes (and the mother's). One way to do this is to ensure that the child's father is clearly identified so that the father might be called upon for support—a goal that is perhaps best achieved with female monogamy, so that the paternity of the woman's children is certain (or at least unquestioned).

Cultural, social, and political development in most societies has been largely androcentric. The reasons for this may also hearken back to how families are raised. Most humans require close supervision until at least age seven if they are to become successful agents in the world.[12] Because childcare is tied to females biologically (via breastfeeding), most societies have transitioned to a policy of continuity: The mother continues to care for the children until their point of independence. In some instances these tasks are shared, but these exceptions tend to occur among the rich via hiring expensive (female) nannies, and among the poor by sending children to live with (female) relatives. The middle class uses daycare (staffed mostly by females). Though social generalizations have many exceptions, for the most part these dynamics indicate that a disproportionate share of child rearing typically falls on women, which in turn means that women are at a competitive disadvantage vis-à-vis men in access to the goods of agency, especially in political and economic arenas. This very great responsibility conveys a power disadvantage in a highly competitive economic theater. To continue the metaphor, the final bow to the audience is generally performed by a man.

The final area of discrimination falls biologically from the fact that most women are smaller and less strong than most men. This does not mean that some women are not stronger than some men, but for the most part men hold a strength and physical power advantage. Were this not the case, then (aside from weapons) there would be no rape or domestic violence in the world.

Discrimination by Sexual Orientation

Sexual orientation, be it homosexual, transsexual, or any other biological expression, remains one of the least understood phenomena in the world. Many people use the following argument to form their judgment that such expression is an indulgence in perversion:

1. All human action is governed by a strong sense of free will—Fact
2. Sexual orientation is an action—Fact
3. Sexual orientation is freely undertaken—1, 2
4. Homosexual or transgender orientation is an action—Assertion
5. Homosexual or transgender activity is freely undertaken—1–4
6. Homosexual or transgender activity is an indulgence in perversion—Assertion
7. All sexual activity must follow a mainstream heterosexual model—Assertion
8. [An indulgence in perversion is, by definition, a freely chosen action that is contrary to a mainstream model]—Fact
9. [That which is freely undertaken and is contrary to a mainstream model is wrong and should be avoided and prosecuted]—Assertion

---

10. Homosexual and transgender activity should be avoided and prosecuted—5–9

There is a second common argument, which references fidelity to nature. It goes like this:

1. All societies ought to respect sexual responses that follow "according to nature"—Assertion
2. All people's sexual orientation is a hardwired genetic orientation (nature)—Fact

3. "Acting according to nature" means acting according to a hardwired genetic orientation—Fact
4. One's sexual response should reflect his or her hardwired genetic orientation—1–3
5. Homosexual and transgender activity constitute a sexual response—Fact
6. Homosexual and transgender activity is natural—3, 4

---

7. Homosexual and transgender activity should be supported by society—1, 4–6

Both arguments are simple, but they point to a huge difference in attitudes about these issues: Either sexual orientation is entirely in one's power or sexual orientation is genetically determined. If the latter is true, and it seems it is—both on the basic science scene and in social science contexts[13]—then most traditional models of moral acceptance and blame would take these scientific facts into account in making judgments about sexual orientation (under realistic models of ethics). What is scientifically shown to be genetically driven is out of one's control, and thus no blame can attach itself to that trait. For example, if one were born tall or short, it would be wrong to hold the person to be morally responsible for being tall or short. The first argument is defective because it overemphasizes our control over nature. One cannot will to be tall or short. Instead, a person finds him- or herself to be tall or short and then tries to find self-fulfillment given those parameters. However, many of the major religions of the world—especially Christianity, Judaism, and Islam—view homosexuality and transsexuality as violating God's word, an objection that assumes that people can freely choose their sexuality. The problem of discrimination exists in large part because there is no general social consensus on the origins of sexual orientation. I encourage you to look carefully at the premises of the arguments and discuss their truth or falsity as a way of working through the causal factors at work.

Again, this is an instance of the way we accept novel normative theories (Chapter 2). Real consideration of a claim requires that one enter the realm of overlap and modification.

Possible Solutions

Discrimination by Race

If it is correct that racial discrimination has biological and cultural causes, then the solutions must address these barriers. First, we cannot change our biology (save for experimental calls for genetic engineering).[14] But though biology may *incline* us in certain attitude directions this does not mean we are determined to accept those attitudes. Biology may create impulses for unreflective responsive action based on these attitudes, but because of the power of reason and the will people can overcome these impulses to accept racist attitudes. The attitudes are *not* hardwired (as, say, sexual orientation is). This is because biological determinism exists in sexual orientation. *Inclinations* toward some attitude are different from hardwired determinism. For example, say you are a physically strong individual and a good street fighter and you walk into a pizza shop to get some pizza. The clerk says your pizza might take twenty minutes. Well, you don't want to wait twenty minutes. There are people in the shop eating pizzas right now! You could walk up to any one of them and take their pizza. If they objected, you could knock them out with one punch. Perhaps you have an impulse to do just that based on a biologically based inclination. But most people who have such strength and impulses have learned to control themselves and wait their turn. (The others are serving time in jail.)

To have a biological or culturally motivated impulse is not sufficient to conclude that an action following that impulse will take place. The same holds true for the xenophobic kin-selection inclination. You may have an inclination that is biologically based to favor those who look like you, but you need not act on it. One way to control this impulse is to examine other senses of similarity. This turns kin selection on its head! For example, a European-descent American might find that his value system is closer to an African American than to another European-descent American. This is what made the Reverend Martin Luther King Jr. so effective. King and his message of racial equality resonated more strongly with mainstream America than did the oppressive and brutal tactics of many of the Southern policemen who opposed King and his followers (see Chapter 2 on overlap and modification). When the civil rights protesters were marching in their Sunday best, singing hymns familiar to many Christian Americans, many European-descent Americans said to themselves, "We sang that hymn just last week in church." When the police came out with their fire hoses and knocked these peaceful protesters down and brought vicious dogs who tore the protestors' flesh, then the same people said, "That isn't right. Why are they doing that?" Reverend King appealed to their sense of common humanity—of *similarity*.[15] This similarity is not morphological but is related to moral character. Moral character supersedes morphology to most people, and moral character is not racially linked (except among the pathologically racist).[16]

The biological response to impulse is mirrored in the cultural response. When the shared community worldview and extended community worldview say that discrimination is not only a permission but also an obligation, this constitutes a powerful motivation for behavior—but it is not determinate. As in the King example, the phenomenon of *overlap* (of community and personal worldviews) and *modifica-tion* (or community and personal worldviews) is still a possibility—though it may take transformational leaders, such as Dr. King, to make it happen. Thus both the biological and the social causes of racism can be overcome.

Discrimination by Gender

In principle, gender discrimination should be the easiest sort of discrimination to overcome. This is because reproductive autonomy would counter many of the sources of problems mentioned earlier. Women can (with the use of birth con-trol) decide not to become pregnant—without consulting a man. Women can (with the use of sperm banks and in-vitro fertilization [IVF] clinics) decide to become pregnant—without consulting a man. If the biological basis of female discrimination is about reproduction, then the theoretical grounds of respond-ing to that exist right now. The problem is that these options are only available to a few. For example, to get birth-control pills (the most effective contraceptive method), one must be able to go to a doctor and be prescribed them. Going to a medical doctor is expensive. Those who are poor may not be able to afford the cost of the physician's appointment to get a prescription, much less the cost of the pills themselves. In various countries in the world, reliable birth control for women is often not readily available.[17]

Likewise, choosing to become pregnant by artificial means is expensive. Women who want to bypass an interpersonal sexual relationship with a man in order to procreate are dependent upon IVF or traditional artificial insemination techniques using sperm banks. This leads many to question whether procreation is a human right. Some international organizations and entities have been lean-ing this way. But if it is a right, then what level of right is it (relative to the Table of Embeddedness)? In my opinion it would fit into the level-one secondary good of being able to actualize a personal life plan according to one's wishes. This means it is less essential than food, water, sanitation, clothing, shelter, protection from unwarranted bodily harm, and basic health care: level-one basic goods. It is also less than primary and secondary education and human liberties on par with the U.S. Bill of Rights: level-two basic goods. It is embedded at level three (the highest of the secondary goods). It is above level four—materially "keeping up with the Joneses," or level five—materially surpassing one's peers. This does not mean it is not important, but that it fits into one's quest for self-fulfillment, which only can begin once the other two basic levels have been met.

However, is reproductive equality enough to solve the problem? Childcare is also essential. In theory this should be an issue for both men and women. How-ever, because around the world there are far more females taking care of children than men, the burden has fallen to women. In G-8 countries (the eight richest countries in the world), the solution might be to bring primary education down to a lower level—say to three years old with employment security to the parent caregiver and government support to the parent caregiver (be it a she or a he). Under such a system, some sort of extended maternity or paternity benefits might exist for those critical first three years (ideally shared by the parents in shifts with their respective jobs). After that point, state-run education would begin in ways shown to be educationally and emotionally beneficial to the child. This might be an effective policy for the richest nations, but in the rest of the world (almost three-quarters of the people on earth), the situation is rather more difficult. These governments cannot support such programs. For these countries, macro community solutions will always be underfunded. It will be a necessity that micro communities take up the slack along the lines of "it takes a village." No one policy can be set out because each village will deal with the problem differently.

Finally, there is the issue of male strength and physical power, which is a fact of biological dimorphism that has been a part of the species for thousands of years. If X is physically more powerful than Y and there is an irresolvable difference, then it is very likely that X will force his solution upon Y. For many couples this is the case. It is the source of domestic violence and general violence by men against women. The shared community worldview is the only plausible way to restrain male violence against women: Men and women in the community must make it perfectly clear that these aggressive actions will not be tolerated. Such community standards are only as effective as those within the micro community who are willing to enforce these maxims through effective intervention.

Discrimination by Sexual Orientation

Discrimination on the basis of sexual orientation has been fostered by historical attitudes that are founded upon a false notion that people have no biological inclinations regarding sexuality (save heterosexuality). Such attitudes assume that those whose sexual orientation is different choose to be that way, counter to social and religious norms. But this attitude is patently false (as noted earlier). The solution to this aspect of the problem would be to ensure that primary, secondary, and tertiary schoolbooks were peer reviewed by those knowledgeable about the basic science. This approach will work with those in the population who are forming their opinions. The young are often the most open to considering an alternative point of view. Moving the personal worldviews of this group is very important in instigating social and political change—both nationally and internationally.

However, this is not enough. The *dissonance and rejection* worldview response (see Chapter 2) to scientific facts that runs contrary to one's beliefs is very strong.

When the audience is entrenched within a culturally based mindset that sexual orientation is subject to one's dispositional will, this audience will not be won over by tolerance and equal rights. Why is this? Because they think any counter-evidence is slanted by some empowered media plot to subvert basic values (meaning the reinforcement of their own worldview; this is an example of *coinciding and amplification*). On this level, the only real hope is the appearance of transformational leaders who show others that equal rights for everyone cannot wait any longer. In various countries at different times there have been scapegoats (such as Oscar Wilde) and martyrs (such as Harvey Milk), but what the nations of the world need are transformational leaders who will engage in the *overlap and modification* approach used effectively by Gandhi and King. Such statesmen and -women put their lives on the line. But then, many gays, lesbians, and transgendered souls put their lives on the line every day. They are wrongfully beaten and abused. The cultural hurdle may only be surpassed when such a figure steps forward who the mainstream identifies with on one level, but who also engages the progressive call for equal rights. Until this happens, the discrimination and victimization of this social group will, sadly, continue.

General Conclusion

Some might say, "What's the point?" In accord with the extended-community worldview imperative, we must educate ourselves about the plight of others outside our own immediate spheres. If we don't educate ourselves, then various marginalized groups remain invisible to the other social groups within the population.

One common policy recommendation that might help all three of the featured groups in this chapter is the collection and dissemination of statistics that confront various aspects of life in terms of race, gender, and sexual orientation. For example, one might collect statistics concerning population percentage, deaths, deaths by cause, victims of violent crime, access to basic medical care, primary education enrollment, secondary education enrollment, tertiary enrollment, incarceration rate, employment rate, employment sector participation, percentage in the government, and so on. The intent of these categories is roughly to capture the participation in the goods of agency as measured by the Table of Embeddedness—basic goods (levels one and two) and secondary goods (level one). This is one way international agencies, the UN, or transparent NGOs can become involved. Using internationally recognized statistical standards of gathering, analyzing, and disseminating data, these groups can discover and reveal an ongoing image on how these three groups are faring within societies. If the society in question has any commitment to being responsive and responsible to its citizens, it will take these statistics seriously as a measuring device to track and drive social change. The twofold challenge is first, to engage the personal and community worldview change according to the process of worldview modification (how we confront novel normative theories; see Chapter 2) and, second, to engage our newly modified worldviews via the community and extended community worldview imperatives so that we might address these important issues of morality and global justice.

Key Terms

discrimination, marginalization, victimization, race, psychological screening, gender, homosexual, transsexual

Critical Applied Reasoning Experiment

Choose a country in the world. Next, choose a group that is subject to discrimination and/or victimization (by race, gender, or sexual orientation). Engage your choices in the following scenario: You are head of the new United Nations Statistical Task Force on Discrimination and Victimization. You are assigned to create a two-page questionnaire that asks what you feel are crucial questions that will allow the country you have chosen to identify its problem and then measure progress over time.

Notes

1. Pamela Constable, "Afghan Law Ignites Debate on Religion, Sex," *Washington Post* (April 11, 2009): A-1.
2. On the "other" read a social viewpoint and a scientific one: Michael Omi and Howard Winant, "Thinking Through Race and Racism," *Contemporary Sociology* 38, 2 (2009): 121–126; and Lanny Fields and Michelle Garruto, "Optimizing Linked Perceptual Class Formation and Transfer of Function," *Journal of Experimental Analysis of Behavior* 91, 2 (2009): 225–252.
3. One champion of this approach is Derrick Bell, *Silent Covenants: Brown v. Board of Education and Unfulfilled Hopes for Racial Reform* (New York: Oxford University Press, 2004). For other books offering a broad background, see Dorothy Brown, *Critical Race Theory: Cases and Problems*, 2nd ed. (Eagan, MN: West, 2007); and Adrien Wing, *Global Critical Race Feminism: An International Reader* (New York: NYU Press, 2000).
4. These two categories of discrimination and victimization apply equally to race, gender, and sexual orientation.
5. Anders Nilsson and Felipe Estrada, "Victimization, Inequality, and Welfare During Economic Recession," *British Journal of Criminology* 42, 4 (2003): 663.

6. Partha Dasgupta, *An Inquiry into Well-Being and Destitution* (Oxford: Clarendon Press, 1993); and Amartya Sen, "Gender and Co-Operative Conflicts," in *Women and World Development,* ed. Irene Tinker (New York: Oxford University Press, 1990).

7. Ibid.

8. Amartya Sen, "More than 100 Million Women Are Missing," *New York Review of Books* (December 20, 1990).

9. U.S. Department of State, "Trafficking in Persons" (Washington, DC: U.S. State Department, 2010).

10. Like rape statistics, these are very difficult to obtain and are subject to error (generally on the low side). For a flavor of some of these issues, see Edward Dunbar, "Race, Gender, and Sexual Orientation in Hate Crime Victimization: Identity Politics or Identity Risk?" *Violence and Victims* 21, 3 (2005): 323–338; Lisak Waldner and Julian Berg, "Explaining Anti-Gay Violence Using Target Congruence," *Violence and Victims* 23, 3 (2008): 267–288; and Thomas M. Lampinen, Keith Chen, Aranka Amema, and Mary Lou Miller et al., "Incidence of Risk Factors for Sexual Orientation-Related Physical Assault Among Young Men Who Have Sex with Men," *American Journal of Public Health* 98, 6 (2008): 1028–1036.

11. The classic statement of this is by Richard Dawkins, *The Selfish Gene: 30th Anniversary Edition* (Oxford: Oxford University Press, 2006).

12. In wealthy societies this age increases to around eighteen (the modal age whereby children finish compulsory secondary education—at least in the United States).

13. From the basic science scene, work on fruit flies seems to confirm this: D. Yamamoto, H. Ito, and K. Fujitani, "Genetic Dissection of Sexual Orientation," *Neuroscience Research* 26, 2 (1996): 95–107; see also a general discussion in Cheryl L. Weill, *Nature's Choice: What Science Reveals About the Origins of Sexual Orientation* (London: Routledge, 2008); and in social science, Deborah T. Meem, Michelle Gibson, and Jonathan Alexander, *Finding Out* (Thousand Oaks, CA: Sage, 2009).

14. Some of my thoughts on this are found in my coauthored book (with Kevin Brown) *Genetic Engineering: Science and Ethics on the New Frontier* (Upper Saddle River, NJ: Prentice Hall, 2002).

15. I set this relationship out in more detail in Michael Boylan, ed., *Public Health Policy and Ethics* (Dordrecht: Kluwer/Springer, 2004): 10–14.

16. And there are pathological racists. Many of these individuals were involved in the large-scale lynching phenomena during pre–World War II America—see Phillip Dray, *At the Hands of Persons Unknown: The Lynching of Black America* (New York: Modern Library, 2003).

17. This is a huge topic area. Some useful places to start are: R. Stephenson and M. A. Koenig et al., "Domestic Violence, Contraceptives, and Unwanted Pregnancy in Rural India," *Studies in Family Planning* 39, 3 (2008):177–186; D. G. Foster and

D. P. Rostovseva et al., "Cost Savings from the Provision of Specific Methods of Contraception in a Publicly Funded Program," *American Journal of Public Health* 99, 3 (1999): 446–451; M. L. Meldrum, "'Simple Methods' and 'Determined Contraceptives': The Statistical Evaluation of Fertility Control: 1957–1968," *Bulletin of the History of Medicine* 70, 2 (1996): 266–295; C. S. Klima, "Unintended Pregnancy: Consequences and Solutions for a Worldwide Problem," *Nurse Midwifery* 43, 6 (1998): 483–491; and E. Matasha and T. Niembelea et al., "Sexual and Reproductive Health Among Primary and Secondary School Pupils in Mwanza, Tanzania: Need for Intervention," *AIDS Care* 10, 5 (1998): 571–582.

CHAPTER 10

Democracy, and
Social and Political Dialogue

A central problem to global morality and justice is the nature and operation of national governments. A *government* can be viewed as an über-institution within a society: an institution that rules other institutions. Classical Western political philosophers often listed the forms of national government something like this:

> Aristocracy, meaning the rule of the best (after *aristos* the superlative form of *agathos*, good)—generally a benevolent monarch with or without hereditary succession
>
> Democracy, meaning (to ancient philosophers) the rule of the landholding males
>
> Oligarchy, meaning the rule of the few—generally a powerful clique around a symbolic leader
>
> Tyranny, meaning rule by a powerful strongman[1]

Because this tradition was enunciated in the West it is possible to view most Western governments within these large abstract categories. (It is my conjecture that these broad categories are not confined to merely the West but may be extended universally.)

In order to begin our discussion, it is important to distinguish political systems from economic systems. For example, the USSR was a communist government (a tyrant) within a version of socialism as an economic theory of distributive justice. The present-day People's Republic of China is also a communist government (a tyrant), but within a form of capitalism (an economic theory of distributive justice).

135

Often it is the case that people believe that market economies (capitalism) automatically equate to democracies. This is far from the case. Nazi Germany and fascist Italy also had versions of market economies under tyranny. Though proponents of the automatic connection between capitalism and democracy (such as Milton Friedman) thought that capitalism tended to promote democracy, and vice versa, history has not shown this to be the case.[2] Much of Western Europe in the post–World War II era has been democratic and socialist.[3] The only way to make such an argument is to beg the question and insert the conditions of a thriving democracy into one's definition of capitalism (such as extensive human rights, freedom to enter and exit markets, public institutions that are responsive to and representative of the population, and a rule of law that is independent of the government). When this is done, naturally the adoption of capitalism will entail the adoption of democracy, because the two are merged into one entity. But this merely asserts the conclusion and so is not an acceptable argument.

However, this chapter is not about economics (that subject will be the focus of the next chapter). Instead, this chapter examines a metatheoretical norm about government: the *fair government principle*. The fair government principle adopts the analogy of moving from the personal worldview to the shared community worldview concerning autonomy. The underlying notion is that the individual values personal freedom highly (as a second-level basic good of action). If communities are groups that reflect many of the same characteristics of the individuals who make up the communities, then it seems reasonable to say that individuals qua community members would also desire autonomy. However, the fair government principle does not set out what particular government will satisfy this, but rather dictates how it should operate:

> The fair government principle says that for a government to be fair it must both permit and encourage formal and informal social/political institutions that will allow for an interactive exchange (consistent with the personal worldview imperative) between micro communities and the ruling macro community government in a meaningful way that is protected by a governmentally independent rule of law.

By *meaningful* here is meant that whatever the process, the government will listen to, seriously consider, and act upon the input based on the merit of the suggestion and not on the self-interest of the rulers themselves.[4] A rule of law should be independent of the executive and legislative functions of government. It is a referee that makes everyone play by the rules.

This chapter examines national governments in a global context against the standard of the fair government principle.

The Problem

If we hold the fair government principle as the judging base, then most of the world fails the test. Why is it that most of world does not have an interactive opportunity to influence its government? Throughout the world there are human rights failures (at the low end) and atrocities (at the high end) due to governments that do not measure up to the reciprocation called for by the fair government principle.[5] Often these problems begin from the bottom up. For example, every year the Carnegie Endowment for International Peace jointly analyzes and scores countries on twelve social, economic, political, and military indicators of national well-being.[6] The report for the year 2007 lists the following countries as constituting the bottom twenty: Somalia, Sudan, Zimbabwe, Chad, Iraq, Democratic Republic of the Congo, Afghanistan, Ivory Coast, Pakistan, Central African Republic, Guinea, Bangladesh, Burma (Myanmar), Haiti, North Korea, Ethiopia, Uganda, Lebanon, Nigeria, and Sri Lanka.

By failing to provide their citizens with the basic goods of agency (especially level-one goods), the central governments of these countries put themselves at risk. With one exception, the "failed governments" identified by the Carnegie Endowment are in Africa (11) and Asia (8). The instability of those countries threatens their neighbors and the world. In Africa, the failure of the fair government principle has contributed to the Darfur genocide and the Hutu-Tutsi genocide, as well as to civil unrest in Ethiopia, Somalia, Congo, and Kenya. In Asia—China, Burma (Myanmar), Iraq, Afghanistan, Pakistan, Saudi Arabia, the Central Asian states, and Russia—instances abound with unresponsive governments that permit human rights abuses such as imprisonment without trial, religious persecution, political jailing, degradation of women, sex trafficking, slave trading, and in many places a breakdown in civil order, all without an effective mechanism for redress. North Korea has atomic bombs and is experimenting with ballistic missiles to deliver them. Pakistan is on the brink of civil war and also has the Bomb. Iran (not on the list) is developing the Bomb and has used incendiary rhetoric against Israel. Many of the countries in Latin America are not democracies.[7] In fact, some countries (such as Ecuador, Peru, and Argentina) have transitioned from democracies to despotic rule, but this did not really change the responsiveness of government[8] because robust social institutions that parallel the political system still managed to accommodate popular input. What this means is that in the day-to-day lives of the peoples in these countries, the power of the central government is matched by micro and macro social institutions. These institutions include businesses, the Roman Catholic Church, music and the arts, and soccer clubs. These institutions are powerful and can be responsive to popular needs even when the government may not be. Such an alternative is acceptable to the fair government principle. For the most part, North America and Europe fare much better on the democratic reciprocity meter—though problems sprout up now and again.[9]

Human rights abuses and the authoritarian imposition of power over dialogue means that either oligarchs or tyrants rule most of the world. When this happens, all basic goods (levels one and two) are at risk if the totalitarian government reneges on its moral duty to provide those goods reliably to its citizens. In some cases this failure reflects the neglect of a ruling clique that has contempt for the bulk of its citizens, but in worse cases age-old grudges are played out to disenfranchise or ethnically "cleanse" a region, a process also known as genocide.

The governments that allow such activities are morally dysfunctional. Their existence may call for an international response (see Chapter 13). But the down and dirty is this: Governments are not living up to the fair government principle and are causing their citizens to be bereft of the basic goods of agency (not to mention level-one secondary goods). According to the argument for the moral status of basic goods and the Table of Embeddedness, this is immoral. As such, it constitutes a monumental international problem.

The Causes

If we accept the moral imperatives implied by the fair government principle, why is it that most of the countries of the world are falling short? This is a complex question that could warrant a book of its own. However, let us tease out a few common causes that tend to block governments from being responsive to popular input in a reciprocative fashion.

The first cause is that many countries of the world have weak central governments. The real power lies with tribes or gangs (sometimes known as militias). Each tribe is a small macro group run by a strongman (tyrant). The central government is almost a feudal affair with a weak leader trying to maintain order among warring factions. Oftentimes, the reason for this factionalism is colonial in origin. European colonial armies were able to gain power over much of the world in the sixteenth through eighteenth centuries. They created artificial countries with boundaries drawn for their own extrinsic advantage rather than for the intrinsic benefit of the members of the colony. Thus, for example, Britain created the country of Nigeria containing incompatible tribes that had always been separate: the Yoruba, Ibo, Hausa, and Fulana.[10] These historically antagonistic macro communities were brought together by extrinsic colonial interests. The result today is enmity between groups and a longing for autonomy and separation (for religious and social reasons). Much of this artificial statesmanship occurred via the agency of nonexperts such as Flora Shaw, who became the wife of Baron Frederick Lugard, the British governor-general of Nigeria. State lines reflected the interests of contending European conquistadors rather than those of the peoples. It is no wonder that this would create problems. When the Sykes-Picot Agreement of 1916 took on the reorganization of much of the Middle East by France and Britain, new maps were constructed by foreigners whose cultural ignorance set the scene for later warfare. For example, the creation of Kuwait out of whole cloth eventually led Iraq to invade in 1991.

Those states that were able to form central governments tended to be authoritarian—whether tyrants or oligarchs. Such governments originate in their ability to wield power effectively. Thus, from the beginning, these sorts of government see the task of governing as holding onto and expanding their power—first nationally, second regionally, and finally throughout the world. If government is about the establishment and growth of power, then from the outset there is going to be trouble. This is because the citizens of their country are only viewed as instruments of their power. Citizens have extrinsic worth only.

If one accepts that citizens have extrinsic worth only, then obviously one would treat them any way that would ensure their continued instrumental value. When the source of power is from the barrel of a gun, a country is really ruled by the gun. The person holding the trigger is somewhat irrelevant.

The second cause of government unresponsiveness to popular input lies in the nature of the micro and macro communities within the country. Do these communities have agendas that cut out large segments of the society from political participation for reasons of gender, ethnic group, religion, or intellectual beliefs? These are communities that are built upon the two-tiered community worldview model of (1) coinciding and amplification, and (2) dissonance and rejection (see Chapter 2). The two-tiered model will turn out to be very intolerant of social/political difference. Their mantra is, "get onboard or get off the train." In contrast, the fair government principle advocates that the way people confront novel normative theories is to give them a chance via overlap and modification, subject to the stage-three dialectical process of imaginatively viewing a new and different community that is in accord with the highest standards of the rational and affective good will—generalized to the community (and extended community).

The third cause is the international environment of the country. Does the region have special problems of its own that put pressure on the domestic political structure of a country? For example, a country in the Middle East that is almost exclusively Muslim may exert pressure on other states in the region to be Muslim. When a state that is not Muslim emerges—such as Israel—there is regional pressure to remove "the other" so that regional "purity" might be maintained. Such views encourage governments that are the majority in the region to marginalize or act with violence against the other as the majority uses coinciding and amplification along with dissonance and rejection to form an agenda for regional purity by the "true believers."

The phenomena of true believers supported by intolerant governments do not support rational examination of community worldviews—even those across regions. Instead, they foster irrational hatred that is an anathema to peace.

Possible Solutions

John Rawls in his book *The Law of Peoples* discusses traditional principles of international justice:[11]

Peoples are free and independent, and their freedom and independence are to be respected by other peoples.

Peoples are to observe treaties and undertakings.

Peoples are equal and are parties to the agreements that bind them.

Peoples are to observe a duty of nonintervention.

Peoples have a right of self-defense but no right to instigate war for reasons other than self-defense.

Peoples are to honor human rights.

Peoples are to observe certain specified restrictions in the conduct of war.

Peoples have a duty to assist other peoples living under unfavorable conditions that prevent their having a just or decent political and social regime.[12]

For Rawls, the international order is a dialogue between the good guys (what he refers to as liberal democracies) and the almost good guys (decent societies). The liberal democracies tolerate some unjust organization of the decent societies in order to further the causes of development and peace. The other societies are not tolerated but kept in check by the two morally superior types of government. This is the roadmap to positive change.

Much of Rawls's vision is consistent with the fair government principle, though there is one important difference: It tends to be utopian. For this reason, it is less useful as a solution. For example, though Rawls's book was written before the September 11, 2001, terrorist attacks and the resulting response by the Bush administration, I believe it is fair to provide a note of caution to his rosy assessment of American democracy. For example, Rawls declares that democracy alone will make a nation nonaggressive, but history has repeatedly demonstrated the opposite. From the Athenian democracy of Pericles to the Republic of Rome to the British Empire to the U.S. activity in Central and South America, and more recently, U.S. involvement in Southeast Asia and the invasion of Iraq (which even the CIA agreed had nothing to do with the September 11 attacks), world democracies with power have used that power for their own advantage—including aggressive armed conflict.[13] This undercuts the idea that democracy *alone* is a panacea for peace and prosperity.

I set Rawls out for consideration because his theory of justice and the formation of governments and their associated institutions have been very influential. It is against his utopian prescription that the more modest fair government principle should be examined. Where Rawls calls for the creation of liberal democracies throughout the world, the fair government principle merely sets out a procedural objective—the establishment of and respect for interactive social and political institutions for change, considered disinterestedly within the context of a politically independent rule of law. Because this is a lower bar to meet, it is more aspirationally possible. In order to attain the real interactive relationship between a government and its people, a third element of the individual and shared community worldview must be added: *overlap and modification.* As was mentioned earlier, it is an essential element in the fair government principle that the people have a venue by which sincere and authentic *exchange* can occur (consistent with the personal worldview imperative). This venue must be within social institutions or the local or national government structure. But what is crucial here is to break out of the rigid mold of the true believers who only employ the responses of *coinciding and amplification* and *dissonance and rejection.* What makes overlap and modification different is that it is open to change. As was shown in Chapter 2, it progresses to a third stage of confronting novel normative theories and tries to imagine what the projected change would be for the individual, shared, and extended communities. Only with the addition of this important worldview tenet (protected by an independent judiciary) can there be any realistic hope for a government that fits the fair government principle.

On Rawls's scale there might only be eight countries or so in the world that would qualify as liberal democracies. The "decent societies" might number a dozen or so. But that leaves most of the world in one of the other categories.[14] Because the fair government principle only stipulates institutional responsiveness to public interests as opposed to Rawls's eight points, it might make future membership easier to attain. For example, under the fair government principle one can envision a dictator who might (in his own self-interest) allow for social input. Some dictatorial theocracies give political credence to religious leaders who *may* also reflect the feelings of the population or to social or recreational movements (as per the examples from South America). If the micro communities within the national macro community are listened to in some practical fashion, then the dictates of the imperative have been met (albeit in a superficial way)—even if there is no ballot box.

Also, one can imagine the flip side: a democratic country whose leaders rig the system so that real representation does not occur. Even in the United States, which prides itself as the world's oldest continuous democratic republic, there have been controversial instances of thwarting the idealistic vision of its founders through unfair elections, undue influence of special interests, graft, and corruption. Creating a good government, whether it is scored on Rawls's card or on the fair government principle, is not easy. Yet it is a goal that we must strive for both nationally and internationally.

Fair government is difficult to achieve in the face of warring factions within a political entity. Probably the first strategy, then, is to recognize these political realities and try to bring the various factions into a legitimate political process through a federated devolution of power. In other words, all factions would recognize and give allegiance to the central state, and in return they would be given recognized, enhanced autonomy in their own affairs. In cases where this proves utterly impossible, the ideal solution is to spin off the discontented entity into its own country. This was the strategy that Mikhail Gorbachev followed in dissolving the former Soviet Union: He granted independence to discontented polities in a time of crisis within the Soviet Union so that the core state, Russia, could operate more effectively. Of course, when there are valuable minerals or oil in the discontented's landmass, it is not realistic to expect a happy divorce.

Another obstacle to fair government is found in an authoritarian central government ruled by a strongman. The only way to keep this sort of government in check is a well-entrenched, independent, and protected legal system. Such a legal system is given the power to override *anyone* in the society. It was the power of the rule of law in the United States that caused Richard M. Nixon to resign the presidency in 1974. A vibrant independent and protected court system can act as check and balance against excesses of the executive and (in cases of democracies or quasi-democracies) the legislative branch.

But this may be more difficult than it might seem. When the court system in Pakistan stood up to President Pervez Musharraf, he suspended the chief justice. Such a response indicates that there is no politically independent rule of law in the country. This is a common response that dictators employ against a judiciary that opposes their will. In such cases, the international community can censure or impose other sanctions on the offending state.

Another way to foster political openness and responsiveness is through education that follows a liberal model, teaching skills such as reading and writing along with discussion of literature, mathematics, history, art, and science. The emphasis of this type of education is on becoming an independent, autonomous critical thinker. In contrast, the sectarian model of education teaches everything in terms of a politicized theology. Whether it is in the United States or the Middle East or Africa, politicized theology is not real education. It works against being an independent, autonomous critical thinker, instead emphasizing the community to such an extent that the individual is lost in the equation. I have always argued for a balance between individualism and radical communitarianism.[15] If the nations of the world committed to providing liberal education at least to the secondary level to all citizens (male or female), a great step forward would be achieved: Level-two basic goods would be enjoyed by everyone.

The final major division is the international environment. This is the uniquely internationalist component to the equation. The most common regional problem is and has been various theocratic conflicts. In the history of Europe this evidenced itself in the Crusades, which pitted Christians against Muslims, and later in the Reformation, in which Protestants and Catholics struggled with one another. In the Middle East today, the state of Israel is at risk largely because it isn't Muslim. One way to fix this problem would be for governments to separate themselves from theocracy. Governments should be ruled by ethical and social/political criteria that are grounded on externalist features (such as the Table of Embeddedness) and that are open to all for scrutiny.[16] Theism, though, is internalist and private. When it mixes with government it is open to those who wish to exploit it as a personal power tool (either deviously or sincerely: both the same). The fair government principle requires that various social institutions are able to petition and interact with the government to instigate an inquiry on social change (i.e., overlap and modification). When religious leaders wield political power, the development of an effective sincere and authentic questioning of novel normative theories becomes very unlikely. Without the third tier, regional conflicts seem headed toward armed conflict to no one's advantage.

Conclusion

From a nationalist viewpoint, the government is the ruling institution of society. For governments to be effective ruling institutions, they must allow and nurture interaction with other social institutions and the micro communities within the country. Without this commitment, the government will become despotic and lead the way to a failed state that brings harsh consequences upon its citizens. How the international community should respond to such failed states will be the subject of subsequent chapters.

Key Terms

fair government principle, political versus economic systems of government

Critical Applied Reasoning Exercise

Pick a country from the list of twenty that appears earlier in this chapter. Read about this country on the Internet. Now, imagine that you have been named

minister of education for this country. Given the situation of the country today
and the internal and external problems facing the country, create a two-page primary and secondary education outline for that country that will move it from a
two-tiered (coinciding and amplification + dissonance and rejection) country to
a three-tiered country incorporating overlap and modification.

Notes

1. Aristotle, *Politics* IV; Plato, *Republic* 554b–570e.

2. Milton Friedman, *Capitalism and Freedom* (Chicago: University of Chicago
Press, 1962): ch. 1. Of course, one could beg the question by defining capitalism as
only having perfectly free laissez-faire markets and other trappings of a liberal democracy, but this only obscures the relationship between economics and politics.

3. In reality, no country is purely one economic system. There is always a mixture. For a discussion of some of the mixtures see Michael Boylan, ed., *Public Health
Policy and Ethics* (Dordrecht: Kluwer/Springer, 2004): ch. 7.

4. Please be aware that "to act upon" does not necessarily mean "endorse." Person X can act upon Proposal Y by denying it. This is not a pro forma denial but an
authentically reasoned judgment.

5. Some of the resulting atrocities are documented in Ifa Kamau Cush, "One Law
for the Powerful," *New Africa* (April 2009): 39–40; Owen Fiss, "Within Reach of the
State: Prosecuting Atrocities in Africa," *Human Rights Quarterly* 39, 1 (2009): 59–70;
Annapuma Waughray, "Caste Discrimination: A Twenty-First Century to UK Dis-
crimination Law," *Modern Law Review* 72, 2 (2009): 182–184; Barbara Frey, "Woman
Human Rights," *Human Rights Quarterly* 40, 3 (2009): 383–402; up-to-date on sex
trafficking of women, online at www.acf.hhs.gov/trafficking/abort/fact-sex.pdf; and
Amartya Sen, "The Power of Declaration," *New Republic* 240, 1 (2009): 30.

6. Fund for Peace and the Carnegie Endowment for International Peace, "The
Failed States of 2008," *Foreign Policy* (July/August 2008).

7. See Larry Diamond, Marc F. Plattner, and Diego Abente Brun, eds., *Latin
America's Struggle for Democracy* (Baltimore, MD: Johns Hopkins University Press,
2008); and the well regarded Scott Mainwaring and Matthew-Soberg Shugart, *Presi-
dentialism and Democracy in Latin America* (New York: Cambridge University Press,
1997).

8. Moisés Naim, of the Carnegie Endowment for Peace, writing in the *Financial
Times* (April 26, 2002).

9. For example, eastern Europe and the Balkans have had difficulties, as has Mexico with the powerful drug lords.

10. John N. Paden, *Muslim Civic Cultures and Conflict Resolution* (Washington,
DC: Brookings Institution, 2005).

11. John Rawls, *The Law of Peoples* (Cambridge, MA: Harvard University Press, 1999).

12. Ibid., 37.

13. A. H. M. Jones, *The Later Roman Empire* (Baltimore, MD: Johns Hopkins University Press, 1986); Wendy Webster, *Englishness and Empire: 1939–1965* (Oxford: Oxford University Press, 2007); P. J. Marsall, *The Cambridge Illustrated History of the British Empire* (Cambridge: Cambridge University Press, 2001); Walter Nugent, *Habits of Empire: A History of American Expansionism* (New York: Knopf, 2008).

14. The figures on this are in constant flux according to the sourcing agency. For a picture in time see the websites of Amnesty International and Human Rights Watch.

15. Boylan, *Public Health Policy and Ethics,* ch. 6.

16. Ibid., ch. 5.

CHAPTER 11

Globalization

Is the world flat? Can globalization become that common element that brings the world together in unified vision under the aegis of market-based capitalism? For some, this is the vision of a progressive future. Because making money for rationally interested individuals around the world seems to be a disinterested methodology (that is, one that acts mechanically without partisan preference) and because "disinterested" is a property of most moral theories, it would seem that globalization might be a positive strategy toward positive international development.

Let us start with some definitions: *globalization* will be taken to mean the unfettered free-market capitalist economic trading between countries (without tariffs) seeking the most efficient means of production and distribution to the world's consumers. Proponents believe that capitalism is the most efficient system of economic development in the history of humankind, and that such development will lift more people out of poverty by providing basic goods and level-one secondary goods to more people than ever before. If it is the case that unfettered market-based capitalism creates the conditions for democracy (a responsive form of government that fulfills the fair government principle), and if democracies are not prone to war, then globalization can significantly reduce poverty, create responsive governments, and instigate world peace: quite a promise.

Detractors are not so optimistic. They claim that while there are some groups that are lifted out of poverty (as defined by the United Nations), there are other unintended consequences that cause more harm that benefit. This chapter will attempt to paint a broad picture that will help your formulate your own personal worldview stand on globalization.

The Problem

Of globalization's three goals—significantly reducing poverty, creating responsive governments, and instigating world peace—the goal most often discussed is poverty reduction. In order to assess the problem we return to the theme of Chapter 7. One way to describe poverty is to follow the World Bank and set an income of $2.50 a day ($912.50 per year) as the defining upper limit of poverty. Using this measure, more than half the world—three billion people—are in poverty.[1] According to the methodology of this volume, a better measure of the problem is the access to the basic goods of agency. UNICEF offers some bleak assessments.[2] In 2005 there were 2.2 billion children in the world. Of these, 640 million (about one in three) did not have adequate shelter, 400 million (about one in five) did not have access to safe water, and 270 million (about one in seven) did not have access to basic health care. The result is that 10.6 million children in the world die before the age of five (the same number of children as all who live in France, Germany, Greece, and Italy combined). As dismal as these numbers sound, is poverty nonetheless diminishing? And if so, has it been the result of globalization?

Maybe, and maybe not. In a sphere as complex as the society, so many events are occurring all the time that drawing singular causal connections is too ambitious. However, some conjunction between events at least rises to the level of statistical correlation. And that is the best explanation we have. For clarity's sake, I will use the time frame from 1980 onward as a point of reference. The starting date is significant because it was then that the United States began encouraging a more relaxed regulative environment regarding trade and market policy. In general, from 1980 to 2005 there was a general trend downward in the amount of poverty in the poorest countries in the world—particularly in China and India (almost half the world's population together). This lessening of poverty worked dialectically with the associated states of famine and disease (see Chapter 7) so that the basic lot of many people was improved. This era also represented a time in which foreign companies were invited in to build factories for export overseas. The weak Yuan (Chinese currency) also made China particularly attractive to foreign investment. Such a general trend would seem to support the notion that globalization helped to reduce poverty. However, recently (at the writing of this book, albeit in the midst of a global economic recession) the successes of the past have begun to reverse themselves. Most of these negative trends have focused on access to food (and the 500-calorie per day minimum to stay alive). Some blame this on the worldwide economic recession, whereas others say the policy of using corn (a basic foodstuff) to make ethanol drove up the cost of corn and effectively reduced its presence in the food chain. As per above, it is impossible to cite exact cause-effect relationships.

Other measures of poverty, such as access to clean water, sanitation, and protection from unwanted bodily harm (from military violence to inoculation against infectious disease), have gotten progressively worse—even before the recession hit.[3] For example, access to primary and secondary education (a level-two basic good) also has declined from 1980–2000.[4]

Another sort of problem concerns the status of women during globalization. Women are an important group to focus on because they are overrepresented among the ranks of the poor and are more likely to be the caregivers for young children (see Chapter 9). For example, during the late 1970s in Sri Lanka, the government created various export-processing zones to attract multinational corporations. Subsequently, a large number of young rural Sri Lankan women moved to the new urban zones to get the new jobs. One recent study shows that instead of gaining what they sought, these women suffered occupational health problems, mental health problems, malnutrition, abortion, and the increased risk of sexually transmitted disease.[5] Another example is from China, where proponents of globalization cite the general reduction in starvation deaths that coincided with the globalization period of 1980 onward. However, one recent study (while admitting the lower starvation levels) argues that the struggle against entrenched sexism in Chinese society under the "unisex model of Red China" has gone backward. Women who engage in factory work in Jiangsu and Shandong are worse off than before globalization. Though these women earn higher wages for their work, they nonetheless face severe gender-based wage discrimination. In addition, their financial gains have been obliterated by the loss of social status due to not being able to complete domestic and other community obligations that are firmly woven into the shared community worldview. The result has been a net loss of self-esteem by women. Because the shared community worldview considers self-fulfillment as a level-one secondary good, loss of self-esteem is a significant downside to globalization.[6]

These and other social disruptions constitute a *cost.* When one looks at the process of social change, there is always a cost. The question is whether the change is *worth* the cost. This is a difficult normative question and thus is subject to the way we confront novel normative theories (Chapter 2). After initially assessing the logical plausibility of the claim (stage one), three sorts of reactions occur in the second stage: (1) coinciding and amplification, (2) dissonance and rejection, and (3) overlap and modification. Virtually all confrontations to the shared community worldview (as well as to the personal worldview) will choose (1) or (2) and be done with it. Very little cost is incurred. But the interesting cases are when there is (3) overlap and modification. When this comes from the people who formed the intrinsic structure of the community and are permitted responsively to act within society (fair government principle), the seeds of real progressive change have been sowed (subject to the final stage that matches worldview against the new community that will probably be created). When this process begins within people about whom the changes will affect and who have power to make their judgments known and acted upon either through the government or through societal institutions, one has a positive ongoing process (see Chapter 10). However, it can occur that the impetus for change comes from without (from multinational corporations, for example) and that these provocateurs do not consider the following level-two basic goods:

- The assurance that those you interact with are not lying to promote their own interests
- The assurance that those you interact with will recognize your human dignity (as per above) and not exploit you as a means only

When women are cast out of their community by desperate circumstances and a culture that assumes that they will bear a disproportionate share of the burden, they often must fend for themselves. This has led to a great expansion of the tourist sex industry in many countries that have been so changed by globalization.[7] These sorts of consequences rend the fabric of the community and make responsive government less likely.

Because dictators are often attractive customers to global businesses (because of their willingness to relax minimum age requirements; occupational, health, and safety guidelines; and environmental concerns), globalization can have the unintended consequence of undercutting the fair government principle by keeping repressive regimes in power.[8] When this is combined with the increase in arms trade among these countries, the result can destabilize a region. When such an outcome occurs, one wonders whether the costs of globalization exceed the benefits.[9]

The net result of globalization has not been beneficial to all parties equally. If this were the case, then according to the maxim that "a rising tide lifts all ships," all parties in globalization should be sharing in the benefits at an equal rate. This is far from what has resulted. The income gap between the countries in the top quintile and those in the lowest was thirty times in 1960, sixty times in 1990, and seventy-four times in 1997.[10] This means that the richest nations are making out much better than the poor nations in globalization. Such a state of affairs smacks of exploitation (which is prohibited as a second-level basic good).

This may be due to the fact that many of the international trade agreements are not meant to benefit the populace of a nation in equal measure with either the multinational companies or the ruling clique of the host country.[11] Because dictatorships are rarely responsive to their citizens, a multinational company can set up business with little to no health and safety standards and the lowest possible wages (sometimes made lower by child and prison labor). The two parties—multinational companies and the dictator—enter into a symbiotic relationship that benefits them both, promotes their mutual interests at the expense of the people in the country, and works against the creation of good, responsive government.

If the promise of globalization is the reduction of poverty, the creation of responsive governments, and regional/world peace, then the scorecard is definitely mixed. In order to be able to evaluate how this situation might be improved, let us next consider the underlying causes.

The Causes

The single most prominent cause for the failures that have occurred under globalization is the nature of unfettered capitalism as an incomplete theory of distributive justice.[12] An incomplete theory is one that does not fully describe mode of operation. Instead, it may hide pragmatic realities in utopian assumptions about human nature and the operation of social institutions. In the case of unfettered capitalism this lacuna lies at its core. The theory is based principally upon unabashed selfishness. Proponents say that if everyone is selfish, the group will keep free riders (those who do not contribute their fair share) and crooks (those who try to cheat others who play by the rules) in check if for no other reason than to protect and promote their own selfish interests. This is often repeated as if it were a religious dogma. The systematic expression of this is referred to by the metaphor of the *invisible hand* (an inscrutable force that rights imbalances).

As I have suggested earlier, capitalism by itself is an incomplete theory of distributive justice and when it is alone within a society it leads to the rule of the powerful—in a word, kraterism. Kraterism works by rewarding the powerful and turning things over to them. When the powerful are skillful, some sort of equilibrium can be maintained (albeit an unjust one). However, when these power brokers border on pathological narcissism (meaning that they really believe they are the "masters of the universe"[13]), they feel they are immune from all normal constraints and do as they please. They have become Nietzsche's *übermenchen*. Even free-market true believer Richard Posner has recently recognized this point.[14]

The reason that the market players in fact seldom police each other is because keeping your opponents in check is a rational strategy only in a zero-sum game. In a zero-sum game when an agent, A, takes x (where x is a valuable good), it comes at the expense of all other players because there are only a limited number of such goods to be had. It is a "zero-sum" game because A's gain (x) exactly equals the loss of the other players ($-x$), such that $x-x = 0$. This game situation is called a zero sum: The quantities are limited, and there are more people desiring goods than there are goods to go around. It is like the children's game of musical chairs where there are y number of chairs and $y + 1$ number of contestants. In such situations it is likely that the players will try to keep the cheaters in check (a form of the invisible hand). However, when the players believe that the zero sum is no longer operable within the market, everyone can make money and all can become enriched at no one's expense! In such a situation, it is irrational for Agent A to keep other players in check because that task would merely take time away from his making more money for himself. After all, someone else's gains do not come at Agent A's expense as they would in a zero-sum game. In such a perceived situation, the attitude can become (according to one recent example), "Turn on the printing presses in the name of mortgage-based securities and credit-default swaps!"

The second problem area is that dictators, who fail miserably at the fair government principle, rule most poor countries. As was mentioned in the problems section of this chapter, there are structural reasons why a multinational business might prefer to deal with a politically stable dictatorship than with some other form of government. This is because there are fewer people to please. Because dictatorships are rarely responsive to their citizens, a multinational company can get off with little to no health and safety standards and the lowest possible wages (made lower by child and prison labor). The two parties enter into a symbiotic relationship that benefits them both and promotes their mutual interests at the expense of the people in the country. Contracts like the preceding are all too prevalent in subsistence and developing societies. They work *against* the creation of good, responsive government.

The final problem is globalization's potential impact on regional stability and peace. Because it is in the best interests of multinational companies to support the government in power (be it a democracy, a benevolent monarchy, or a dictatorship), and because many countries in the world find themselves in politically hostile relations with their neighbors, it is natural that part of the arrangement between multinationals and their cheap source of labor is to look after the security of the country that is home to their factories in order to ensure that they can continue to provide a predictable, steady stream of products. Creating such civil stability may require that the multinational corporations provide military weapons for the country's self-defense (directly through upfront sales or more likely indirectly via a secured link to international arms dealers). The problem is that "self-defense" often takes a *preemptive* turn that leads to border fighting and, possibly, regional instability. This is especially prevalent in Africa, the Middle East, and South Asia.

These problem areas threaten to undercut the valuable contribution that economic interdependence can bring to help reduce poverty, encourage responsive government, and create the conditions for a more peaceful world.

Possible Solutions

The solutions presented in this section follow three paths: (1) no globalization, (2) more globalization on unfettered free-market principles, and (3) a restructured globalization. Let's look at these in order.

No Globalization

The first possible solution is to put the brakes on globalization. How would one do this? The easy answer is by changing government policy to include tariffs and government subsidies of domestic industry. Tariffs are taxes on imported goods. Tariffs help protect domestic industry by making the imported goods of foreign producers more expensive. Tariffs that are set at high-enough levels can greatly reduce foreign trade. In the extreme, if everyone levied tariffs on all imports in order to protect and promote their own domestic industries, then a trade war would begin in order to counterbalance the tariffs, and most international commerce would cease. This outcome would severely disrupt the global economy, causing more people to starve, and creating instability that in turn might foster more dictatorships.

Another government policy to dampen foreign trade would be to pay direct subsidies to domestic industries so that they can out-compete foreign traders. This is a de facto restraint on foreign trade because it is often hidden within larger government programs. Subsidies are the most-used form of protectionism by the wealthy countries of the world and one of the most cited reasons for World Trade Organization complaints. Subsidies are anticompetitive in a similar way that tariffs are, but they are harder to detect. They are often very popular within nations because they are a positive response to competition (giving some industry money so that it can compete but not reveal the true costs of production—which competitors, in theory, must absorb themselves). This often sounds better to a domestic audience because tariffs are negative like taxes whereas subsidies seem like encouraging incentives. But both work against global markets in the same way and with the same ultimate effects: They cheat against a fair system of competition. These rules about tariffs and subsidies apply to wealthy nations who seek unfair competitive advantage.

However, it should also be noted that when the international community acts to help a subsistence society that cannot compete on the world market, this is not an instance of domestic subsidy to gain an unfair advantage. Rather, it is an instance of the world community banding together to help a country get on its feet developmentally. In this situation the world community might create a two-tiered system with one tier applying to wealthy countries that already have developed markets that are able to compete without aid on the world market, the G-20 nations. The second tier will apply to the other 175-plus nations of the world who are not yet at a stage of development in which they can fairly compete.

If either tariffs or subsidy protectionism were successful among the G-20 nations, then one might envision a world where isolationism were the rule. This would be a very poor end result for any of the three goals addressed in this chapter: poverty reduction, encouraging responsive government, and promoting world peace. For these reasons, it is my opinion that "no globalization" solutions to the problems of globalization would be worse than the status quo.

More Globalization

A second solution to the ills of globalization is to pursue *more* globalization on unfettered free-market principles. Advocates of this position say that globalization has not failed, it's just that it was never implemented in a *pure* form. If unfettered free-market capitalism were to be put into place according to strict laissez-faire principles, then the global market would correct the excesses of the status quo, and the goals of globalization (poverty reduction, encouraging responsive government, and promoting world peace) could then be achieved.

It is difficult to assess this claim because it has never been tried. Indeed, it is difficult to imagine it ever being tried within the international arena given all the diversity of governmental systems and the shared community worldviews within nations. I believe that no amount of empirical data will convince either globalization's proponents of the strategy's probable failure or globalization's detractors of its possible success. This is because the question really rests upon whether the assessment of capitalism as incomplete, tending to kraterism, and depending upon a zero sum is correct. As with many thorny questions in philosophy, one can only marshal likely explanations and then depend on the personal worldviews of the audience to achieve assent or dissent. From my earlier remarks in this chapter, it should be clear that I am a dissenter to this solution.

Restructured Globalization

The last sort of solution is to continue down the road of globalization, but under international guidelines that will seek to prevent the excesses of the status quo. In order to get a handle on just what these guidelines might be, let us look more carefully at the problems. First, there is the initial incentive to create foreign factories. A true spirit of globalization ought to include some sense of egalitarianism. This means treating all peoples everywhere with equal concern. All workers everywhere ought to be able to work for locally comparable wages in a safe workplace free from gender, religious, and ethnic discrimination. If international standards can be adopted similar to those in the United States and the other G-6 nations by these subsistence societies, then the cost of the goods produced in those subsistence and developing countries will be more expensive. But these health and safety standards are a must. Manufacturers in the United States must look after their workers in this way as well as adhering to environmental regulations that are aimed at slowing down the general degradation of the planet's air, water, and other natural resources. For example, we could imagine three scenarios for the ABC Widget Company, as shown in Figure 11.1.[15]

FIGURE 11.1. A Fictional Example of Two Globalization Strategies

---

Scenario One: Operations in the United States (or Other Home Country)

Material and pure manufacturing costs—raw materials to factory/actual
    nonlabor manufacturing costs per widget = $5
Labor costs per widget = $1
Health care costs = $0.1
OSHA (occupational and health safety costs) = $0.3
Environmental regulations costs = $0.3
Bringing goods to market costs = $0.1
Taxes = $ 0.1

Total per-widget cost to wholesaler = $6.90

Scenario Two: Status Quo Globalization

Material and pure manufacturing costs—raw materials to factory/actual
    nonlabor manufacturing costs per widget = $5
Labor costs per widget = $ 0.01
Health care costs = $0
OSHA (occupational and health safety costs) = $0
Environmental regulations costs = $0
Bringing goods to market costs = $0.2
Taxes = $0 / Bribes $0.5

Total per-widget cost to wholesaler = $5.71

Scenario Three: Restructured Globalization

Material and pure manufacturing costs—raw materials to factory/actual
    nonlabor manufacturing costs per widget = $5
Labor costs per widget = $0.1
Health care costs = $0.1
OSHA (occupational and health safety costs) = $0.3
Environmental regulations costs = $0.5
Bringing goods to market costs = $0.2
Taxes = $0.1 / Bribes = $0

Total per-widget cost to wholesaler = $6.30

NOTE: All costs are per widget; annual production 500 million widgets. This is a fictional example meant to emphasize how globalization under different assumptions can still operate at a comparative profit—but only half as much. The relative valuation of figures is an approximation from my experience at the Center for American Progress, 2007–2009, as a visiting fellow.

Looking at Figure 11.1, if we assume that the annual output of widgets is 500 million per year from these factories, then the total cost of operations in the United States is $3.45 billion, compared to a cost of $2.85 billion in Scenario Two (the current state of globalization) and $3.15 billion in Scenario Three (a restructured state of globalization). The restructured state of globalization cuts the current cost savings in half ($595 million to $300 million). This means that the status quo globalization saves home country manufacturing 17.2 percent while the revised globalization saves only 8.6 percent.

The difference between Scenarios Two and Three is that in the latter, some accommodation for health, safety, wages, and environmental regulation are taken into account, and there are absolute prohibitions on child and prison labor. These are significant. I contend that the future of globalization must be one that diminishes the blatant exploitation of workers and the environment (a level-two basic good on the Table of Embeddedness). If different areas of the world have different wage scales, then the implementation of Scenario Three will be to create a responsible presence by international business such that relative quintile wages for the same work performed in the home country will be researched, and the salaries in the new country will be pegged at the same relative quintile level. Thus, if widget assembly-line workers in the United States are paid in the sixtieth percentile of all manufacturing workers, then manufacturing workers in the new country should also be paid in the sixtieth percentile of all manufacturing workers in that country. The wages paid will still be less than in the home country, but the relative importance of this sort of manufacturing wage level will be established. In time the cost differentials will cease as development in the source country raises the general gross domestic product and the consequent costs of goods and services. In this way, revised globalization has as its goal its own elimination. It seeks to end the preferential, exploitative relationship with subsistence economies by helping them develop into wealthy and responsible nations. Whether the goals of responsive government and regional peace follow suit is too difficult to determine. The complication of the systemic model makes us resort to vigilant monitoring. Under the right conditions, this dream (properly controlled) may become a reality.

Key Terms

globalization, restructured globalization

Critical Applied Reasoning Exercise

You are a management consultant hired by the ABC Widget Company to evaluate a possible move of manufacturing operations to Country X (choose a real country). Write a 2–4 page report that focuses on three scenarios: (1) staying in the home country, (2) moving to the new country under status quo globalization, and (3) moving to the new country under restructured globalization. Be sure to base your report both on practical issues (as per Figure 11.1) and ethical principles. Give a clear recommendation to the board of directors

Notes

1. The World Bank's Development Indicators, 2008. Statistics cover the year 2005. If one uses the figure of $10 a day ($3,650 a year), then 80 percent of the world's population is below this mark.

2. *State of the World's Children*, UNICEF, 2005.

3. Michael Boylan, "Clean Water," *International Public Health Policy and Ethics,* Michael Boylan, ed. (Dordrecht: Springer, 2008): 273–288.

4. Mark Weisbrot, Dean Baker, Egor Kraev, and Judy Chen, "The Scorecard on Globalization 1980–2000: Twenty Years of Diminished Progress," Center for Economic Policy and Research (August 2001).

5. C. T. Attanapola, "Experiences of Globalization and Health in the Narratives of Women Industrial Workers in Sri Lanka," *Gender, Technology, and Development* 9, 1 (2005): 81–102; compare this to S. Hawthorne, "Wild Politics: Beyond Globalization," *Women's Studies International Forum* 27, 3 (2004): 243–259.

6. F. MacPhail and X. Dong, "Women's Market Work and Household Status in Rural China: Evidence from Jiangsu and Shandong in the late 1990s," *Feminist Economics* 13, 3 (2007): 93–124; compare this to C. Wichterich, "The Re-Discovery of Gender Inequality: EU-China Trade," *Development* 50, 3 (2007): 83–89.

7. Thomas Pogge, "Assisting the Global Poor," *The Ethics of Assistance: Morality and the Distant Needy,* ed. Deen K. Chatterjee (Cambridge: Cambridge University Press, 2004): 260–288, reprinted in Thomas Pogge and Keith Horton, *Global Ethics: Seminal Essays* (St. Paul, MN: Paragon, 2008).

8. Ibid., 542–544.

9. Ibid., 546–549.

10. United Nations Development Programme, *Human Development Report 1999,* 3, sec. 38.

11. Pogge, "Assisting the Global Poor," 549.

12. Michael Boylan, ed., *Public Health Policy and Ethics* (Dordrecht: Kluwer/Springer, 2004): ch. 7.

13. I am referring to the attitudes described fictively by Tom Wolfe in *Bonfire of the Vanities* (New York: Farrar, Straus and Giroux, 1987).

14. Richard A. Posner, *A Failure of Capitalism: The Crisis of '08 and the Descent into Depression* (Cambridge, MA: Harvard University Press, 2009); compare this to

the work by Nobel Prize economist Daniel Kahneman on the irrationality of market players and to George A. Akerlof and Robert J. Shiller, *Animal Spirits: How Human Psychology Drives the Economy and Why It Matters for Global Capitalism* (Princeton, NJ: Princeton University Press, 2009).

15. The following figures are fictional for the purposes of the thought experiment, but do reflect my two years on the economic team at the Center for American Progress, a public policy think tank in Washington, D.C.

The Environment

"Drill, baby, drill!" was a recent cry among individuals and organizations who sought a solution to the energy crisis via more onshore and offshore drilling. Because (from the point of view of the United States) most of the onshore fields have been leased except in legislatively protected national forests and parks, the real pressure has been to increase offshore drilling in both shallow and deep waters. At the writing of this book, the spill from the Deep Water Horizon oil-drilling rig operated in the Gulf of Mexico by BP (formerly British Petroleum) threatens to be the worst environmental disaster in history, because the shut-off machinery for blowouts did not function as designed. Some say that, in their drive to drill quickly and perhaps save costs by cutting corners, the various companies involved were not as careful as they should have been about the reliability of their devices. Who knows the ultimate result of this event, but if there is not some closer regulation of petroleum extraction, then it is reasonable to expect that the BP–Gulf of Mexico disaster will be repeated time and again around the world.

One of the few issues that scientists and most world leaders agree on is that the environment is too polluted and this fact is causing human harm right now. Some scholars declare that we face the danger of environmental catastrophe within fifty to one hundred years.[1] Though there is great agreement that air, water, and soil pollution have reached high levels, there is not a consensus about what to do about it. Instead, a number of questions arise: Is the problem already at a crisis level? What methods of pollution-control work? How much do they cost? Who should bear the financial responsibility for global cleanup? Is global warming caused by human activity, or is it part of a natural climate cycle? These are difficult queries, and disagreements over the answers stand in the way of effective response.

The Problem

The United Nations Statistics Division parses the problem of pollution via *air, water,* and *ground* (waste treatment).[2] Let's examine these in order.

Air Pollution

The problem of *air pollution* takes at least two forms: (1) a cause for global warming, and (2) a medical threat to those breathing the air, causing and exacerbating asthma and other respiratory ailments.

Air pollution principally consists of sulfur dioxide (SO_2), nitrous oxide (N_2O), carbon dioxide (CO_2), and methane (CH_4). Together, these chemical compounds in the air create greenhouse gasses that contribute to global warming and climate change.

The average surface temperature on earth rose 0.6 degrees Celsius (1.08 degrees Fahrenheit) during the twentieth century (mostly post–World War II). Though a rise of roughly 1 degree might seem hardly noticeable, and inconsequential, it is in fact quite significant. From ecosystems to biomes, the balance of life is finely calibrated. Increasing earth's temperature even a small amount can have major affects on reproduction cycles, genetic clocks, migration patterns, and so on. When one thinks about the increased surface air temperature, various convection patterns that shape weather patterns are also subject to change. New air and water temperatures have created more severe weather patterns for hurricanes and tornadoes.[3] Such storms cause great environmental and societal destruction.

In addition to global warming, air pollution creates health problems of its own. For example, the sulfur dioxide concentrations in the air can be transported over long distances and will increase the acidity of rain, which, in turn, can ruin crops, harm the soil, and damage buildings. Air pollution in the form of ozone, fine particles in the air, and other airborne toxicants also increases the incidence of respiratory disease. A long-term study on residents in six U.S. cities conducted by the National Institute of Environmental Health Sciences at the National Institutes of Health (NIEHS) conclusively established a link between common air pollutants and the risk of pulmonary and cardiovascular disease.[4] Recent ongoing studies in Southern California by NIEHS also suggest that exposure to fossil fuel emissions may hinder child lung development and may thus impair individuals for their entire lives. Clearly, air pollution constitutes a health problem right now. It is more than "smelly air." It can kill and handicap people. As pollution gets worse, so will these health problems.

Water Pollution

There are two general ways to think about *water pollution.* The first is via the adulteration of natural fresh and saltwater by the activity of humans. The most common form of adulteration is via the activity of industry (including agriculture). The Chesapeake Bay Foundation cites as most pernicious the rising levels of nitrogen and phosphorus from sewage treatment plants, agriculture, and power plants. In some areas in the world PCB compounds from lubricants and the manufacturing by-products of plastics also constitute a major problem. The wholesale dumping of waste by-products into local waterways has been very common since the beginning of the industrial revolution in the nineteenth century. But because the amount was relatively small compared to the expanse of water, many of the effects could be absorbed—especially in large water systems (long rivers, sizeable lakes, and the oceans).

However, in particular regions of the world post–World War I, the effects of this sort of water pollution have killed the wildlife within certain rivers and lakes. Things in the United States, for example, got so bad that in 1969 the Cuyahoga River in Ohio actually caught on fire!

When a waterway receives new chemicals, it is rather like a science lab in which you dump some chemicals into a beaker full of water and then test the resultant solution. What has happened is an alteration creating a new solution (cases in which the chemicals dissolve), a new mixture (cases in which the chemicals stand in an active suspension—separate but together), or a new colloid (cases in which the chemicals stand in a static suspension—separate but more fixed together). In any of these cases a *change* has occurred. The body of water in question is now different. If the body of water is the environment of living organisms from the unicellular to aquatic mammals, then this change can pose obstacles for future survival.

Some of these adulterations can come about secondhand. For example, the burning of fossil fuels elevates the amount of carbon dioxide in the air, some of which is absorbed into the oceans and mixes with water to form carbonic acid $[CO_2 + H_2O => H_2CO_3]$. The creation of this acid in large quantities is affecting the pH-levels in the oceans (the scale that measures acids and bases).[5] This change in acidity has been documented to affect reproduction (by slowing down the speed of sperm cells) and altering the Krebs cycle within living cells so that it is not as effective—meaning that organisms are less energetic and cannot act as effectively. This consequence is huge because the eco-environments of the four principal levels of the ocean (sunlight zone [to 200 m], twilight zone [to 1,000 m], midnight zone [to 4,000 m], and the abyss [greater than 4,000 m]) are carefully calibrated according to existing conditions. Significant changes constitute a challenge to all organisms living within that zone.

Thus, the direct and indirect adulteration of the oceans and other waterways are a major concern for the first form of water pollution.

The second general way to think about water pollution is by the effects of global warming on water reserves around the world. In this context we will think about temperature alteration in a way analogous with how we conceptualized chemical adulteration. Each constitutes a human-generated change in the environment. Global warming contributes to rising water temperatures, which in turns leads to several problems. Three of the most troublesome areas are: (1) growing scarcity of potable water, (2) melting ice caps, and (3) an increase in the average potential energy in the oceans. The first and perhaps the most pressing problem is the growing scarcity of water due in part to increased water temperatures. When the average surface temperature of a body of water rises, this means that the rate of evaporation increases. Thus, marginal reservoirs disappear and semiarid regions become arid. This creates a crisis for agriculture and for providing potable water for human consumption. The result is a growing scarcity of clean water to support life on earth. This growing scarcity also is a factor in exacerbating infectious disease. As we saw in Chapter 8, various diseases are caused by polluted and scarce water: water-borne, water-washed, water-based, and water-related insect vectors. These are also a big part of the environmental profile of potable (so-called blue) water in the world.

Second, the ice caps are melting at alarming rates. Average Arctic temperatures are warming twice as fast as anywhere else in the world.[6] One casualty is the Ward Hunt ice shelf, which has been intact for 3,000 years. It began cracking in 2000 and is now breaking into small pieces. The loss of Arctic ice will accelerate general global warming because the ice caps had acted as a counterbalance to warming. Thus, the result is an accelerating feedback system that promotes warming: (1) in stage one there is x amount of Arctic ice that moderated the global temperature; (2) in stage two x is decreased by 10 percent and thus its ability to moderate temperatures is also decreased by 10 percent, making the planet warmer; (3) in stage three x is decreased by 12 percent (the normal progression plus the compounded effect of less polar push back, etc.) This demonstrates how the cycle will accelerate exponentially over the long term unless intervening action is taken.

Likewise, Antarctic ice is also melting at an alarming rate, as documented by scientists from the British Antarctic Survey (BAS).[7] Professor Chris Rapley, director of the BAS, believes that 13,000 square kilometers of sea ice from Antarctica has been lost over the period of 1950–2000. This sea ice used to act as a buffer against the movement of Antarctic glaciers. Now these glaciers, too, are flowing into the sea and melting. Rapley explains that if these events were due to natural fluctuations over time, then one would expect spotty variability in this effect. But because it is occurring everywhere (e.g., in all three measured streams in West Antarctica), there is something happening beyond normal meteorological cycles. The three most egregious losses are the Larsen A ice shelf, measured at 1,600 square kilometers (1995), the Wilkins ice shelf, measured at 1,100 square kilometers (1998), and the Larsen B ice shelf, measured at 13,500 square kilometers (2002). The result of these and other anticipated losses will be a rise in global sea levels by 77 centimeters (30.3 inches) by 2010! In the short run, rising sea levels will start to encroach upon coastal property on shorelines around the world. In the longer term, severe flooding will result. Can we build sea walls high enough to keep out the floods?

A third issue is that the increase in the temperature of the oceans creates an enormous pool of potential energy ready to be tapped whenever a hurricane is created at sea. The potential energy of the warmer oceans is transferred to kinetic energy in the storm, giving the storm's power a boost that can promote it from (for example) a level-three storm to a level-four or level-five storm. Thus, the increased water temperature can create storms that are more intense, harming both the environment and human civilization.

Ground Pollution

Ground pollution generally refers to the degradation of the soil and all that is in it (including ground water). There are two forms of ground waste. First is regular municipal waste that includes day-to-day household waste and other residential wastes such as yard waste, grass clippings, litter containers, disposable diapers, and used appliances (washers, dryers, dishwashers, refrigerators, ranges, computers, and any number of large durable goods). This category also includes waste from small businesses, hospitals, and schools, as well as city government. It also often contains various categories of recyclable waste that is generally lumped into city dumps. These dumps are filling up faster and faster, causing some municipalities to buy new land or to resort to bizarre measure such as filling decrepit railroad cars and dumping them full of garbage into the ocean. This solution, of course, only moves the problem from point A to point B. As such, it is no solution at all. At the present pace, we have fewer and fewer landfill sites.

The second form of ground waste is hazardous waste. This sort of waste is toxic because it is infectious, radioactive, and/or flammable, or because it has other chemical properties that will severely harm the health of human and animal populations should these chemicals seep into the ground water (as was the case in the infamous Love Canal incident that caused hundreds of individuals to contract cancer as a result).[8] The precise range of this problem is hard to gauge because it is a sensitive political issue within countries. Instead of using the reporting categories of the Basel Convention on the definition and reporting of hazardous wastes, many countries resort to their own idiosyncratic definitions.[9] This makes international assessment of the problem difficult at best. However, one thing is sure: With some toxic wastes—especially radioactive wastes, which possess a half-life of 10,000 years—this is a form of ground pollution that once initiated can be around a long time. In the United Nations statistical reports, virtually all of the seventy countries surveyed from 1990 to 2004 have had significant increases in hazardous waste within their boundaries. Most observers think that the real figure is actually higher (for the reasons mentioned earlier).

The problem of pollution in all three areas—air, water, and ground—pose significant health hazards to populations both domestic and international.

The Causes

Air Pollution

Numerous gasses contribute to air pollution. For example, sulfur dioxide is caused by fuel combustion in diesel and conventional engines but particularly from coal-powered energy plants, the largest source of sulfur dioxide emissions.

Nitrous oxide is formed in urban areas with high traffic intensity. Especially when trapped under an ozone layer that prevents it from dissipating, nitrous oxide may reach unhealthy concentrations that exacerbate human respiratory problems.

Carbon dioxide (CO_2) is by far the largest contributor to global warming. Most CO_2 is produced by the combustion of fossil fuels. The biggest culprits here are power plants and factories that burn coal and lignite. Automobile exhaust is another great contributor. A third cause for rising carbon dioxide levels is deforestation. Because trees and other plants take in CO_2 during photosynthesis, forests actually decrease the amount of CO_2 in the air. So when logging decreases the total forest acreage, a consequence is that less CO_2 is removed from the air.

There are other more minor causes of greenhouse gasses: metal industry, enteric fermentation, manure management, rice cultivation, and solid waste disposal on land.

Water Pollution and Water Shortages

The causes of water shortages and pollution are numerous. For simplicity let us focus on nature, humankind's basic activities, and social/political entities.

Nature

Genuine water availability is a function of the hydrological cycle. The cycle works this way: The sun's heat evaporates water into the atmosphere. The heat of the sun, the dryness of the prevailing air, and the wind control the speed of this process. As the water vapor rises in the atmosphere, it cools, condenses, and returns as precipitation to earth—on both land and sea—where it begins the cycle again. The water returns to terrestrial land, striking the soil, streams and lakes, and man-made coverings. The water also returns to marine (ocean) locales. Marine water is returned by evaporation while terrestrial water is also returned by flora in the form of transpiration.

The total amount of water on earth is fixed. It is continually changing from solid to liquid to gas in a self-renewing cycle. The water on the planet is distributed thusly:[10]

> Marine: 1,400,000 sq. kiloliters = 96 percent
> Everything else: 60,202.6 sq. kiloliters = 4 percent

By far most of the water on the planet is marine saltwater (not proximately useful for domestic activities of life). For human needs, the most important of these water reservoirs is surface terrestrial water (lakes), rivers, and underground terrestrial water. These are the primary, proximate sources of potable water. The large geographic regions that support these rivers, lakes, and underground terrestrial water are called water basins.[11] For example, a single water basin that supports Lake Superior extends across the states of Minnesota and Wisconsin and into Ontario, Canada. The geography of the land creates the conditions that make rainwater and melted snow move in particular directions. This geography does not recognize artificial man-made boundaries such as nations and intranational divisions. Because water basins are commonly quite extensive and frequently extend across even international boundaries, water-basin management can be complex.

Smaller divisions within water basins are called watersheds. Because of their more limited scopes, watersheds are generally more amenable to local water-management programs. The strategy for water management of watersheds is to focus on the particular ecosystem that supports it. Because an ecosystem is naturally self-sustaining and interactive, it provides a good model for adaptation and management. By beginning with the natural sustainable dynamic, we have a pattern or goal to try to re-create or approximate. Water basins are more difficult because they are affected by many different ecosystems and may cut across more than one biome. This means that many different strategies must be undertaken (according to the circumstances) and that the interaction between these may result in counterproductive outcomes.

We should not be overly anthropocentric about water management. It is not only humans who need water. There are three other natural classes that depend upon water to maintain their identity. The first of these is the land itself. The structural integrity of hills, topsoil, and even mountains over time can be altered by too much or too little water. If one considers the problem from a land ethics point of view, then water management is important to maintain the land as it is.[12] In the United States, the needs of the land itself have rarely been considered.

Strip mining and poor agricultural practices have often had the effect of altering the character of the land—and the character of the land is a crucial element in the creation of ecosystems and biomes.

Sometimes the land can be a source of pollution. This often occurs due to extreme weather conditions in which large areas of land mix with water and block out sunlight and possibly affect the oxygen content of water. However, this is a sporadic rather than a regular occurrence.

The second natural class that depends on water to maintain its identity is the flora. Plants need water, minerals, and sunlight to survive. Minerals are a function of the land's character. Water availability is determined by the water basin and watershed dynamics. Sunlight is sensitive to the atmospheric medium that separates plants from sunlight entering the earth's exosphere. Without adequate water, plants will die. When plants die they affect the land because they cease to fix minerals into the soil as well as to maintain topsoil. Again, the entire ecosystem or biome can significantly alter.

The third class is the fauna. Animals need clean water to stay alive and complete their life cycle. Animals provide nourishment to plants through their excretions and the decomposition of their bodies. They also help plants to pollinate and promote vigorous growth by their eating habits.

Both flora and fauna can contribute to water contamination. In the first case dead trees (for example) can become habitats for bacteria that are harmful to other ecosystem members. In the second case, animal defecation and animal carcasses provide more virulent host opportunities for parasites and bacteria to thrive. These events can work to the detriment of other animals that drink from the stream or pond.

It is most often the case that the question of water is viewed from the anthropocentric viewpoint, but it is important to see the biocentric position as well.

Humankind

Of course, humans (like other animals) require clean water to support their life activities. Humans use far more water than do other animals, not just for domestic uses (such as drinking, cooking, bathing, washing, and so on) but also for industry and agriculture. Table 12.1 shows how various regions of the world allocate their water usages.

What Table 12.1 tells us is that most of the water that humans use is not directly concerned with the activities of day-to-day living—that is, domestic uses. Other animals only consume water for domestic purposes and those purposes are limited to primarily to drinking. Because an average of some 90 percent of freshwater worldwide is involved in agriculture (most often for the purpose of irrigation) and industrial uses, this may provide an area of hope for the future if better and more efficient practices are developed.

TABLE 12.1. How Water Is Used Around the World

	Agricultural (%)	Domestic (%)	Industry (%)
Europe	40	15	45
North America	50	10	40
Australia/Oceania	60	28	12
South America	62	25	13
Africa	80	15	5
Asia	70	10	20

Source: Jill Boberg, *Liquid Assets: How Demographic Changes and Water Management Policies Affect Freshwater Resources* (Santa Monica, CA: Rand Corporation, 2005): 24.

At present, both agriculture and industry are great sources of pollution. In agriculture, fertilizers mix with the water. In terms of traditional fertilizers—that is, manure—this means human and animal fecal matter is dissolved by rain that will run off into either ground water or into local streams and lakes. This mixture of water and fecal matter creates a breeding ground for parasites, bacteria, and viruses that will constitute a threat to the health of humans and animals.

When farmers use chemical fertilizers the situation is not much better. Chemical fertilizers can also affect the ecosystems of rivers, lakes, and marine bodies of water. These chemicals can poison large numbers of animals and affect human health as well by increasing the risk of cancer and other diseases.

Industrial wastes are much like the chemical runoff from farms except the by-products are often more toxic. Some extreme cases, such as Love Canal, can cause epidemic illness that is often fatal.[13] Thus the impact of the activities of humans on the supply of clean water exponentially exceeds the impact of the land or fauna or flora.

Social/Political Entities

Because humans deleteriously affect water so much, it is useful to identify certain combinations of humans and their behaviors as key actors in the tragedy of water contamination. These entities are the social and political constructs of human culture. Beginning with the largest, they include international organizations such as the United Nations and its various operational bodies, such as the World Health Organization, and the policies and treaties that flow from these. Other international bodies such as the World Bank can also play pivotal roles in the financing of public health initiatives that otherwise might not occur.

Next in terms of size are international companies whose business ventures within a country often play a pivotal role in water pollution and water shortages.

Because corporations are often loath to lower their bottom line by making investments that have no direct shareholder value (such as voluntary pollution controls), government oversight is important for regulating water pollution and water usage.

At the third level are the international relations between countries. Water basins are often situated over extended geographic regions that overlap to two or more countries, and what happens in one place can have an immediate effect in another. This requires cooperation. But what if relations between the countries are strained? The result, sad to say, is often close to the worst possible outcome.

Last is the role of intracountry local government. Local populations see water as an asset to their own communities. Their interests may be different from other localities. This is similar to the problem between countries with the exception that within one nation it is often easier to find some sort of peaceful, political resolution of the problem.

Solid Waste

The two most important causes of solid waste as a problem are (1) its explosive growth, leading to a problem of finding the space to contain it, and (2) the toxic nature of some of the waste by itself and in combination with other waste.

Unlike air pollution and water pollution, solid waste tends to be a national rather than an international problem. Exceptions include the Great Pacific Garbage Patch, a collection of human litter in international waters in the north Pacific Ocean. The patch is almost the size of Texas and is composed of pelagic plastics (which do not degrade), chemical sludge, and other nonbiological degradable garbage from the North Pacific Gyre.

In national terms municipal waste is collected on behalf of the citizens of a town and is generally taken to a landfill facility or an incineration plant. Most common in this mixture are household waste that is biodegradable (such as food scraps and yard waste) and waste that is not biodegradable (such as plastic diapers, plastic bottles, Styrofoam cups, and so on). In many cases a large hole is made in the earth and the garbage is put inside and then covered up. A cheaper strategy is to simply pile up the garbage into a sort of mountain. Depending upon the wealth of the community, this sort of strategy will require at some point a closing off of the dump with dirt on top or a vinyl cover of some sort to avoid a public health disaster (as a breeding ground of rodents and associated virulent bacteria).

Toxic waste is (or should be) treated separately. This category includes biomedical wastes, radioactive wastes, and all other wastes that by themselves or in contact with other wastes will create an environmental crisis to the health and safety to those living around the site. Because there is so much unknown about hazardous waste, the treatment of such poses a tremendous problem. The poster child of these is waste from nuclear power plants. This waste is harmful for a long time, and communities tend not to want it in their vicinity just in case there is some sort of leakage that causes cancer or some other fatal or disabling result.

Possible Solutions

Before we can entertain solutions to this problem we first have to find a way to analyze it conceptually. Let's begin with two prominent philosophers: John Broome and Henry Shue.

Broome's reasoning is driven by an economic analysis. So, for example, when analyzing the bedrock environmental concept of whether there is a duty to future generations, Broome begins by accepting Derek Parfit's claim that equal harms to well-being count the same whenever they occur.[14] But how we are to understand this and quantify it require further analysis.

> Some commodities represent a constant quantity of well-being whenever they occur; let us call them constant-well-being commodities . . . Saving people's lives is plausibly another example of a constant-well-being commodity; on average, saving one person's life in one hundred years will presumably add just as much well-being to the world as saving one person's life now. Granted that well-being ought not to be discounted, constant-well-being commodities ought not to be discounted . . . Lifesaving in the future will make the same contribution to well-being as lifesaving in the present. Certainly future lifesaving is cheaper than present lifesaving, but this is not a reason for valuing it less.[15]

Thus, Broome sees the desired goal as well-being. This is a broad goal, comparable to a combination of level-one and level-two basic goods and level-one secondary goods (see Table 3.1) that in turn create a positive state of mind: well-being. Broome next poses a paradox about our duties to future generations:

> If we can convert a quantity of lifesaving now into a greater quantity next year, and if the lifesaving next year is just as valuable as lifesaving now, the conclusion we have to draw is that lifesaving should be deferred. We should withdraw resources from lifesaving today, and apply them to saving more lives next year. We should also defer lifesaving next year in order to save yet more lives the year after . . . We will end up postponing all lifesaving to the indefinite future, which never comes. So we will end up saving no lives at all.

Broome's analysis demonstrates a problem for those wishing to create public policy for environmental or any other sort of area of concern that pits present generations against future ones. It rests upon the following argument:

1. Future lifesaving is cheaper than present lifesaving—Fact (from economics and the cost of present v. future goods investment)
2. [We should always direct public policy in the most economically efficient fashion]—Assertion
3. [Well-being is an economically quantifiable good]—Assertion
4. To choose any particular temporal lifesaving component—t_n there is always a subsequent temporal lifesaving component—t_{n+1} such that all claims to t_n should go to t_{n+1}—1–3
5. [The inference at premise #4 implies an infinite sequence since once identified, t_{n+1} implies a successor function that by the power set axiom creates a t_{n+2} => fs (successor function) $t_{n+3} \ldots t \aleph_1$]
6. [$t \aleph_1$ refers to an infinite set (without integration or any sort of definitive quantitative result]—Assertion
7. [Public policy cannot make definitive decisions without definitive quantitative results]—Fact

---

8. One cannot make life-saving policy regarding well-being to current or future generations—4–7

This paradox is set up to force us to reexamine how we are to understand duties to future generations. Broome's answer is that "lifesaving may not be a constant well-being commodity."[16] He goes on to say that this may be age determined (a young life demonstrates more potential well-being than an older life, say a twenty-year-old versus a ninety-year-old). This response points to well-being as a commodity that can be multiplied by expected longevity. Such a model would be consistent with a utilitarian point of view so long as the well-being coefficient is set on a limited scale. When this is the case, longer projected longevity will weigh more heavily and will thus define social justice.[17]

For some critics of this standpoint (such as myself), a rights-based deontological approach would argue that in premise #1 the suggestion of "cheaper" versus "more expensive" is rather beside the point except as it applies to the "ought implies can" caveat of any moral imperative. The more important central question asks what any living human agent (at this moment) rightly claims as a good in the Table of Embeddedness. For example, protection from unwarranted bodily harm, a level-one good, would apply here. This right claim against all other members of society (proximately) and the world (remotely) requires from those others the reciprocal duty both to refrain from promoting harm and to rescue others from such harm. In the case of the environment, this means that individuals in their activity, industry in its activity, and government in its activity should all agree to examine their behavior according to the shared-community worldview imperative and the extended-community worldview imperative. The result would be a concerted effort to limit all environmental causes of unwarranted bodily harm within a hurry-up timetable (such as cutting carbon emissions by half in the next five years, recycling and reusing whenever possible, and replanting forests). These and other policy objectives would move us toward sustainability: the holy grail of environmentalism.

In this view, then, how ought these substantial obligations to clean-up be allocated? Henry Shue has addressed this question. He argues[18]:

1. There are two principal approaches to progressive environmental policy: a comprehensive approach (advocated by Steward and Wiener)[19] and the focused, targeted approach (advocated by Drennen)[20]—Assertion [A] (p. 208)
2. The answer to premise #1 comes from four sorts of questions: (a) allocating the costs of prevention, (b) allocating the costs of coping, (c) allocating background and fair bargaining, and (d) allocating transitions and the goal—A (pp. 208–209)
3. The costs of prevention fall disproportionately vis-à-vis the rich and poor [heavier on the poor]—F (p. 211)
4. [Public policy should be progressive]—A
5. The rich should make more sacrifices than the poor—3, 4 (p. 212)
6. The costs of coping are dominated by (a) "to each his own" and (b) "wait and see"—A (pp. 214–215)
7. 6-a offers a too small perspective while 6-b incorrectly separates coping and prevention costs (cf. Great Seawall of China)—A (pp. 215–216)
8. Neither 6-a nor 6-b are sufficient by themselves—6, 7 (p. 217)
9. Fair bargaining depends upon the agents holding equal shares—A (p. 219)
10. Internationally the parties are unequal—F (p. 218)
11. Fair bargaining offers a challenge to environmental policy—9, 10 (p. 219)
12. Transitions require a goal—A (p. 219)
13. A goal requires some notion of an ultimate ceiling—A (p. 220)
14. At present it is a few rich nations with small population that pollute the most CO_2—F (p. 220)
15. The compromises necessary for transitions and meeting ultimate goals are challenging—12–14 (p. 221)
16. Two further questions can give greater direction to the four from premise #2: "from whom" and "to whom" [since the four questions are inconclusive]—5, 8, 11, 15 (p. 221)
17. The answers to the two further questions will be a "fault criterion" or a "no-fault criterion"—A (pp. 223–224)

18. The "fault criterion" offers a clearer answer than the "no-fault criterion"—A (pp. 224–226)
19. The "fault criterion" should be used—17, 18 (p. 226)
20. The comprehensive approach aligns itself with the homogenization [and the no-fault approach]—A (p. 228)
21. Homogenization fails to distinguish between genuine and frivolous needs—A (p. 228)
22. [The homogenization approach should be rejected]—3, 4, 21
23. The comprehensive approach should be rejected—19, 20, 22 (p. 229)
24. The targeted approach can specify the greatest needs along with strategies to make the costs progressive—A (pp. 230–231)

---

25. The targeted approach should be the policy direction of choice over the comprehensive approach—1, 23, 24

Shue's argument poses four key questions of distributive justice relevant here: (a) allocating the costs of prevention, (b) allocating the costs of coping, (c) allocating background and fair bargaining, and (d) allocating transitions and the goal. Because public policy should be progressive, the rich countries should pay more than the poor in setting up a solution to the problem of environmental pollution.[21] This ultimately comes back to a fault criterion. The rich nations are largely responsible for creating the problem in the first place, so they should be largely responsible for paying for the clean-up. It is not enough to ask every country to bear an equal share. This is as unfair as a flat tax (because it is regressive). On the principle of being progressive and on the principle of retributive justice (asking the biggest sinners to take the largest burden of getting back to balance), the richest nations of the world—perhaps the G-20—should take it upon themselves to make environmental change happen.

The practical problem with Shue's position is that it flies in the face of the special interests who constitute the engine that generated the problem in the first place. I support the basic thrust of Shue's argument, but with the following conceptual and concrete refinements.

Conceptual Refinements to Shue's Argument

1. Environmental policy should be guided by morality (e.g., valid claim rights against other members of society and the world in general).
2. There should be a general acceptance that clean air, sustainable ground-level waste disposal, and clean water are level-one basic goods. Because all basic goods constitute claim rights that entail correlative duties, the entire world must accept its duty to provide all people on the planet

with clean air, sustainable ground-level waste disposal, and clean water. This is a strong moral ought.

3. There should be a general acceptance that the interests of all people—including the poor, women, children, and the sick and disabled—are included in #2.

4. There should be a general acceptance that natural environmental systems be respected. The principle of precautionary reason should always be applied when tampering with any ecosystem, biome, watershed, or water basin.

5. All interruptions in the natural order should be required to meet the burden of proof that the intervention will create a sustainable outcome. This thesis should be subjected to public and scientific scrutiny before proceeding.

6. Economic development should not be mixed up with executing moral duty. If Option A will give more economic development at the expense of the poor and if Option B will give less economic development but recognize the societal duty to provide clean water and sanitation to all, then B should trump A.[22]

Concrete Refinements to Shue's Argument

In addition to these conceptual givens, a few more concrete steps can be taken:

1. International organizations, such as the World Bank, should not try to mix evangelical capitalism in their development grants to subsistence societies.

2. Competition and commercialization of water as a resource should be avoided until all citizens within a society have access to clean water and sanitation.

3. An international body with stature, such as the United Nations, WHO, the International Monetary Fund, or the World Bank, should monitor all new major development projects concerning air pollution (power plants and manufacturing), waste and toxic disposal, and new water projects with respect to the principle of precautionary reason and environmental sustainability (above).

4. The wealthy nations of the world should devote substantial resources (progressively: according to their ability to pay) toward the capitalization of substantial sanitation and water purification projects at both the national and local levels in subsistence societies (monitored as per #3).

5. Wealthy societies should look within their own countries in order to clean up regional air pollution, recycle and reuse regular ground waste,

and avoid compromising the availability of water for domestic use (including the monitoring of agricultural and industrial pollution). They should also create a climate fund to retro-fit power factories and waste disposal plants in order to move toward the goal of sustainability.

6. A binding system of arbitration should be established to adjudicate international disputes concerning air, water, and ground pollution (especially toxic wastes) along with watershed/water basin management as well as verifiable alterations in the hydrological cycle within a region.

Some naysayers claim that we'll never make global progress on the environment. Our very future existence depends upon proving these pessimists wrong.

Key Terms

air pollution, water pollution, ground waste disposal (regular and toxic)

Critical Applied Reasoning Exercise

Pick one area from this list: air pollution, water pollution, ground waste disposal (regular and toxic). Go to the United Nations site on environmental pollution, http://unstats.un.org/unsd/environment. Examine the statistics and see if you can spot a trend in your chosen area for a particular country. Then look at the UN's analysis and think about the problem from your own personal worldview perspective. Make one policy recommendation to solve a single identifiable problem. Be sure to address who will execute the policy and how it will be paid for.

Notes

1. For an overview on this, see Keith Smith and David N. Petley, *Environmental Hazards: Assessing Risk and Reducing Disaster* (London: Routledge, 2009); and Robert L. Nadeau, *The Environmental Endgame: Mainstream Economics, Ecological Disaster, and Human Survival* (New Brunswick, NJ: Rutgers University Press, 2006). For a very engaging overview of these and related issues, see the special issue of the *Journal of Social Philosophy: The Global Environment, Climate Change, and Justice* 40, 2 (Summer 2009).

2. These statistics are annually updated and are available online at http://unstats.un.org/unsd/environment.

3. The science on this can be found in Allan J. Clarke, *An Introduction to the Dynamics of El Nino and the Southern Oscillation* (St. Louis, MO: Academic Press, 2008).

4. A copy of this study can be obtained from their website on the principle of open source: www.niehs.nih.gov/health/impacts/respiratory.cfm.

5. This process is set out by Victoria J. Fabry, et al., "Impacts of Ocean Acidification on Marine Fauna and Ecosystem Processes," *ICES Journal of Marine Science* 65, 3 (April 2008): 414–432.

6. National Resource Defense Council, http://www.nrdc.org/globalwarming.

7. For this and the latest, turn to the British Antarctic Survey at www.antarctica.ac.uk/bas_research.

8. Craig E. Colten and Peter N. Skinner, *The Road to Love Canal: Managing Industrial Waste Before EPA* (Austin: University of Texas Press, 1995); and Elizabeth D. Blum, *Love Canal Revisited: Race, Class, and Gender in Environmental Activism* (Lawrence: University Press of Kansas, 2008).

9. The Basel Convention is an international protocol adopted in the late 1990s for dealing with toxic waste. To view the document, see www.basel.int/text/documents.html.

10. National Resources Canada, "Weathering the Changes: Climate Change in Ontario," *Climate Change in Canada: Our Water,* http://adaptation.nrcan.gc.ca/posters/articles/on_05_en.asp?Region=on&language=en.

11. Jill Boberg, *Liquid Assets: How Demographic Changes and Water Management Policies Affect Freshwater Resources* (Santa Monica, CA: Rand Corporation, 2005).

12. Aldo Leopold, *A Sand Country Almanac: And Sketches Here and There* (Oxford: Oxford University Press, 1949).

13. Jennifer Bond Reed, *Love Canal* (New York: Chelsea House, 2002).

14. Derek Parfit, *Reasons and Persons* (Oxford: Clarendon Press, 1984): 356ff.

15. John Broome, "Discounting the Future," *Philosophy and Public Affairs* 23, 2 (1994): 128–156.

16. Ibid.,150.

17. A similar critical response was made to this argument by Muireann Quigley and John Harris in "Personal or Public Health?" in *International Public Health Policy and Ethics,* ed. Michael Boylan (Dordrecht: Springer, 2008): 15–30.

18. Henry Shue, "Subsistence Emissions and Luxury Emissions," *Law and Policy* 15, 1 (1993): 39–59; reprinted in Thomas Pogge and Keith Horton, *Global Ethics: Seminal Essays* (St. Paul, MN: Paragon, 2008). Page numbers to Shue refer to the reprinted edition.

19. Richard B. Stewart and Jonathan B. Wiener, "The Comprehensive Approach to Global Climate Policy: Issues of Design and Practicality," *Arizona Journal of International and Corporate Law* 9 (1992): 83–113.

20. Thomas Drennen, "After Rio: Measuring the Effectiveness of the International Response," *Law and Policy* 15 (1993): 15–37.

21. Shue, "Subsistence Emissions and Luxury Emissions."

22. There are some further nuances to this in Michael Boylan, ed., *Public Health Policy and Ethics* (Dordrecht: Kluwer/Springer, 2004): ch. 8.

CHAPTER 13

War and Terrorism

The origins of war are an enduring theoretical problem in political philosophy and an endemic practical issue for the world at large. At the writing of this book there is considerable tension around the world that gives rise to non-state terrorism. There is also a constant echo of war or the rumor of war. This is an unpleasant but realistic look at how these ever-present realities shape the way the rest of morality and global justice go forward. Before we begin our brief exploration into this topic area, let us agree to some definitions:

- *War* is an aggressive act by one state against the territory or sovereignty of another state for the purposes of gaining land, resources, or strategic advantage according to internationally recognized rules and constraints governing such action (both *ad bellum* and *in bello*).
- *Just war theory* is a moral account of when it is morally permissible to go to war (*ius ad bellum*) and how the war may be conducted (*ius in bello*).
- *Belligerent kraterism* is an aggressive act by one state against the territory or sovereignty of another state for the purposes of gaining land, resources, or strategic advantage without regard to any constraint.
- *Terrorism* is using violence and mayhem to make a public message that creates fear so as to convince a population via *argumentum ad baculum* (argument from coercion or force). Because terrorism uses violence (generally against civilians), terrorism is the violation of the criminal laws in any given country. These include murder, arson, and the destruction of property. The actors are generally (though not necessarily) non-state agents whose purpose can be either profit motive (to enrich the criminals) or

177

political ideology to vent frustration or anger against a nation, institution, or some identifiable social group. Sometimes the author of terrorism is the government itself in an effort to control the civilian population within its borders.

- *Genocide* is an intranational event in which a deliberate slaughter of civilians occurs due to ethnic or religious reasons. The Ku Klux Klan in the United States is an example of this. Hitler's massacre of the Jews is another. The Hutu-Tutsi bloodbath in Rwanda is a third.
- *Guerrilla warfare* is an act by a non-state group (though it may be other-state sponsored) that uses tactics that incite fear and mayhem within a given country as part of a strategy of overthrowing the sitting government and establishing a new one.

For our purposes, each of these terms must be considered in the context of various statistics measured by Uppsala University's Data Program and Oslo's International Peace Research Institute (PRIO) that track international violence in the following categories:

- *Interstate*—generally traditional and unbridled krateristic war
- *Intrastate*—including both sorts of terrorism as well as government-sponsored terrorism and guerrilla warfare
- *Extra-state terrorism*—an outside state sponsors factions within a country with the intent to fuel violence (meant to describe colonialism)
- *Internationalized internal conflict*—an intrastate conflict sponsored by an outside state that also lends warriors to help fight the fight

These terms have various definitions in different contexts, but for simplicity let us agree to use these here in this context.[1]

The Problem

War

VI

Papiols, Papiols, to the music!
There's no sound like to the swords swords opposing,
No cry like the battle's rejoicing
When our elbows and swords drip the crimson
And our charges 'gainst "The Leopard's" rush clash.
May God damn for ever all who cry "Peace!"

VII

And let the music of the swords make them crimson!
Hell grant soon we hear again the swords clash!
Hell blot black for always the thought "Peace"![2]

The ethics of war vary in their historical and cultural expression. St. Augustine and St. Thomas had a few things to say about it, though they gave us no comprehensive treatise. There are also Jewish and Islamic thinkers who wrote on establishing rules of war.[3] On the one hand, it seems absurd to talk about *rules* of war, when *war* seems to be all about doing whatever it takes to win the day: unfettered kraterism. Is all this talk about rules just a sham that covers up our understanding that when war occurs, *anything goes*? Michael Walzer in his greatly influential book *Just and Unjust Wars* provides arguments for the proposition that despite the appearance of amoral havoc, most of us retain moral attitudes about war.[4] For example, when a massacre is perpetrated and then is widely condemned, that condemnation places the massacre in a moral context. Even if a potential massacre is averted, such as to spare innocent civilians, the decision to give quarter to the noncombatants is made within a moral context. When the conduct of soldiers can be described as treacherous or dishonorable, those are moral evaluations of their conduct in war. Likewise, when political and military leaders resort to hypocrisy to create false depictions of war, the very use of the word *hypocrisy* incorporates a moral judgment. As Walzer correctly argues, the use of moral language in and about war means that at the very least those who employ such terms and those to whom such language is meaningful believe that war thus exists within a moral context.

I believe that Walzer's argument is conclusive against those who argue that war is merely a normal prudential expression of action. For example, Karl von Clausewitz contended that because war is limitless and because morality requires limits, there is no morality in war.[5] One's personal worldview will be quite different when considering war as either a normal prudential reaction to some situation (in the kraterist mode without restraint) or as encompassed within moral limits.

If we accept that war exists within a moral context, and if morality requires limits, then *there can be no such thing as unlimited war!* But this may sound queer because surely there have been butchers who have seemed to stop at nothing. What does this say? Merely that they have gone beyond the measure of the way actual people use language to describe actions in war. It would be more accurate to say that there *are* limits to war and that when this reality is ignored, mere lawless anarchy (unbridled kraterism) ensues. Perhaps this comes close to begging the question because it says that complete limitless behavior ensues when one goes beyond the limits of war to a state of unbridled kraterism. I would reply that this is not begging the question but merely stipulating how we are to use language. The term *war* is to be reserved for those morally encompassed cases in which the proper causes of going to war *ad bellum* are observed and then separately the behavior in war *in bello* is also observed. War properly regards restraint. When this restraint reaches a commonly accepted threshold, we may go further in our identification of the conflict as being a *just* war. When some (but not enough) restraint is observed in armed conflict (according to a commonly accepted threshold), the war is unjust. Unbridled kraterism does not accept limits and so is always morally reprehensible and unfit for any national or cosmopolitan standard. This gives war (within the moral context) some legitimacy.

But what constitutes such a context? The so-called domestic analogy is the most compelling. When John attacks Jamal (a morally innocent person) with a knife, Jamal has permission to thwart John's attack using the minimal force necessary (measured by prudent man guidelines).[6] When attacked, we may defend ourselves using the minimal force necessary according to our skill at self-defense. This can include lethal force. If John kills Jamal, then John is a murderer. If Jamal kills John (under the stated conditions), then Jamal is legally and morally innocent.

When applied to nations, it works this way: Nation X attacks Nation Y. Nation Y may defend itself against Nation X. All the killings by Nation X against Nation Y constitute unjustified killing of innocents, or murder. However, all the deaths incurred by Y against X (using the standards of minimally necessary force and proportionality) are permissible under moral and international law.

One added amendment to self-defense that makes the claim murkier is self-defense on behalf of others. Going back to the domestic analogy, if I see Monica being attacked by Ahab, I may justifiably intervene against Ahab on behalf of Monica. Even though I personally am not being attacked, the legal account in the American/British criminal law tradition allows me to rescue another entity using minimal force to stop the attack. When this is applied to the international sphere, this caveat becomes rather slippery. For example, in Vietnam, the United States used this sort of argument to defend its intervention on behalf of South Vietnam against North Vietnam, because the latter was attacking the former (a similar argument was also used in Korea). It is difficult to evaluate such claims because the intervening party might not be acting purely disinterestedly but might be pursuing interests of its own under cover of its professed altruism. Thus, in the cases of Vietnam and Korea, the United States[7] had interests in stopping the spread of communism, which it viewed as a real threat to its existence. Thus, whereas the United States claimed to be defending the underdog (South Vietnam), a very strong argument can be made that the United States was actually acting on behalf of its own perceived national interest. Using war as a normal tool of diplomacy is not permitted under just war theory. Therefore, whenever invoking this sort of justification of self-defense on behalf of another, a large measure of careful scrutiny ought to be employed in order to determine whether the claim isn't really a self-interested aggressive act in disguise.

These sorts of dynamics refer to the moral issues involved in going to war, *ius ad bellum*. A further complication can occur when Country X feels threatened by Country Y because Y had gathered armies at the border (or other such provocative activity) and looked as if it were about to attack. Should X wait until Y actually invades before engaging in military activity? Or should X engage in a preemptive strike that technically makes it the aggressor but gives it a strategic advantage for acting *first*? This is a very difficult question. I think that the proper response for X is to engage in a similar military build-up while also using diplomatic avenues to their fullest extent. Here is an instance where one's moral theory will generate public policy. If one were a utilitarian consequentialist, then the way to answer the preemptive war question would be to balance out the projected utility consequences for both approaches (assuming that these can be reasonably approximated). Because utilitarians count everyone equally, the deaths of one's enemy will count the same as allied deaths. Virtue ethics advocates will try to discern what critical moral virtues are at stake and then try to act accordingly. The antirealist camp will look to some sort of tradition or history of military response that has been publicly accepted and then try to be consistent with that (e.g., contractarians might be very interested in multilateral treaties as the sole determination).

Because I support a deontological rights-based approach that follows generally from the application of the relevant worldview imperatives along with the cosmopolitan application of the Table of Embeddedness, I would *not* support preemptive strikes as being instances of self-defense.

Thus, the answer to whether preemptive military strikes are instances of self-defense and thus allowable under just war theory or whether they fail to reach the acceptable standard and become unjust wars is answered via the accepted moral theory that drives public policy.

The second sort of traditional category to judge the morality of war is *ius in bello*, the body of law governing the manner in which war is carried out. These standards are more complicated: They conscribe just *how* one carries out war (from either point of view—attacker or defender). These sorts of questions address the sort of weapons that are allowed—such as prohibitions on biological, chemical, or nuclear weapons. They also examine the status of civilians and noncombatants. Some civilians are actively involved in the war effort such as making munitions and tanks. Those civilians not actively involved in the war effort are generally thought to be immune from military force. In many cases noncombatants, such as medics and doctors—even though they are in uniform—are exempt from violence because their mission is not to kill but to protect. Another category in the rules of carrying out war covers the taking of prisoners, their care, and the limits on their interrogation (such as prohibitions against torture).

The judgment about how one carries out a war is separate from whether one was guilty in starting the war in the first place. It is possible, for example, to be innocent in questions of *ad bellum* (meaning that you are fighting in self-defense), but guilty in questions of *in bello* (meaning that once the war began you targeted noncombatants and engaged in torture, for example). The reverse is also possible: to be guilty as the initial aggressor *ad bellum* but to comply with the rules of carrying out a war *in bello*. Thus, the questions are separable, but in all probability the community worldview that would step outside the rules in either event singly would probably do so in both.[8]

Countries that seek the advantages of armed aggression against others may often decide that they will simply act as they feel they *must* in order to attain the said advantage from their aggression. These sorts of actions declare a lack of obedience to the developed protocols of justification to war (*ad bellum*) and the way to fight it (*in bello*). This conspicuous lack of self-control is reminiscent of Aristotle's description of the incorrigible person, the un-self-controlled (*asophrosune*).[9] In personal action (personal worldview) and in group action (shared community worldview) the uncontrolled entity that knows that it is uncontrolled and doesn't care in its thirsty power-seeking is a sort of entity that belies any reference to just war theory. These countries are usually (but not always) ruled by dictators who baldly assert power to get what they think they can get. Sometimes they are successful, such as Joseph Stalin; sometimes they fail, like Saddam Hussein. The point is that kraterists engage in a Nietzsche-like will to power as they create their own rules in order to affect an outcome that is advantageous to them. Because the kraterists thumb their noses at ethics and international law, there is little that can be *said* to them. They believe ethics to be a hoax to keep the herd in order. In these cases, responding countries ought (under my account) to obey the conventions of just war even if their opponents do not. This was the attitude of the Allies during World War II (for the most part) and should continue to be the case based on one's chosen ethical theory (in my case, a rights-based deontological approach).

In a more complete treatment we might think about *ius post bellum*, the moral context of the aftermath of war. How should the conventions of war treat the losers? The Treaty of Versailles that ended World War I is a famous case in point. Germany was burdened with such punitive measures by the victorious allies that it stoked German resentment and made possible the rise of a demagogue such as Hitler. In contrast, the Marshall Plan after World War II, in which the United States led an effort to rebuild war-ravaged Europe, offers a better model for *post bellum* conventions. The history of almost sixty-five years of peace in Western Europe proves this to be a superior strategy.

War should be undertaken as an explicit national response to a direct attack upon its territory, resources, or sovereignty by another state. It should not be undertaken lightly but should be the last resort after diplomatic negotiations fail. Level-one basic goods (protection from unwarranted bodily harm) and level-two basic goods (the protection of basic liberties) demand that the protocols of just war theory be observed.

The good news is that in the swing of historical trends, since 1990 interstate conflicts have gone down. From the time of World War II until 1960 these conflicts remained relatively level. Then they peaked for the Vietnam War and again after the break-up of the Soviet Union. Since 1990 these interstate conflicts have been on a low trend.[10] Looking at the period from the present to 1946, the most war-prone countries (meaning that they have participated in the most interstate wars or conflicts) are the United Kingdom (21), France (19), the United States (16), and Russia (9).[11] When we change our purview to the theaters of war (inter- and intrastate) the picture is rather different (participating in one conflict equals a conflict year, so that if a country has multiple conflicts, then multiple conflict years are ascribed): Burma/Myanmar (232), India (156), Ethiopia (88), Philippines (86), Israel (79), the United Kingdom (77), France (66), Iraq (60), Vietnam (60), Russia (51), the United States (49), and Iran (48). These events include all categories of conflict. Another interesting statistic is that the dollar value of major international arms transactions fell by 33 percent between 1990 and 2003.[12] A final statistic of note is that in 2000–2009, interstate conflicts amounted to only 11 percent of all violent conflicts.[13]

Conventional war is on a downward trend. The principal actors in such conflicts are the major economic powers in the world. Why is this the case? The quick answer is that international business interests operate on the principle of unbridled kraterism and seek their ends as expediently as possible without regard for constraints (unless this constitutes a cost component). Though the number of interstate conflicts is currently on a downtick at the writing of this book, who knows what the future will bring?

Terrorism

For Americans, terrorism became especially real on September 11, 2001, in the terrorist attacks against the World Trade Center in New York, the Pentagon, and whatever was the intended target of the downed plane (many say the Capitol or the White House).[14] But terrorism has been around a long time. Terrorism is generally classified in PRIO's *intrastate* category, but (as with the case of September

11) this is not always an accurate characterization. Some scholars even suggest that terrorism may have legitimate moral expressions.[15] Since 1960, intrastate conflicts have dominated the numbers of violent conflicts, nearly doubling in the forty-two-year period ending in 2002.[16]

In order to understand terrorism in its contemporary context, let us analyze a few of our definitions and then see where this conceptual analysis leads us. First, this book suggests that terrorism begins with a rogue group engaged in criminal activity (judged via national standards against an international backdrop via the United Nations). In the first instance we have criminal groups that seek to enrich themselves. A prime example of this is the international drug trade. The mafia and other criminal organizations also engage in lawless activities for their own profit motive. They use lawlessness and horrific scenes—such as gangland-style killings—to strike fear into the hearts of the local community in order to gain compliance with their profit schemes. The various drug cartels in Colombia and Mexico, for example, use this principle: They kill those who might stand in their way in dramatic fashion in order to cow the local, regional, national, and international forces who might stand against them. It is appropriate to call these individuals and groups terrorists, as well. These are the first sort of terrorists. A second group of terrorists are also criminals, seeking to express their anger or dissatisfaction with the current order. They employ means that kill civilians, and they use publicity techniques that promote their ideas. These terrorist organizers are not about revolution. They do not seek to create a new government (cf. guerrilla warfare). Instead, their goal is to proclaim some point about the current situation in their country or in the world. It is because of this depiction that terrorism (so defined) is more closely aligned to common criminality than to an international event—such as war. But criminals of this sort break national laws because they want to make an ethical, political, or religious point. In the first two instances an example might be the Bader-Meinhof Group (later known as the Red Army Faction) in post–World War II Germany or the Red Brigade (1970s in Europe); both sought to make political points without an agenda for revolution and an alternative government.[17] These entities should be understood nationally rather than internationally. They should be judged as national law-breakers: criminals. As such, these criminals need to be tracked down and brought to trial under the prevailing laws of the country in question.

Another example might be Timothy McVeigh's bombing of the Alfred P. Murrah Building in Oklahoma City. He thought that America was passing him by. This was because McVeigh's understanding of what the country stood for was not the country he watched on the evening news. Like the Bader-Meinhof Group or the Red Brigade, he sought the venue of terrorism to express his discontent, so he bombed an office building and killed 168 people. A similar example is Scott Roeder, who murdered Dr. George Tiller, an ob-gyn physician, because the doctor agreed to perform legal late term abortions. These acts of terrorism (like so many others against abortionist clinics) illustrate an act of lawlessness for the sake of making a political point. A final example is al-Qaeda, which has claimed responsibility for destroying valuable real estate in the financial district of Manhattan and the murder of around three thousand people on September 11, 2001. The group acted because of various political points, such as its opposition to the U.S. presence in military bases in Saudi Arabia. These splinter groups take on special importance when the results of their actions gain wide attention.

But the most common form of intrastate violence is based upon ethnicity.[18] In this case, the leaders prey upon ethnic hatred to gain popular support for acts of violence within their country—sometimes leading to genocide. Darfur (Sudan), Angola, Rwanda, Burma (Myanmar), and Kosovo are contemporary examples.

Whether the law-breaking group is mafia, al-Qaeda, "ethnic cleansing groups," or the government itself, the approach is similar. None of these terrorist organizations seek to create an alternative government. They simply want to cause havoc and distress in the populace for the purpose of material gain, making a political point, or gaining nonspecific national influence.

Guerrilla Warfare

Guerrilla warfare must be distinguished from the goals and activity of terrorists. Guerrilla warfare begins with a small group of individuals within some state who think that their government should be changed. Because their numbers are small they cannot directly challenge the government and its military forces straight on. Instead, they hide in remote regions; they often do not wear uniforms; and they blur the distinction between combatants and noncombatants. They also typically adopt a hit-and-retreat strategy against military targets, though they also sometimes attack civil and civilian targets perceived as supporters of the current regime. As the guerrilla forces increase in size they may take on trappings of a regular military operation, using heavy weapons and engaging in actual battles against the government's troops. In this later stage a legitimate civil war is engaged. And the relevant conceptual construct is of the *in bello* rules from just war protocols.

Examples of guerrilla wars that have proceeded in just this way include the American Revolution, the Russian Revolution, the Red Chinese Revolution, and the Cuban Revolution. When there is popular support for the movement and when the ruling regime is out of touch with the concerns of its citizens, this sort of response can be very effective. Guerrilla war can be viewed as a sort of "bloodied ballot box" in an attempt to initiate the fair government principle: achieving a responsive ruling body.

From this presentation, *motive* is the key difference in how one is to judge whether an act of terrorism is from a profit motive, from an ethical, political, or religious motive, or from a real desire to create a new country because the existing government does not respect the fair government principle. Each case poses a different problem.

The Causes

War

Gone are the times when warfare consisted chiefly of confrontations between two tribes who would gather and act in menacing ways toward each other. These dramatic posturings would sometimes lead to real combat and killing, suggesting that aggression as a response to anxiety, threat, or desire might be a cause for taking more land or other resources for oneself. The seventeenth-century philosopher Thomas Hobbes theorized that competition based upon envy and desire fueled many to continue to seek more than their share. Hobbes called this reaching beyond one's grasp (*huperarchein*).

What is particularly toxic to the cause of peace is *memory*. In my opinion, a large majority of wars occur because communities *remember*. They remember the wrongs of the past. For example, in Ernest Hemingway's short story "Under the Ridge" the narrator (someone like Hemingway) is a filmmaker documenting the Spanish Civil War of the late 1930s.[19] The narrator is retreating after filming a key battle about to be lost by the antifascists. He pauses in a semi-protected rock formation for a little rest among warriors fighting for his cause. There in this brief moment of time, the narrator is confronted by a man who hates various peoples including the Moors, English, Russians, and North Americans. The reasons for the xenophobe's hatred stem from acts committed against his community before he was born! This *memory* filled with hatred is central to one reason why there is war. People don't forget; people don't forgive.

Very few people who feel autonomy and some measure of self-fulfillment (judged against a community/national scale of expectations) are inclined to be violent. But when the international venue is added, more confusion is caused, because the expectations and results of one community worldview against another may cause dissonance, commonly through new economic expectations. Wealthier nations may be envied by those of more modest means, and cultural differences may also create social friction that politicians can use to whip up support to bear arms. However, when people are content with what they have and when the government reflects this contentment, it seems there is less reason to engage in war.

Terrorism

The causes of terrorism are subtler. Terrorism has many guises, and each has its own causes. For example, someone who is disaffected because he thinks that the community-sanctioned economic system will not compensate him properly may go outside the system to convey his public messages of fear as part of an economic scheme to make money illegally. Such individuals eschew the distribution schemes of their societies in order to garner *more* than that system would ordinarily allot to them. Some criminals stop at that. But many decide they have to protect their income stream. Thus, the drug cartels and the mafia will go to any length necessary to protect their income. This includes murder and mayhem—but it has a purpose: to stop those who would curtail their profits.

A second type of criminal terrorists (those who have ethical, political, or religious motives) is more difficult to understand. Because so many people in society do not engage in the personal worldview imperative, it is the case that many people walking on earth do not even consider the four conditions of the imperative (discussed in Chapter 2): consistency (inductive and deductive), completeness (the rational and affective good will), connection to a theory of the good (a moral theory), and something that they can *really* live out in their lives. These sorts of terrorists are mere discontents, acting out of passions rather than any commitment to a rational reshaping of the world for the better. They are not interested in creating a new society or world order in any practical sense. What models they do espouse are commonly impossibly utopian schemes that also incorporate very intolerant personal worldviews. Thus, an anti-abortionist might feel that he or she *must* bomb the abortion clinic or kill the doctors who work there. Or a Timothy McVeigh might be so upset that the United States has more than a minimalist government that he will blow up a government office building to make his point. Or Osama bin Laden might be so upset at America's presence in the Middle East that he would plan horrific murder and destruction to make his point. Or some group within a country is so filled with ethnic hatred that it seeks a vision of genocide to purify the fatherland. Or a dictator feels his grip on power loosening so he creates a reign of terror (like the Chinese Cultural Revolution) to solidify his position of power. These are some of the causes of the second sort of terrorism.

Guerrilla Warfare

Guerrilla warfare comes about when the fair government principle is violated. Thus, when states fail to be responsive in some meaningful way to the desires of their people (by ballot or other means), they leave themselves open for demonstrations and, ultimately, armed rebellion. The motto "live free or die"[20] often means in practice "throw the bums out and put someone else in there." When there are no peaceful institutions to bring this about, the alternative is a hit-and-run style of warfare—the only sort that has a hope of succeeding against the established order. The guerrillas seek to set up a new and better government. Unfortunately, the new regime is often not much different than the old one: "meet the new boss, the same as the old boss."[21] In the history of the world some guerrilla wars end in a changed government that meets the fair government principle (like the United States of America). Others fail utterly (like the French Revolution or the Russian Revolution). Still, guerrilla wars begin on a regular basis.

Possible Solutions

War

Let us focus on two primary causes of war: (1) ancient grudges, and (2) *huperarchein* (overreaching for gaining land, resources, or strategic advantage).

Grudges are an important cause of war. In the Bosnian war of the 1990s, there were references made to grudges that went back 300 years or more. In the Middle East, talk of the Crusades has often been a barrier to the progress of peace for nearly a thousand years. The wounds of memory also fester in various other tinderboxes in the world: Ireland (concerning the British), United States (concerning slavery and concerning the conquered native populations), Korea (concerning Japanese invasions over the centuries), India (concerning British rule), Tasmania (concerning the British genocide), and most of Africa and South America (concerning European colonialism and neocolonialism).

Because grudges arise out of the emotions of hatred and revenge, it is important to conceptualize a framework that might be a part of the shared-community and extended-community worldview imperatives for everyone. The model I'm suggesting is the *three-generation rule*. This rule sets an agreed-upon statute of limitations on unjustified acts of extreme violence and oppression. The rationale for the statute is that if X commits an action in 1860 (such as purchasing a slave in the United States), then X's children (X_2) and grandchildren (X_3) may have benefited from X's actions in some way, but by the death of X_3, the last vestiges of X's direct influence will have ceased, and the victims of X's actions (contemporaries, children, and grandchildren) will be gone. At this point it is time for a new start. Though Hebrew law supports my general goal by setting a three-generation rule at forty years in the Exodus (due to low life expectancy), I think that the modern standard might be closer to 150 years. Thus, if people around the world were to accept this standard, then there might be an agreed-upon endpoint for historically based grudges.

Such a suggestion will require lots of worldview changes via overlap and acceptance. The task is enormous such that it borders on the utopian.

The overreaching (*huperarchein*) cause of war is even more difficult. This is because the very reason that a ruler is able to come to power in the first place is that he or she is adept in overreaching to get to this position. Only the driven overreachers can make it to the top of the political process. Depending upon the size of the country (smaller countries tend to be less competitive in their scramble for power), it is almost guaranteed that those who get there are seriously distorted. Why might we suppose that those whose personal worldview is so corrupted might be able to step outside and seek moderation? For the most part, I think that the cessation of war from this cause is impossible. So long as there are leaders whose grand vision requires implementation by force, we will have war. We can hope that popular support of such wars wanes when national and regional distributive justice are based upon a blended model that emphasizes cooperation models over competitive ones (see Chapters 3 and 6)—and when popular support for military action is weak, the effectiveness of the war effort is mediocre (because the soldiers are focused on staying alive rather than meeting military objectives). In these cases, the wars will not accomplish their purpose, and the ruler (if he remains in power) may be less inclined to use war to accomplish his competitive, aggressive purposes.

The next best bet is to create strong international agreement about adherence to just war standards that will create limitations on how wars are fought. If these international standards (such as the Geneva Conventions) have local and regional acceptance, then there is damage limitation. However, there is no guarantee that a rogue state might not just thwart these limitations or that an established member might violate various key provisions (such as torture) in the name of necessity.

The cessation of war sadly is not practically possible from the present world situation. There will be war. Perhaps international protocols will make it more controlled so long as the leading nations (i.e., the G-20 nations) strictly abide by the war conventions. Failure to do so will undermine the entire enterprise.

Other central future events may also affect the occurrence of war as time progresses. Certainly the possibility of a nuclear war raises other questions. Could nuclear deterrence among an ever-increasing number of nations with the Bomb change the way war is engaged? Can deterrence work if international terrorists also acquire a nuclear device?

And then there is the emergence of robotic warfare. There are fewer combatant deaths when drone warriors take on the battle. But will the noncombatant numbers go down? If these drones are intelligent enough to fight, might they in time acquire moral status of their own (assuming that potentiality of action is the grounding of human rights as per *The Moral Status of Basic Goods* argument)? An offshoot of robotic warfare is cyber warfare, in which computers are created to disable other computers in other countries so that the attacking country might gain economic or strategic advantage. It is certainly possible that warfare in one quadrant might be virtually solved while it flares up in another area.

Terrorism

The first category of terrorism concerns criminal activity for profit. Criminal terrorism in the first instance is a law enforcement activity against those seeking profit from illicit activities. In the case of the international drug trade, this requires cooperation between various states. National sovereignty is compromised when drug lords are able to act with impunity, thwarting the police to do as they please.

International organized crime is a vexing problem because of bribery and corruption that thwart political will. Another issue is that in the case of the drug trade, often the dynamics pit a rich country (such as the United States) that is the user against a poor country that is the provider. In such a case there is in many peoples' minds a sort of natural justice at work: Why should the poor country go to great lengths to protect its rich neighbor? They might say that drug addiction is a sign of affluent decadence. They might say that the solution of the problem lies in the moral fiber of the wealthy country's population: If they give up drugs, the problem vanishes!

These two opposing worldviews (supporting international organized crime for its economic value to a poor country versus the internal degradation of the fair government principle as the de facto government passes over to the criminals) pose very troublesome options. In the aforementioned case, if one were to assume that most people would like to earn an agricultural livelihood producing healthy crops, then an option to thwart the economic value argument would be to give opium or marijuana farmers a more lucrative market planting corn, wheat, or soybeans. Again, such a solution would not work unless there were multilateral support for such crop subsidies. It should be noted that this would go against the pure unbridled laissez-faire model for world trade that has been advocated over the past three decades. Other sorts of economic development can offer the farmers other alternatives. However, as mentioned in Chapter 11 on globalization, this strategy can also carry high social costs via cultural disruption. Unless something is put in its place to protect the disenfranchised people (the other: racial minorities, the disabled, women, and children), development will be no panacea. If one solves the development issue, then the second worldview issue of maintaining the existing government according to the fair government principle will be solved (because there is no natural affinity to those challenging the rule of law).

Beyond varieties of ordinary criminal behavior, terrorism might also be perpetrated for reasons of ethical, political, or religious motives; ethnic hatred, with a possible goal of genocide; or governmental action against its own people to maintain power and control.

Ethical, political, and religious dissidents have been and always will be a reality. An active primary and secondary education system that features discussion of all sides of an issue (as opposed to indoctrination) creates options for open ethical, political, or religious dissent. This may help ease the problem, though it will never cure it. Theocracies based (as they must be) on internalist epistemology are an anathema to the fair government principle.[22]

Ethnic hatred can only be overcome by the *overlap and modification* outcome of the way we accept novel normative theories (see Chapter 2). This requires the emergence within the country of a peacemaker, such as Mohandas Gandhi, Martin Luther King Jr., or Desmond Tutu. There is no recipe for this. Until such leaders emerge, these sorts of intrastate violence will continue.

Government violence against its own people is all about the existence of outlaw governments that abjure the fair government principle. When a government embraces true representation of popular sentiment (via the ballot box or some other means), another level of the rule of law is created that is respected above individual egoistic inclinations. This is a very difficult journey for countries without this cultural and political history.

Guerrilla Warfare

Guerrilla warfare is generally a national rather than an international problem. However, this is not always the case. In the struggle between the Irish Republican Army (IRA) and Northern Ireland, significant funds for the IRA were raised in the United States. Also, in the Palestine-Israel conflict, many foreign governments have weighed in on one side or the other. Sometimes this sign of support has come in the form of outsiders who engage in suicide bombings that target noncombatants (civilians) who are not key players in the conflict.

Like war, guerrilla activities seem like they will be around forever. These actions might be fewer if the fair government principle is instigated in greater numbers of countries. When people find that they have some influence in their government (by ballot or social custom), they are less likely to become so frustrated that they vow to "live free or die." It is unclear how we can promote the fair government principle. This is because it is involved in a paradox:

1. X (a country) is under a repressive regime—Fact
2. Y (another country) wants to help X get out of its repressive regime—Fact

3. Y takes action on X's behalf to make X a country in which the citizens can have significant input on the creation of public policy (the fair government principle)—Fact
4. People can only have significant input on the creation of public policy when they act autonomously—Assertion
5. When someone acts on behalf of another and unilaterally sets the conditions of solution, paternalism, and not autonomy, exists—Assertion

---

6. No country can act on behalf of another to make it autonomous and thus able to solve its problem of repression—1–5

The Paradox of Paternalistic Policies to Create Autonomy

Now, it may be true that no country—the United States included—can paternalistically bring another country to adopt democracy or some variant that complies with the fair government principle. Paradoxically, the act of intervening to help another country achieve fair government might undermine the very autonomy of the recipient country that the helping country seeks to bolster. What might be more helpful would be resources that could be made available upon the request of the country in question for infrastructure upgrades, the building of schools and hospitals, and support for human rights. Such assistance would be better from the United Nations or established NGOs. These groups are separate from any one single government, and there is less a sense that accepting help might come with strings attached. The marketing of this sort of assistance should aim at enabling a broad coalition of groups and institutions in the country (as opposed to going directly into the pocket of a dictator).

Conclusion

Of all the topics treated in this book, the prospects for success in creating a peaceful world are the most daunting. War in its many guises seems to be with us for the foreseeable future because it is based upon the dual realities that (1) leaders of most countries become leaders based upon their krateristic skills, and (2) kraterism is the number-one cause not only of war but of unbridled aggression. It's often easier to maintain power when there is a "bad guy" that everyone loathes and fears. This also increases the ethnic hatreds that are also causes of war.

Terrorism's many guises will present differential potential for hope. However, without a strong international community via an empowered United Nations and transparent NGOs, there is little hope for success in reducing its prevalence. Internal change must start internally. Men and women of peace must come to the fore and try to become transformational leaders. Strong international action against genocide is absolutely necessary—even in states that are not economically important to the G-20. International sanctions against governments that use violence against their own peoples is also a must. But these are all difficult goals to achieve. On the flip side, the ordinary criminal terrorists (whether for money or to express grievances for ethics, politics, or religion) are likely to be with us forever. The best we can do is to try to acquire procedures that can thwart these criminals and to capture them, fairly prosecute them, and then sentence them. These aberrant individuals can best be tamed when confronted by a fair and equitable justice system. The disparity between the two approaches will sustain public opinion against these criminals.

Guerrilla warfare seems to be most amenable to modification via the availability of resources from the United Nations and prominent NGOs. This can be a tangible achievement because it would indicate that the world is closer to implementing the fair government principle.

Key Terms

war, just war theory, belligerent kraterism, terrorism, genocide, guerrilla warfare, three-generation rule, *huperarchein*

Critical Applied Reasoning Exercise

Pick an area of concentration: war (in one clearly defined guise), genocide, guerrilla warfare, terrorism as criminals out for money, or terrorism as criminals out to prove an ethical, political, or religious point. Find a case study for your chosen area. Use the library or the Internet to get details about your case study. Then, write a three-page policy proposal that seeks to solve the problem—first ideally (utopian), and then modify your solution, making it practical in the world we live in (aspirational). Be sure to label all steps in the process.

Notes

1. These definitions are very controversial and generally equate to the way one thinks about the question. Particularly contentious is the definition of terrorism. I would direct readers who would like to research this further first to the special issue of *Ethics* 114, 4 (2004), esp. the articles of Kamm, Rodin, and Coady. For a more recent and succinct discussion of these evolving understandings of defining terrorism, see Seumas Miller, *Terrorism and Counter Terrorism* (Malden, MA: Blackwell, 2009): ch. 2.

2. Ezra Pound, "Sestina: Altaforte," from *Personae* (New York: New Directions, 1926). Pound was convicted of making pro-Italy fascist broadcasts in World War II and served a term in St. Elizabeth's mental hospital in Washington, D.C.

3. For a good background on this, see Gregory M. Reichberg, Henrik Syse, and Endre Begby, *The Ethics of War: Classic and Contemporary Readings* (Oxford: Blackwell, 2006).

4. Michael Walzer, *Just and Unjust Wars,* 4th ed. (New York: Basic Books, 2006 [1977]).

5. Karl von Clausewitz, *On War,* tr. Michael Howard and Peter Paret (Princeton, NJ: Princeton University Press, 1976): 76; cf. in a more general worldview context that is not at issue, Sun Tzu, *The Art of War,* tr. by Ralph D. Sawyer (New York: Basic Books, 1994).

6. Prudent man guidelines refer to what a representative prudent man (or woman) might do in similar circumstances. For example, if a karate expert were attacked with a knife, he might be expected to be more expert at disarming the attacker without using lethal force. However, if the victim of the attack possesses no expert skills, then he may (as a result of this lack of knowledge) pick up a cudgel and deliver a potentially fatal blow.

7. Technically the United Nations intervened in Korea, but this is a bit artificial. Had the Soviet Union not boycotted the UN Security Council, the resolution would have never passed. The United States was the dominant force in that military action. The "cover" of the nascent United Nations is rather misleading.

8. Walzer in *Just and Unjust Wars* believes the two can be separated. Jeff McMahan demurs in "The Ethics of Killing in War," *Ethics* 114, 4 (2004): 693–733. My position is that the separability question is rather artificial. Those inclined to flaunt internationally recognized rules will probably do so in both events. It will in practicality be an all-or-none choice—though conceptually they can be separated.

9. Aristotle, *Nicomachean Ethics,* ed. Otto Apelt (Leipzig: Teubner, 1903): 1146a 23–24.

10. Peace Research Institute Oslo (PRIO), 2004. From Credo Reference, www.credoreference.com/entry.do?pp=1&id=844851 (not a free site; generally accessed via libraries).

11. According to PRIO. It should be noted that all interstate conflicts are counted here including those that are resolved rather quickly and given the euphemism of *minor military engagements.*

12. Arms Transfer Database, PRIO, 2004.

13. This statistic employs the same PRIO categories used for the earlier data (from Credo Reference).

14. These are discussed by the National Commission on Terrorist Attacks, *The 9/11 Commission Report: Final Report of the National Commission on Terrorist Attacks upon the United States* (New York: W. W. Norton, 2004).

15. The argument being that within countries without an effective fair government principle, there is no other outlet save for organized guerrilla warfare to overthrow the government.

16. PRIO 2004 (from Credo Reference).

17. A recent book that is heavy on important detail on Bader-Meinhof and the Red Army Faction is Stefan Aust and Anthea Bell, *Bader-Meinhof: The Inside Story of the R.A.F.* (New York: Oxford University Press, 2009).

18. CREDO Reference, 2009.

19. Ernest Hemingway, "Under the Ridge," in *The Fifth Column and the First Forty-Nine Stories* (London: F. F. Collier & Son, 1938).

20. This is the motto of New Hampshire in the United States; at the writing of this book it is inscribed on the state's automobile license plates.

21. A song lyric from the rock group The Who, "Won't Get Fooled Again."

22. Michael Boylan, ed., *Public Health Policy and Ethics* (Dordrecht: Kluwer/ Springer, 2004): ch. 4.

CHAPTER 14

Immigrants and Refugees

An offshoot of war, economic hardship, political oppression, and environmental catastrophe is the creation of a mass of people whose lives were based upon a premise that is no longer viable. People who are desperately challenged in these ways are often faced with a question of whether they should stay where they are or leave. In an ideal world, each person on earth could make such a decision and go wherever he or she wanted to. There would be no agents preventing entry. People could *emigrate* from the place where they lived and *immigrate* to wherever they thought would be better. The sorts of goods involved on the Table of Embeddedness might include basic liberties (such as a liberty to travel—a level-two basic good derived from the basic human rights category) and exercising of autonomy (the ability to pursue a life plan according to the personal worldview imperative—a level-one secondary good). For much of human history this was the way it was. By foot, by horse, or by boat, people were allowed to go where they pleased. Before 1924 the United States of America thought that there was so much value in attracting those with the fortitude to leave the past behind because they had a vision for the future that a plaque was installed on the pedestal of the Statue of Liberty making the following bold declaration:

"The New Colossus"

Not like the brazen giant of Greek fame,
With conquering limbs astride from land to land;
Here at our sea-washed, sunset gates shall stand
A mighty woman with a torch, whose flame
Is the imprisoned lightning, and her name

197

Mother of Exiles. From her beacon-hand
Glows world-wide welcome; her mild eyes command
The air-bridged harbor that twin cities frame.
"Keep, ancient lands, your storied pomp!" cries she
With silent lips. "Give me your tired, your poor,
Your huddled masses yearning to breathe free,
The Wretched refuse of your teeming shore.
Send these, the homeless, tempest-tost to me,
I lift my lamp beside the golden door!"

—EMMA LAZARUS, 1883

Sadly, open immigration to the United States, and to most of the world, is no more. But should this policy continue?

The Problem

In Chapter 6 it was asserted that states are conventional entities that marshal collections of micro and macro communities into artificial units generally through the potential or actual use of force. One might look at the level-two basic good of a liberty to travel where one wishes and the level-one secondary good of living the sort of life one wishes as initial levels that must be trumped by a more embedded good if one is to move away from this *prima facie* argument for there being open borders around the world.

The argument for open borders rests on expression of the above-mentioned rights to goods on the Table of Embeddedness. These might express themselves as *the ability to flee* (emigration) and *the ability to move into* (immigration), as shown in Table 14.1.

The ability to move away and the ability to move into constitute the right to emigrate and the right to immigrate.[1] The two rights are linked, of course, because the right to emigrate entails a right to immigrate—one cannot leave one country without being able to enter another country (unless there were areas of the world that were uninhabited—Antarctica perhaps?).

Where do the arguments pertaining to displaced peoples—for open immigration and the right of emigration—fall on the Table of Embeddedness? When one is fleeing war, sickness, or abject poverty, a level-one basic good is at stake. When one is fleeing an oppressive dictator, a level-two basic good is at stake (basic liberty rights). When one is moving away to seek better recompense for the work one does, a level-one secondary good is involved.

What does this analysis of embeddedness to action tell us? Namely, that the right claims for various parties seeking to emigrate and immigrate vary. Those

TABLE 14.1. Arguments for Emigration and Immigration

Ability to Flee (Emigration)

- Ability to flee a war-torn region for one that is peaceful
- Ability to flee a disease ridden area for one that is not so stricken
- Ability to flee an oppressive dictator
- Ability to flee a poor country whose resources do not allow for one to survive with any certainty
- Ability to flee an environmental disaster such as a hurricane or earthquake

Ability to Move Into (Immigration)

- Ability to join a community that supports one's political, religious, or cultural outlook
- Ability to sell one's labor in the most conducive market to it
- Ability to move to where one believes life will be better

claims that are more embedded should be considered before those that are less embedded.

This sounds reasonable, except that it is often the case that there might be more than one category involved. One example of this is in the case of strategic war rape. Strategic war rape occurs when one side of a conflict (international or intranational) feels that it can demoralize the other side by selecting random women and publicly raping them. This has the effect of demoralizing the side whose women have been raped. There are no reliable statistics on the frequency of war rape because the victims who come forward are ostracized and treated as if they were guilty. However, because they were publicly victimized, their only option is to flee to another venue. Thus, the numbers of those women who flee war zones gives an indirect measure of strategic rape: 17 percent in Sierra Leone, for example, and even higher numbers in the Democratic Republic of Congo.[2] For example, Suzie may want to leave her country in Africa because she has been the victim of strategic war rape. She had been living in a community in which she had sufficient level-one and level-two basic goods. But then the strategic war rape occurred. Because it was done publicly before her village, her husband has ostracized her. She now must leave (with or without her children)—but to where?

In a personal interview with Sylvie Mbanga, a trained lawyer and human rights worker concentrating on strategic war rape in the Democratic Republic of Congo (across from Rwanda), I learned much about the horrific situation that these women faced and are still facing fifteen years after the genocide took place.[3] The rapists rarely are given any punishment. When it does happen (in extreme flagrant cases) a couple months in jail is all they get. When Sylvie was able to get an NGO to look after the medical health of these rape victims, her home was firebombed and her father and extended family had to flee to Uganda.

But what if Uganda had not accepted these people? Here we have a situation in which a university philosophy professor (Sylvie's father) is fleeing with his family. Why should Uganda accept him? Might they claim closed borders so that the "riff-raff" of the Congo would stay where it was? After all (Uganda might claim), these immigrants are troublemakers or they wouldn't be trying to flee.

The plight of displaced peoples is both an international issue and an intranational issue. Sometimes, people merely want to move about in their own country, but in much of the world (especially in the majority of countries that do not recognize the fair government principle) even intrastate migration is prohibited. Internal migration within some countries, such as North Korea, Burma (Myanmar), Sudan, and China, is limited by political fiat.

However, even democratic countries can experience difficulties in internal migration. For example, following the destruction of Hurricane Katrina in the United States, there was some contention that those displaced from New Orleans ought not be relocated into Texas (because of the added cost on Texas taxpayers).[4] A problem was recognized: thousands without a place to live due to natural disaster. But the solution was unclear. The "not in my backyard" principle seemed to kick in. Allowing internal refugees to move about might mean additional and potentially burdensome economic costs to the host locale. Many people were not willing to pay the price (in higher taxes or decreased general services) to accommodate this relocation.

These dynamics lead us to the principal arguments *against* open emigration and immigration in an international venue, as shown in Table 14.2.

The arguments outlined in Tables 14.1 and 14.2 are diametrically opposed. At this preliminary stage in the presentation it is enough to be aware of the positions presented and the personal worldview that would be behind each. I would advise against forming a clear opinion for either position, for as in the case of war and terrorism, there may be no clear-cut answers but rather some sort of continuum against which public policy can be formulated. This formulation must be made by referring to foundational principles—such as the Table of Embeddedness.

The Causes

The causes of displaced peoples via emigration and immigration follow from the categories delineated in Tables 14.1 and 14.2. When people are displaced from their homes, they have to go somewhere, either in their own country or in a different country.

TABLE 14.2. Arguments Against Emigration and Immigration

Emigration

- [Political] Allowing open emigration will allow people to leave an oppressive regime and thus show the government's weakness and thereby demoralize the resident population.
- [Economic] Allowing open emigration will lessen the skilled labor pool and hurt the native country of the emigrant.

Immigration

- [Economic] Immigrants coming into a country will add to the labor pool and thus depress wages.
- [Economic] Immigrants will tax the existing welfare system: health care, education, disability, and so on.
- [Cultural] Immigrants will change the character of existing communities in the host country regardless of whether the residents in these communities want such changes.
- [Security] In a world of terrorism and war, the security of each country depends upon its ability to screen and deny access to criminal elements.

For purposes of clarity, let us categorize emigrants who flee their present country (or their place within their country) and immigrants who move toward another country (or to another place within their country) due to the lack of basic goods as *refugees*. In either case the focus should be on being displaced and why populations feel compelled to move.

The first cause is violence. We saw in Chapter 13 that by far the most prevalent sort of violence today is intrastate violence. This has been on the rise since 1990 whereas interstate violence has actually decreased over the same interval. As one might expect, the population of refugees (externally and internally displaced people) over the same period reflects these statistics. In 1990 there were around 17 million refugees in the world. In 2002 this figure dropped to under 10 million. (This figure has increased by 4.7 million due to the war in Iraq.)[5] In 1990 there were around 18 million internally displaced persons, a figure that increased to around 25 million in 2002.[6] Intrastate violence is largely ethnically driven. This phenomenon when carried to extremes has been called "ethnic cleansing." The causes of interstate and intrastate violence give rise to *displaced people* (see Chapter 13).

The second cause is economic. Since 2008, the world has experienced a severe economic downturn. This has hurt those at the very bottom of the socioeconomic ladder the most.[7] One must distinguish two sorts of economic causes: (1) loss of level-one basic goods (food, water, sanitation, clothing, shelter, protection from unwarranted bodily harm, and health care), and (2) loss of level-one secondary goods (basic societal respect, equal opportunity to compete for the prudential goods of society, ability to pursue a life plan according to the personal worldview imperative, and ability to participate equally as an agent in the shared-community worldview imperative). The former are more deeply embedded than the latter.

A third cause is political. Statistics on this are very unreliable because host countries are unwilling to share data (because it would make them look bad) and some countries exaggerate figures to get more international aid. However, with most of the world's countries not following the fair government principle, it is clear that this also is a cause for external displacement. The good at stake on the Table of Embeddedness is a liberty right—a level-two basic good.

A fourth cause is environmental degradation and disasters. Examples of environmental degradation are soil salinity in Western Australia and the Middle East, deforestation of old-growth forests, extinction of animal species worldwide, environmental pollution of water sources, the spread of infectious diseases due to problems in sanitation, and nuclear waste disposal. Environmental degradation makes the land less productive and makes air and water poisonous. It is a cause for internal displacement. The good at stake on the Table of Embeddedness is a level-one basic good.

Examples of recent disasters include the earthquake (2005) in Kashmir that cost 79,000 lives in Pakistan and the Sichuan earthquake (2008) in China that took 61,150 lives; the Mozambique flood (2000); Hurricane Katrina (2005); the Indian floods (2008) affecting the Kosi Basin in Bihar; the African floods (2007) that affected fourteen countries; floods in Bangladesh (seven major floods in fifty-four years), Indonesia (2007), and Malaysia (2006 and 2007, displacing over 100,000 people); the earthquake in Haiti (2010), which killed over 200,000 people; and a horrific flood in Pakistan (2010) whose death toll is still rising but certainly over 2,000. All of these disasters create a necessity for humans to be displaced (generally internally).

Possible Solutions

These four causes of displaced people means that people travel within their own country and in some cases seek asylum from other states. The number of possible immigrants is high. The United Nations estimates that 3 percent of the world's population, or roughly 187 million people, are immigrants.[8]

Those claiming a right to enter another country do so because they have been denied access to goods at one of three levels on the Table of Embeddedness.

- Basic Goods—level-one: food, water, sanitation, clothing, shelter, protection from unwarranted bodily harm, and basic health care
- Basic Goods—level-two: education and human liberties (such as the United Nations Declaration of Human Rights)
- Secondary Goods—level-one: basic societal respect, equal opportunity to compete for the prudential goods of society, ability to pursue a life plan according to the personal worldview imperative, and ability to participate equally as an agent in the shared-community worldview imperative

It is more common for the richest countries of the world, the so-called G-8, to respect requests for asylum from political immigrants over those who seek to immigrate on the basis of obtaining the basic needs of life. A classic case of this occurred during the Reagan administration when refugees from Haiti (then, as now, the poorest country in the Western Hemisphere) were turned away while political refugees from El Salvador (which had a leftist regime that was opposed to the United States) were accepted. The reason for this was that political claims were considered to be higher than economic claims. The Table of Embeddedness suggests just the opposite. Economic refugees who are fleeing starvation to live in a country that can provide them some way to stay alive are seeking a level-*one* basic good. Political refugees who are fleeing a tyrannical regime that does not allow basic human rights are seeking a level-*two* basic good. If one accepts the moral force of the Table of Embeddedness on the basis of the argument for the moral status of basic goods, then the Reagan-era regime should have accepted the Haitian refugees who were just trying to stay alive *first*. The biological ability to act is more fundamental to action than the *preferred* mode of acting, that is, living under a government that recognizes human rights. In this case the United States was wrong not to put the rights claims of the Haitians first.

If we accept the basic cosmopolitan premise of this book that the world is structured nationally but moral rights exist ultra-nationally, then every country should actively work through the United Nations and exert international pressure (including economic sanctions) to permit the free and safe migration of peoples both intranationally and internationally. Further, the wealthiest countries of the world (G-8 to G-20) should commit to accepting immigrants according to the priority of their claims measured according to the Table of Embeddedness.

The argument that there would be economic hardships due to such a policy is specious. This is because the priority of refugees' rights claims incurs a correlative positive duty upon us all up to the "ought implies can" dictum. In this context it means that one should give to another in need up to the point that the giver is in danger of losing the same or a comparable good. One might ask upon whom this duty rests. The answer harkens back to the agents of cosmopolitan change discussed in Part Two of this book: individuals, governments, nongovernmental organizations, and the United Nations and its affiliates. Each of these sources of aid act differently. But when a crisis occurs, all must pitch in together. None is excluded. The effect of this policy would be a radical worldview shift to cooperation rather than competition that currently rules the way the rich countries interact with the poor—which is to say, by exploitation. The fact of this exploitation (from political colonialism to economic neocolonialism) engenders various consequent negative duties as well. Negative duties are those duties that one owes to another whom he or she has injured. The European nations, Russia, and the United States have explicitly, or through corporations licensed to do business in their confines, been guilty of such practices (see Chapter 11).[9] Such facts constitute a parallel justification to assisting people who need to leave where they live to relocate elsewhere.

Counterarguments such as those mentioned in Table 14.2 constitute reasons based upon secondary goods at various levels. When the rights claims of immigrants are basic goods, then only a proximately more embedded good loss would justify turning someone away. Because this duty falls on all states that are economically flourishing (the G-8 to G-20 nations), then each should fulfill this obligation according to its ability to pay, with the United States leading the way as the world's largest economy.

These proposals border on the utopian in that they require a moral awareness on the part of the policymakers of the world (who also personally have the most to lose). It is here that the entire enterprise of global morality and justice rests. Somehow the nations of the world recognize the force of these arguments. How can they get there? Religion and moral suasion come first to mind. And these only become viable once people get together to make their voices heard. In my experience it seems true that public policy only comes about (in nations accepting the fair government principle) as the result of political pressure brought about by concerned citizens. Because the problem is international, the popular pressure must also be international. When the peoples of the world unite to support such a cause, then and only then will cosmopolitanism become more than a phrase bandied about by philosophers.

This book is meant as an educational device to help readers think about their own personal worldviews and how they might fit into just such a cause according to shared-community and extended-community worldview imperatives. These imperatives explicitly command that we must be active agents of positive change according to our best understanding of the issues (sincerity) and according to the sound backing of a recognized theory of morality and global justice (authenticity). I exhort each reader to think carefully about these issues and act accordingly. Make your own decision and do something. The cause is too important to turn away.

Key Terms

ability to flee (emigration), ability to move into (immigration), displaced people, refugees

Critical Applied Reasoning Exercise

Pick a country among the following: United States, Canada, Great Britain, France, Germany, Italy, Brazil, Argentina, South Africa, India, China, Japan. Look up on the Internet an event that has created an influx of displaced people (international or intranational) in another country. Imagine that you are the foreign ambassador of the country you selected. You have been given broad authority to make public policy in this regard. You must respond to the crisis you identified on the Internet with your own country's response. Write a two-page report listing your recommendations and the reasons behind them in a memo to your country's chief executive officer. Be sure to cite moral and practical reasons.

Notes

1. Two excellent essays on this issue that take opposite sides are Chandran Kukathas, "The Case for Open Immigration," and David Miller, "Immigration: The Case for Limits," both in *Contemporary Debates in Applied Ethics,* ed. Andrew I. Cohen and Christopher Heath Wellman (Oxford: Blackwell, 2005): 193–205, 207–219.

2. United Nations, "Investigation by the Office of Internal Oversight Services into Allegations of Sexual Exploitation and Abuse in the United Nations Mission in the Democratic Republic of Congo," January 5, 2005, www.monuc.org/downloads/0520055E.pdf.

3. I met with Sylvie three times in interview before she made a presentation to my college in March 2009 and at the CAAPS peace conference (also at Marymount) in April 2009. I should also note that Sylvie was in Washington to garner support for her cause and was partially sponsored by Pax Christi, a Catholic social action group.

4. For further discussion, see Jed Horne, *Breach of Faith: Hurricane Katrina and the Near Death of a Great American City* (New York: Random House, 2008); and Chester Hartman and Gregory D. Squires, eds., *There Is No Such Thing as a Natural Disaster: Race, Class, and Hurricane Katrina* (New York: Routledge, 2006).

5. Amnesty International, June 15, 2008, www.amnesty.org/en/news-and-updates/report/iraqi-refugees-facing-desparate-situations-20080615.

6. Human Security Centre, *Human Security Report: War and Peace in the 21st Century* (New York: Oxford University Press, 2005): part 3.

7. See *Hunger and Markets: World Hunger Series 2009* (London: Earthscan, 2009).

8. "International Migration 2006," United Nations, Department of Economic and Social Affairs, Population Division, United Nations Publication No. E.06.XIII6, March 2006.

9. For an expression of this argument based upon negative rights and duties, see Thomas Pogge, "'Assisting' the Global Poor," in *The Ethics of Assistance: Morality and the Distant Needy*, ed. Deen K. Chatterjee (Cambridge: Cambridge University Press, 2004).

APPENDIX

 How to Get Involved

So now you've read the book. Perhaps you are motivated to get involved as per the extended-community worldview imperative. There are many ways to do this. One way is to give money to causes that are particularly meaningful to you. All these organizations need money to continue their work, so this is a necessary step in the process.

A second way to make a difference is to give your time and expertise. For younger readers it may be the case that you have more time than money, so this second option may be more attractive to you.

There are different ways to connect to an organization whose mission is one that particularly resonates with your personal worldview. Many colleges and universities have internship centers that can facilitate your application to an organization at the ground floor, where you can help in basic ways to assist that organization in fulfilling its mission.

Another way to get involved is via the Internet and the websites for some of the more prominent organizations. Following is a very small list of organizations that you might want to contact. I have paraphrased or provided some words from their mission statements to give a hint of what they are about. Sometimes ground level internships lead to full time jobs in which you can earn a living and make the world a better place. Good luck!

Idealist.Org
www.idealist.org

A nonprofit action group founded in 1995 with offices in the United States and Argentina, Idealist is an interactive site where people and organizations can exchange resources and ideas, locate opportunities and supporters, and take steps toward building a world where all people can lead free and dignified lives.

Human Rights Watch

www.hrw.org

An independent nonprofit organization dedicated to defending and protecting human rights of the people of the world, Human Rights Watch stands with victims and activists to prevent discrimination, to uphold political freedom, to protect people from inhumane contact in wartime, and to bring offenders to justice.

Amnesty International

www.amnesty.org

An independent nonprofit organization that campaigns for internationally recognized human rights for all, Amnesty International has since 1961 supported those working for a better world via the vehicle of human rights. The organization is present in 150 countries in the world and has 2.8 million members worldwide.

Oxfam

www.oxfam.org

A confederation of fourteen like-minded organizations working to end poverty and injustice around the world, Oxfam was formed in 1995 from the Oxford Committee for Famine Relief (founded in 1942). It is also a world leader in emergency relief.

Médecins Sans Frontières (Doctors Without Borders)

www.doctorswithoutborders.org

Doctors Without Borders is an international medical humanitarian organization created by doctors and journalists in France in 1971. Today its members work in sixty countries with people whose survival is threatened by violence, neglect, or catastrophe due to armed conflict, epidemics, malnutrition, exclusion from health care, or natural disasters.

Save the Children

www.savethechildren.org

Save the Children was founded to create lasting, positive change in the lives of children in need in the United States and around the world. The organization seeks to ensure that children in need grow up protected and safe, educated, healthy and well-nourished, and able to thrive in economically secure households.

International Committee of the Red Cross (ICRC)

www.icrc.org

The ICRC is an independent, neutral organization ensuring humanitarian protection and assistance for victims of war and other situations of violence. It has a permanent mandate under international law to take impartial action for prisoners, the wounded and sick, and civilians affected by conflict. The ICRC coordinates its responses with national Red Cross and Red Crescent societies.

Action Aid International
www.actionaid.org

Action Aid is an international antipoverty agency whose aim is to fight poverty worldwide. Formed in 1972, today it helps 13 million of the world's poorest and most disadvantaged people in forty-two countries worldwide.

Peace Corps
www.peacecorps.gov

Since 1961 the Peace Corps has shared with the world America's most precious resource—its people. Peace Corps volunteers serve in seventy-seven countries in Africa, Asia, the Caribbean, Central and South America, Europe, and the Middle East. Collaborating with local community members, volunteers work in areas of education, youth outreach and community development, the environment, and information technology.

Greenpeace
www.greenpeace.org/international

Greenpeace is present in forty countries across Europe, the Americas, Asia, Africa, and the Pacific. This environmentally focused nonprofit defends our oceans, protects the world's ancient forests, works for disarmament and peace, campaigns for sustainable agriculture, and strives to create a toxic-free future for all.

Transparency International
www.transparency.org

Transparency International is a global civil society organization leading the fight against corruption in order to bring people together in a powerful worldwide coalition to end the devastating impact of corruption on men, women, and children around the world. It has been operating since 1993 and operates through ninety locally established chapters. It is politically nonpartisan.

Brookings Institution
www.brookings.edu

The Brookings Institution is a nonprofit public policy organization based in Washington, D.C. Its mission is to conduct high-quality independent research and based on that research to provide innovative practical recommendations that advance democracy, economic and social welfare, and a secure, open, safe, and prosperous international system.

Carnegie Endowment for International Peace
www.carnegieendowment.org

The Carnegie Endowment for International Peace is a private, nonprofit organization dedicated to advancing cooperation between nations and promoting active international engagement by the United States. It was founded in 1910 and is nonpartisan and dedicated to achieving practical results.

The Center for American Progress
www.americanprogress.org

The Center for American Progress is a nonprofit policy think tank that is dedicated to improving lives via progressive legislation. The center examines domestic and international policy on relieving poverty, conserving energy, stimulating economic growth, and on fair immigration, education, and health care. It also is concerned with issues on global economics and armed conflict.

Hoover Institution
www.hoover.org

The Hoover Institution is a nonprofit policy think tank dedicated to the advanced study of politics, economics, and political economy—both domestic and foreign—as well as international affairs. The Hoover Institution puts its accumulated knowledge to work in the marketplace of ideas from a conservative perspective in defense of a free society.

These organizations are just a brief number of those that are committed in one way or another to the cause of international justice as defined in this book. If you would like to share your experiences with these or other organizations, please e-mail me at Boylan.globaljustice@gmail.com.

GLOSSARY

Ability to flee The attempt to move to another spot within one's own country or to another country. *See also* Emigration.

Ability to move into The attempt of a person or group of people to move into another country. *See also* Immigration.

Action response Part of the extended-community worldview imperative that requires all agents to respond to cosmopolitan need with some sort of action via an individual, the nation, the United Nations, or nongovernmental organizations.

Affective good will *See* Good will.

Agency-based justification of human rights An agent has a right to the goods that are fundamentally necessary for agency.

Air pollution Principally consists of sulfur dioxide (SO_2), nitrous oxide (N_2O), carbon dioxide (CO_2), and methane (CH_4). Together, these chemical compounds in the air create greenhouse gasses. There is also floating particulate matter that can exacerbate respiratory problems.

Antirealist *See* Ethics.

Aristocracy The theory of distributive justice that advocates "to each according to his or her inherited station or bank account."

Aspirational An ethical or social/political theory or goal that is possible to achieve though it may be difficult. *See also* Utopian.

Authenticity A process that focuses and structures foundational investigation into the way ethics and social/political philosophy ought to proceed. This text advocates the personal, community, and extended-community worldview imperatives to perform this function. *See also* Sincerity; Worldview.

Belligerent kraterism An aggressive act by one state against the territory or sovereignty of another state for the purposes of gaining land, resources, or strategic advantage without regard to any constraint.

Capitalism, unfettered The theory of distributive justice that advocates for distribution "to each according to his valued work," without regulation and control.

Charity v. human rights The charity approach makes the response to a situation of a group's lack of basic goods optional and voluntary. The human rights approach makes the response mandatory.

Coherence of worldview Refers both to deductive coherence (one does not explicitly contradict one's self in different situations) and inductive coherence (one does not engage in life strategies that are in conflict and will result in a sure-loss contract).

Collaboration on medical research Policies that might allow open source or other shared research paradigms. This approach requires changes in intellectual property treatises and the status of pharmaceutical corporations.

Communities Social units where people live and interact. *See also* Micro communities; Macro communities, Extended community; Shared-community worldview imperative; Extended community worldview imperative.

Completeness of worldview Refers to the capacity of a worldview to handle all novel cases. The rational and affective good will satisfy this condition.

Confronting novel normative theories A three-stage process. In the first, one assesses the logical argument behind the claim. In the second, one matches the claim against the personal or community worldview, eliciting one of three responses: *co-inciding and amplification, dissonance and rejection,* or *overlap and modification.* In the first two responses there is no change. In overlap and modification one proceeds to a stage in which there is a dialectical interaction with the proposed change and the possible experience going forward. When this is positive (as measured by the rational and the affective good will), the individual or community makes the change. When it is not, the individual or community rejects the proposed change.

Confronting the "other" *See* Other.

Cosmopolitanism The view that nations and their ensuing national interests are morally irrelevant in determining or executing obligations to the people of the world. *See also* Statism.

Cultural relativism The view that cultures vary in what they commend. There are two forms: legitimate cultural relativism (in which the idiosyncrasy of the culture is either a moral prescription or a permission), and illegitimate cultural relativism (in which the idiosyncrasy of the culture promotes ethical prohibitions).

Discrimination Refers to the process of relegating a person or group to the class of *the other,* leading to marginalization (loss of level-one secondary goods) and/or victimization (loss of level-one or level-two basic goods).

Displaced people Those people who feel forced to leave their place in their native country for another place in that country or to another country due to loss of the goods of agency. *See also* Refugees.

Distributive justice *See* International distributive justice; Justice.

Domestic political dynamics and NGOs and UN agencies This refers to the tension between sovereign governments and aid agencies from either nongovernmental organization (NGOs) or United Nations agencies (that represent quasi-world government).

Egalitarianism The theory of distributive justice that advocates "to each according to principle of equal respect and appropriate need."

Embeddedness A term referring to the primacy of some resource to enable an individual to achieve his or her vision of the good through action. The more embedded a good is, the more primary it is. *See also* Table of Embeddedness.

Emigration The attempt by a person or group of people to move to another location within one's own country or to another country.

Ethics There are two general understandings of ethics: the realist conception, in which ethics is the science of the right and wrong in human action, and the anti-realist conception, in which ethics is about meeting social/cultural norms that are relative and thus not objectively real.

Extended community A community in which people within the conceptual space are remotely connected. They don't live together in a single country but are separated across space. The idea behind the extended community is one of the agent learning about and connecting to others around the world.

Extended-community worldview imperative Each agent must educate himself and others as much as he is able about the peoples of the world—their access to the basic goods of agency, their essential commonly held cultural values, and their governmental and institutional structures—in order that he might create a worldview that includes those of other nations so that individually and collectively the agent might accept the duties that ensue from those peoples' legitimate rights claims and act accordingly within what is aspirationally possible.

Extended community relations (extended-community worldview imperative) Individuals should educate themselves and those around them so that they might imaginatively bring others into their personal worldview. This process can create a form of constructed sympathy for the plight of those in other countries. This sort of relationship may occur from one side only: Mr. X can form an imaginative understanding about the peoples of various parts of Kenya even though those in Kenya do not know who Mr. X is. This marks the difference in constructed sympathy from the sympathy found in micro communities and person-to-person interactions.

Fair government principle For a government to be fair, it must both permit and encourage formal and informal social/political institutions that will allow for an interactive exchange (consistent with the personal worldview imperative) between micro communities and the ruling macro community government in a meaningful way that is protected by a governmentally independent rule of law.

Gender The mental identification an individual has as being either *male* or *female* according to that individual's understanding of the same. Somatic characteristics can constitute a secondary (and less important) property for class inclusion. Gender differences (like racial differences) can instigate a categorization of a group of people (in this case the natural majority of individuals, *ceteris paribus*, in any given society) that is then discriminated against. This is a more important aspect of gender around the world than morphological variances.

Genocide An intranational event in which a deliberate slaughter of civilians occurs due to ethnic or religious reasons.

Globalization Unfettered free-market capitalist economic trading between countries (without tariffs) seeking the most efficient means of production and distribution to the world's consumers. *See also* Restructured globalization.

Goods of agency The resources necessary (according to embeddedness) to commit purposive action in order for the agent to achieve his or her view of the good. *See also* Embeddedness; Table of Embeddedness

Good will The mechanism by which we decide how to act in the world. There are two varieties of the good will: (1) the rational good will, in which the criteria of completeness and coherence are paramount via deductive and inductive logic; and (2) the affective good will, in which the criterion of completeness is justified via sympathy—in cases of conflict the rational good will trumps the affective good will.

Government (types of) Traditionally this has meant aristocracy (meaning the rule of the best, after *aristos,* the superlative form of *agathos,* good—generally a benevolent monarch without hereditary succession); democracy (meaning rule of the landholding males); oligarchy (meaning the rule of the few—generally a powerful clique around a symbolic leader); and tyranny (meaning rule by a powerful strongman).

Ground waste pollution There are two forms of pollution: regular waste disposal and toxic waste disposal. The first causes a problem of where to put everything and the second concerns the creation of regional public health problems.

Guerrilla warfare An act by a non-state group (though it may be other-state sponsored) that uses tactics that incite fear and mayhem within a given country as part of a strategy of overthrowing the sitting government and establishing a new one.

Homosexual A person who is born with a sexual orientation toward the same sex. This is a biological fact that cannot be overridden effectively with any environmental conditioning to the contrary.

Human rights *See* Agency-based justification of human rights; Interest-based justification of human rights; Legal justification of human rights; *see also* Charity v. human rights

Huperarchein The tendency of kraterists to overreach. They wish to take more than their deserving share; instead they fulfill their desires by a taking from others.

Imagination The power of the mind that makes real and integrates what is abstract into lived experience, and vice versa.

Immigration The attempt of a person or group of people to move into another country.

Institutions Recognized sets of rules that govern social or political conduct. *Robust institutions* are those whose recognition and power (legally or via culture) are great enough to be able to positively reward (or punish) those who follow (or disregard) their prescriptions for behavior. *Virtual institutions* are those that are recognized by those within some community but lack the power to positively reward (or punish) those who follow (or disregard) their prescriptions for behavior.

Interest-based justification of human rights An agent has a right to the basic means needed in order to achieve well-being.

International distributive justice The theory and mechanism on the way goods and services are parsed within the context of a society and within the context of the world. Various moral, political, and economic systems commend different formulae for the way these goods and services are handed out.

International retributive justice The theory and mechanism that addresses the giving back to aggrieved peoples and nations in the face of wrongs that have been done to them.

Intrinsic attention to poor nations Intrinsic attention refers to the best interests of the object of attention. In the case of poor nations it refers to acting in their best interests and not in the extrinsic interests of richer countries and multinational corporations.

Just war theory A moral account of when it is morally permissible to go to war *(ius ad bellum)* and how the war may be conducted *(ius in bello)*.

Justice The two primary meanings concern distributive and retributive justice. Distributive justice speaks to how goods and services are allocated to individuals. Retributive justice concerns how to reestablish an order when individuals break the law.

Kraterism The theory of distributive justice that advocates "to each according to his ability to snatch it for himself." *See also* Belligerent kraterism.

Legal justification of human rights Legal positivism, legal realism, and natural law fall under this category. In the first case, legal precedent takes the fore. In the second case, the social realities of society take the fore. In the third case, moral principles trump societal legal actions.

Legal positivism The theory that operates on the principle of precedent—first, within the law of the sovereign country, and second, within the law within the historical tradition preceding the country. An example would be U.S. law referencing British law, which in turn references Roman law. *See also* Legal theory.

Legal realism The position that the law should represent the shared community worldview of the significant macro communities within the country. *See also* Legal theory.

Legal theory There are three prominent theories of law in the Anglo-American tradition: (1) legal positivism, (2) legal realism, and (3) natural law. *See* each of these separate entries.

Macro communities Large social units in which people live and interact connected geographically; generally, 501 people or more. *See also* Extended community; Extended-community worldview imperative; Micro communities; Shared-community worldview imperative.

Marginalization Loss of level-one secondary goods as a result of discrimination.

Micro communities Small social units in which people live and interact, ranging from the family to groups of 500 or less. *See also* Extended communities; Extended-community worldview imperative; Macro communities; Shared-community worldview imperative.

Morality *See* Ethics.

Moral relativism The view that there is no science of the right and wrong of human action and that morality is about codifying social/cultural practices that vary according to place and time.

Moral versus prudential approach Moral reasons flow from one of the recognized moral theories: one acts according to the dictates of that theory regardless of its effect upon the agent. Prudential reasons are calculations of personal advantage on the proposed action.

National gatekeeper A national gatekeeper is the legitimate ruling authority within a state.

Nation-states *See* States.

Nations *See* States.

Natural law Asserts a synonymy between legal and moral law; *see also* Legal theory.

Normative According to standards by which we give our assent or dissent. These standards can be based on realist or antirealist criteria.

Novel normative theories *See* Confronting novel normative theories

Other One who is confronted by a social/political power group in such a way that he or she is subject to loss of goods of agency. The status of the other is the basis of discrimination based upon race, gender, and/or sexual orientation (among others).

Personal worldview imperative All people must develop a single comprehensive and internally coherent worldview that is good and that we strive to act out in our daily lives.

Political versus economic systems of government Economic systems concern allocation strategies of distributive justice whereas government systems are the über-institution within a society: an institution that rules all other institutions.

Prevention and treatment of infectious disease Prevention of infectious disease involves both vaccines and nonbiological prophylactic barriers. Treatment includes both cures and methods of containing the disease by slowing down its stages.

Psychological screening Psychological screening occurs when someone believes some fact to be true and, as a result, tends to observe all cases that coincide with this belief as confirming instances and all that do not coincide as outlier cases to be ignored—thus reinforcing his beliefs (often stereotypes), even in the face of contrary facts.

Public versus clinical health analysis Public health analysis views problems from a macro community viewpoint, often through broad group measures. Clinical-health analysis focuses on the one-on-one medical relation between the physician and his or her patient.

Race Any group that is picked out as being *other* on the basis of physical (nongender or disabilities) differences.

Rational good will *See* Good will.

Realism *See* Ethics.

Refugees Emigrants who flee from their present country (or their place within their country) and immigrants who move toward another country (or to another place within their country) due to the lack of basic goods.

Regional sustainable food supply The local, geographical supply (from ecosystem to biome) is deemed to be sustainable if and only if humans take away from the ecosystem an amount that does not diminish the future supply of the agricultural or animal output.

Religion and ethics Religion must act as the follower of philosophy in cases of ethics and social/political philosophy (though it may be a primary source of truth). In cases of conflict, moral philosophy should trump the claims of private religious revelation.

Restructured globalization A model of globalization that requires multinational countries to pay for occupational, health, and safety for foreign employees at the same level as their home country levels. Environmental costs should also be fully borne by the multinational corporation. Child- and prison-labor prohibitions should also be in force. Ultimately, the only advantage will be the cheaper labor (which should be pegged at an analogous quintile for the sort of business involved, e.g., third quintile of manufacturing workers). *See also* Globalization.

Retributive justice *See* International retributive justice; Justice.

Shared-community worldview imperative Each agent must contribute to a common body of knowledge that supports the creation of a shared-community worldview (that is itself complete, coherent, and good) through which social institutions and their resulting policies might flourish within the constraints of the essential core commonly held values (ethics, aesthetics, and religion).

Sincerity An individual commitment toward using one's highest capacities to examine the foundations of ethics and social/political philosophy. *See also* Authenticity; Worldview.

Socialism The theory of distributive justice that advocates "to each according to his or her needs."

Social/political philosophy An amalgam of concerns that raises the level of ethical analysis from the individual level to that of the group. In social philosophy, customs within existing communities are examined to see whether they might be normatively commended or not (according to some extension of a theory of ethics and understanding of the role of culture). In political philosophy, the creation of governing institutions and their operation are the points of concern.

States Cultural/social sovereign macro communities that have established, recognized robust geographical boundaries for the sake of commerce and common purpose.

States and institutions (nature of) States and institutions are social constructions based on some mix of social justice and common agreement in turn based on cultural constructions.

Statism The theory that states are morally relevant in determining or executing duties to people in the world. The strong form advocates a priority stance to the nation's citizens whereas the weak form uses the legalist structure of a state to formulate certain international rights and duties. *See also* Cosmopolitanism.

Table of Embeddedness A hierarchical listing of goods beginning with those most essential to human action and following with other goods in descending order of necessity (i.e., less embedded). Because of the argument on the moral status of basic goods, all people may make justifiable claims against their nation and the world to provide such goods according to the "ought implies can" caveat.

Terrorism Using violence and mayhem to make a public message that creates fear so as to convince a population via *argumentum ad baculum* (argument from coercion or force). The actors are generally (though not necessarily) non-state agents whose purpose can be either profit motive (to enrich the criminals) or political ideology to vent frustration or anger against a nation, institution, or some identifiable social group. Sometimes the author of terrorism is the government itself in an effort to control the civilian population within its borders.

Textile dumping A practice in which the government subsidizes private industry so that companies can gain market share and eventually raise prices in some foreign market; this practice is prohibited by the World Trade Organization.

Theories of ethics Can be realist, swing, or antirealist. Realist theories are comprised of utilitarianism and deontology. Swing theories are ethical intuitionism and virtue ethics. Antirealist theories are ethical noncognitivism and contractarianism.

Three-generation rule Sets an agreed upon statute of limitations on unjustified acts of extreme violence and oppression (e.g., 150 years or three generations, using modern actuarial assumptions).

Transsexual A person who, by nature, has a sexual identification with the opposite sex.

Unfettered capitalism *See* Capitalism, unfettered.

Utopian theory A theory of ethics or social/political philosophy that is practically unrealistic to achieve due to its contradiction with known facts of human communities. *See also* Aspirational.

Victimization Being deprived of level-one or level-two basic goods on the basis of discrimination.

War An aggressive act by one state against the territory or sovereignty of another state for the purposes of gaining land, resources, or strategic advantage according to internationally recognized rules and constraints governing such action (both *ad bellum* and *in bello*). *See also* Belligerent kraterism.

Water-based diseases Diseases that come from hosts that live in water during part or all of their life cycles.

Water-borne diseases Diseases that occur directly as an individual drinks contaminated water.

Water-related insect vectors Diseases spread by insects—such as mosquitoes—that breed in water.

Water-washed diseases Diseases that are spread when unsanitary water is used for hygiene or cooking.

Water pollution There are two general ways to think about water pollution: first, by the adulteration of fresh and saltwater by human activity; second, by the effects of global warming on water reserves around the world.

Worldview The sum total of one's factual and normative understandings about the world. Each of us is enjoined to take ownership of our worldview via sincere and authentic questioning. *See also* Authenticity; Sincerity; Worldview imperatives.

Worldview change *See* Confronting novel normative theories.

Worldview imperatives *See* Extended-community worldview imperative; Personal worldview imperative; Shared-community worldview imperative.

INDEX